MW01626346

MUSEUMS AND THE WORKING CLASS

Museums and the Working Class is the first book to take an intersectional and international approach to the issues of economic diversity and class within the field of museum studies.

Bringing together 16 contributors from eight countries, this book has emerged from the significant global dialogue concerning museums' obligation to be inclusive, participate in meaningful engagement and advocate for social change. As part of the push for museums to be more accessible and inclusive, museums have been challenged to critically examine their power relationships and how these are played out in what they collect, whose stories they exhibit and who is made to feel welcome in their halls. This volume will further this professional and academic debate through the discussion of class. Contributions to the book will also reinforce the importance of the working class – not only in collection and exhibition policy, but also for the organisational psychology of institutions.

Museums and the Working Class is essential reading for scholars and students of museum, gallery and heritage studies, cultural studies, sociology, labour studies and history. It will also serve as a source of honest and research-led inspiration to practitioners working in museums, galleries, libraries, archives and at heritage sites around the world.

Adele Chynoweth has earned her living as a shop assistant, cabaret performer, night club DJ, call centre operator, union organiser, public servant, and teacher in secondary schools and adult vocational education. Adele also studied theatre direction at the Flinders University Drama Centre and completed her PhD with scholarship support. Adele was a Lecturer in the Centre for Heritage and Museum Studies at the Australian National University where she received the Vice Chancellor's Award for Public Policy and Outreach in 2018. In 2020, she was awarded the Medal of the Order of Australia.

MUSEUM MEANINGS

Series Editors: Richard Sandell and Christina Kreps

Museums have undergone enormous changes in recent decades; an ongoing process of renewal and transformation bringing with it changes in priority, practice and role as well as new expectations, philosophies, imperatives and tensions that continue to attract attention from those working in, and drawing upon, wide ranging disciplines.

Museum Meanings presents new research that explores diverse aspects of the shifting social, cultural and political significance of museums and their agency beyond, as well as within, the cultural sphere. Interdisciplinary, cross-cultural and international perspectives and empirical investigation are brought to bear on the exploration of museums' relationships with their various publics (and analysis of the ways in which museums shape – and are shaped by – such interactions).

Theoretical perspectives might be drawn from anthropology, cultural studies, art and art history, learning and communication, media studies, architecture and design and material culture studies amongst others. Museums are understood very broadly – to include art galleries, historic sites and other cultural heritage institutions – as are their relationships with diverse constituencies.

The focus on the relationship of the museum to its publics shifts the emphasis from objects and collections and the study of museums as text, to studies grounded in the analysis of bodies and sites; identities and communities; ethics, moralities and politics.

The following list includes only the most-recent titles to publish within the series. A list of the full catalogue of titles is available at: https://www.routledge.com/Museum-Meanings/book-series/SE0349

Museums and Sites of Persuasion
Politics, Memory and Human Rights
Edited by Joyce Apsel and Amy Sodaro

Museums, Sexuality, and Gender Activism
Edited by Joshua G. Adair and Amy K. Levin

Museum Diplomacy in the Digital Age
Natalia Grincheva

Museums and Social Change
Challenging the Unhelpful Museum
Edited by Adele Chynoweth, Bernadette Lynch, Klaus Petersen and Sarah Smed

Curating Under Pressure
International Perspectives on Negotiating Conflict and Upholding Integrity
Edited by Janet Marstine and Svetlana Mintcheva

Museums and the Working Class
Edited by Adele Chynoweth

MUSEUMS AND THE WORKING CLASS

Edited by Adele Chynoweth

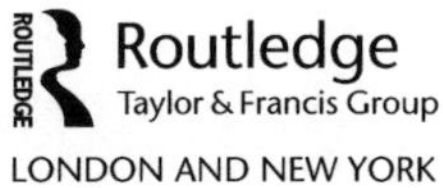

LONDON AND NEW YORK

First published 2022
by Routledge
2 Park Square, Milton Park, Abingdon, Oxon OX14 4RN

and by Routledge
605 Third Avenue, New York, NY 10158

Routledge is an imprint of the Taylor & Francis Group, an informa business

British Library Cataloguing-in-Publication Data
A catalogue record for this book is available from the British Library

Library of Congress Cataloging-in-Publication Data
A catalog record has been requested for this book

ISBN: 978-0-367-46551-3 (hbk)
ISBN: 978-0-367-46547-6 (pbk)
ISBN: 978-1-003-02951-9 (ebk)

DOI: 10.4324/9781003029519

Typeset in Bembo
by Taylor & Francis Books

Cover image (paperback): Union card of canning woman, 1936.
© Museo Marea, Porto do Son, A Coruña, Spain

They say in Harlan County
There are no neutrals there.
You'll either be a union man
Or a thug for J.H. Blair.

Which side are you on?
Which side are you on?
Which side are you on?
Which side are you on?

Oh, workers can you stand it?
Oh, tell me how you can?
Will you be a lousy scab
Or will you be a man?

Which side are you on?
Which side are you on?
Which side are you on?
Which side are you on?

Don't scab for the bosses
Don't listen to their lies
Us poor folks haven't got a chance
Unless we organise

Which side are you on?
Which side are you on?
Which side are you on?
Which side are you on?

Florence Reece, 1931

CONTENTS

FIGURES

CONTRIBUTORS

Meral Akbaş is a sociologist who specialises in gender, social memory, state violence and, recently, critical social heritage studies. After attaining her bachelor's degree from the Department of Sociology at Middle East Technical University, Ankara, Turkey, she began studying prison experiences in Turkey. For her Master's dissertation, she studied memories of female political prisoners who were arrested at Mamak Military Prison after the 1980 military coup in Turkey, which was published as *Mamak Kitabı: Biz Bir Orduya Kafa Tuttuk Arkadaş* [The Book of Mamak: We Challenged an Army My Friend!], as a separate book in Turkish.

Wesley R. Bishop is an Assistant Professor of American History at Marian University in northern Indianapolis. He is currently working on a book about Coxey's Army of 1894, and the influences of populist protests on American politics.

Adele Chynoweth has earned her living as a shop assistant, cabaret performer, night club DJ, call centre operator, union organiser, public servant, and teacher in secondary schools and adult vocational education. Adele also studied theatre direction at the Flinders University Drama Centre and completed her PhD with scholarship support. Her subsequent professional theatre credits led to her work as part of a creative team commissioned to create the Memory Museum for the Centenary of Federation of Australia and later as a curator for the National Museum of Australia. She has also worked as an advisor on museum and community memory projects in Australia and Denmark. Adele was a Lecturer in the Centre for Heritage and Museum Studies at the Australian National University, where she received the Vice Chancellor's Award for Public Policy and Outreach in 2018. Adele is the author of *Goodna Girls: A History of Children in a Queensland Mental Asylum* (ANU Press, 2020) and the co-editor of *Museums and Social Change: Challenging the Unhelpful Museum* (Routledge, 2020). In 2020, Adele was awarded the Medal of the Order of Australia for service to public history. She is also a documentary filmmaker, working with Ronin Films on project development and production.

Silvio Tamaso D'Onofrio has a DSc in Social History from the University of São Paulo. He is the co-ordinator of the REGIONEM research group and a member of the Center for the Study of Epistolography. Internationally: he has published articles and chapters, serves on editorial committees and as a reviewer. His publications include 'A Biographical Essay on Ruth Guimarães: A Black Writer in Brazil in the 1940s' (co-author with Arno Sonderegger) for *Stichproben – Vienna Journal of African Studies* (2020); 'History and historian: Yesterday and today', in *Journal of Comparative Studies* (2019); 'Edgard Cavalheiro, biographer of a generation', in Cavalheiro, Edgard, Valeria Lamego, (eds.), *The correspondence between Monteiro Lobato and Lima Barreto* (2017).

David Fleming is a former Professor of Public History at Liverpool Hope University (UK), having also been Director at Tyne & Wear Museums (UK, 1991–2001) and at National Museums Liverpool (UK, 2001–18), where he was responsible for the creation of the International Slavery Museum and the Museum of Liverpool. He is President of the Federation of International Human Rights Museums, has twice been President of the UK Museums Association, is the former Chair of ICOM's Finance and Resources Committee and former member of ICOM's Ethics Committee and Museum Definitions Committee of ICOM and in Poland, member of the board of Muzeum Slaskie, Katowice. He has advised governments and municipalities around the world on a variety of subjects, including audience development and diversity, urban history, social inclusion, access, ethics, politics, management, leadership and planning, education, activism, marketing and commercial operations. He is a member of the ICOM Committee for Museum Definition, Prospects and Potentials and museum board member in Argentina (International Museum for Democracy, Rosario), and is also a member of the board of the SS Daniel Adamson (a steam-driven working tugboat) and is a member of Liverpool's Beatles Legacy Group.

Martin Hughes is the manager of the Boatbuilding School at the Scottish Maritime Museum, Irvine. In 2015, the School won the Enterprising Museum Award as part of the Scottish Arts and Business Awards. Martin's trainees mentored students at the Prestwick Academy to build a St Ayles Skiff. As a result, the Academy established its own rowing club. The School was also a finalist in the 2019 UK Museums Association Museums Change Lives Awards for its work with local marginalised young people.

Diana James is an Honorary Research Fellow at the School of Humanities and Arts at the Australian National University and the Centre for Aboriginal Studies in Music at Adelaide University. Her research focus is the Indigenous song, story and dance of the Western Desert. Since 1975, she has worked as an applied anthropologist, fluent in Pitjantjatjara, with the Anangu Pitjantjatjara Yankunytjatjara (APY) people in community arts, tourism, oral history translation, local governance and cultural heritage. In 2006, she received her doctorate in anthropology from the Australian National University and has been engaged since as a senior researcher on collaborative projects between the university, museums and Aboriginal organisations. Diana developed with Martu, Ngaanyatjarra, Pitjantjatjara and Yankunytjatjara people the seven-year collaborative research project, Alive with the Dreaming! Songlines of the Western Desert. The research partnership produced several major public outcomes: the Ngintaka Exhibition in 2014 at the South Australian Museum, the Canberra Centenary 2013 performance of the APY traditional opera Kungkarangkalpa Seven Sisters and the nationally acclaimed exhibition Songlines: Tracking the Seven Sisters at the National Museum of Australia in 2017–18.

Jamie Jelinski is an interdisciplinary scholar and PhD candidate in Cultural Studies at Queen's University, where his research analyses the history of professional tattooing in Canada from the 1890s to 1980s. He holds an MA in Art History from Concordia University (2015) and a B.A. in Fine Art from the University of Regina (2013). Jelinski has forthcoming postdoctoral fellowships in the Department of Art History and Communication Studies at McGill University (2019–20) and the Department of History at Dalhousie University (2020–22). His research contributions include published and forthcoming articles in the *Journal of Canadian Studies, Urban History Review, Visual Anthropology*, and *Études/Inuit/Studies*.

Özge Kelekçi is a PhD student in the Department of Philosophy at Middle East Technical University, Ankara, Turkey. She obtained her Master's degree with a dissertation titled *The Disclosure of Petrified Unrest: The Gezi Protests from the Perspectives of Jean-Luc Nancy and Walter Benjamin*. Her focus is on the new subjectivities; bioethics; post-humanity and transhumanity; social/political philosophy; philosophy of death; and queer/feminist philosophy. She has also conducted research studies on memorialisation at the difficult spaces; gender and phenomenology; and new materialism.

Michelle McGrath has worked in museum learning and engagement since 2007. She has worked in a range of museums in London, including Royal Museums Greenwich, the British Museum and the Museum of the Home. In addition to this work, Michelle established the advocacy organisation Museum as Muck in 2018 as a response to the lack of working-class people in the museum sector. Museum as Muck acts as a support network for its members and as a consultancy for museums looking to effect change in the culture of their institution and their recruitment and retainment of working-class talent. Michelle is also a Trustee of the UK Museums Association.

Paolo Magagnoli is a Lecturer in Art History in the School of Communication and Arts at the University of Queensland. He writes widely on modern and contemporary art, with a focus on the history of experimental cinema and documentary photography. He is the author of *Documents of Utopia: The Politics of Experimental Documentary* (Columbia University Press, 2015). His writing has also appeared in *Work: Documents of Contemporary Art* (MIT Press, 2017).

Rabia Nadir is an Assistant Professor and Acting Head of the Centre for Media Studies, Art and Design at the Lahore School of Economics. She has a joint appointment at the Department of Environment Science and Policy Studies where she teaches courses in Urban and Community Studies. She researches contemporary socio-ecological change in urban and rural settlements in Pakistan. Her earlier research focused on the settlement of Pathan migrants in the historic Walled City of Lahore and she is presently looking at development projects, especially for promoting the Walled City of Lahore as a heritage site. Her other fields for urban research include peri-urban villages and small cities of Pakistan. Until 2009, she was a practising architect and instructor in design at the Departments of Architecture and Interior Design, National College of Arts, Lahore.

Philip Payton is Professor of History at Flinders University in Adelaide, Australia, and Emeritus Professor of Cornish & Australian Studies at the University of Exeter in the UK. The author of more than 50 authored or edited books, his recent titles include *The Maritime History of Cornwall* (ed, with Alston Kennerley and Helen Doe, 2014), *Australia in the Great War* (2015), *One and All: Labor and the Radical Tradition in South Australia* (2016), *Emigrants and Historians: Essays in Honour of Eric Richards* (2016), *A History of Sussex* (2017), *Cornwall: A History* (revised ed. 2017), *'Repat': A Concise History of Repatriation in Australia* (2018), *'More than the Last Shilling': Repatriation in Australia, 1994–2018* (2019), *'Cover Plus the Care': A Centenary History of the Defence Service Homes Insurance and Loans Schemes* (2020), *Australia, Migration and Empire* (ed. with Andrekos Varnava, 2019), *The Cornish Overseas: A History of Cornwall's Great Emigration* (revised ed. 2020), *Pictorial History of Australia's Little Cornwall* (revised ed. 2020) and *Cornwall in the Age of Rebellion, 1490–1690* (forthcoming 2021).

Alexander Scott is a cultural historian who specialises in modern urban history. Since 2015, he has been a Lecturer in Modern History at the University of Wales Trinity St David, having previously taught at Lancaster University. His doctoral thesis explored the history and contemporary status of Liverpool's museums, and he has recently had an article on the nineteenth-century exotic animal trade ('The "Missing Link" between Science and Show Business: Exhibiting Gorillas and Chimpanzees in Victorian Liverpool') accepted for publication by the *Journal of Victorian Culture*. Current research projects focus on the politics of housing in 1980s Liverpool and Wales's role in transatlantic slavery.

José Manuel Vázquez Lijó received a PhD in History from the University of Santiago de Compostela (2005). Currently, he holds the position of Associate Professor of History in the Department of History at the Faculty of Humanities and Documentation of the University of A Coruña. He is also the director of the Museo Marea in Porto do Son (Galicia, Spain). He is the author of a number of books and has published more than 20 articles in peer-reviewed journals and conference papers. His principal research interests are social and economic history with a special focus on maritime culture from the sixteenth to the twentieth centuries, which also extends to transatlantic communities and the Galicia region.

Kerry Wilson is Head of Research at the Institute of Cultural Capital, Liverpool John Moores University (UK). She has led a number of research and evaluation projects covering varied aspects of cultural work, its value and impact, for a range of commissioning organisations and funding bodies including the British Council, Arts Council England, the Arts and Humanities Research Council and Economic and Social Research Council. Kerry's research interests, in a cultural sector context, include professional identities, ethics and codes of practice; instrumental value and public policy; and cross-sector communities of practice.

ACKNOWLEDGEMENTS

I grew up in a working-class family in South Australia and became accustomed to external exclusivity. But the capacity to link these experiences to those of others and to a wider socio-political understanding has been supported by many conversations, reading, formal events and networks from my school years and beyond. I am still learning. My rationale for this volume has been nurtured, whether they knew it or not, by Paul Ashton, Richard Benjamin, David Fleming, Françoise McClafferty, Susana Meden, Philip Payton, Jill Sheppard, Laurajane Smith, Jacqueline Z. Wilson, Kerry Wilson and fellow members of the National Tertiary Education Union.

I am also grateful to the Federation of International Human Rights Museums (FIHRM) whose conferences and networks have been an ongoing source of learning and motivation in the pursuit of social justice dialogue and action-based research.

I am indebted to the following scholars who provided expert advice during the process of compiling this volume: Tony Bennett, Joanna Besley, Gary Campbell, Patrizia Cosimo, Elisa DeCourcy, Alexandra Dellios, Cressida Fforde, Gordon Fyfe, Tracy Ireland, Diana James, Mike Jones, Dave O'Brien, Mike Pickering, Laurajane Smith, Matthew Spriggs, Ken Taylor and Kerry Wilson.

Huge thanks to Heidi Lowther, Editor, Museum and Heritage Studies Routledge for generously listening and providing expert leadership in bringing this work to fruition. Thank you, too, to Kangan Gupta, Editorial Assistant at Routledge, for timely and empathetic advice.

It is a privilege to have the support encouragement and inspiration of Series Editors Christina Kreps and Richard Sandell and so to them I extend my profound gratitude.

I extend my heartfelt gratitude to the contributors to this volume, for not only generously sharing their brilliant research but for their persistence amidst profoundly stressful circumstances surrounding an international pandemic. It has been such a pleasure to work with you all.

We are stronger together.

INTRODUCTION

'Which side are you on'? Towards meaningful attention to class in museums

Adele Chynoweth

This volume advocates for a conscious and dedicated awareness, and accompanying practice, of the importance of class in informing the work of all museums. Paying attention to working and poverty classes must not be at the expense of, or instead of, equity in relation to other marginalised characteristics. Instead, class should be understood as a discursive thread that links a range of equity groups and democratic imperatives. The term 'working class' may be somewhat misleading. It is difficult to defend a notion of a single, unified working class, but then again, perhaps it always was. The working class has always been enriched by a diversity of identities. Further, the socio-economic landscape is complex and the study of social class has evolved, but this does not mean that the issue of class is irrelevant. For the purposes of this book, the term 'museums' largely refers to the wider 'GLAM' sector: galleries, libraries, archives and museums. In addition, the policies that inform the conservation, representation and public engagement at heritage sites also have significant implications for the working classes and hence are also included in this volume.

Defining class

Australian scholars Jill Sheppard and Nicholas Biddle identify three waves of social class research. The first is informed by Marx and is largely theoretical, focusing on 'labour, capital, and political power' in class formation and inter-class dynamics,[1] in other words, a theory of social relations within a hierarchy of groups. The second wave, known as the 'Goldthorpe schema' based in sociological theory, concentrates on status of employment. The third wave of social class research is influenced by Pierre Bourdieu's theory of class, which consists of three forms of capital – social, cultural and economic.[2] It is here, through this sociological discussion, that the notion of taste is linked with social groups.[3] As a

DOI: 10.4324/9781003029519-1

result of these scholarly developments, the traditional class categories of 'working', 'middle' and 'upper' class have been revised and broadened. Labour economist Guy Standing identifies several class groups in current existence, among them the 'old' working class and the precariat.[4] Mick Savage et al. also identify seven social classes in Britain today, including the traditional working class, emergent service workers and the precariat.[5] While Australia has prided itself on its 'absence of visible class signifiers',[6] Sheppard and Biddle recognise six classes in Australia, and assert that the study of class is important and relevant.[7] Among them is the precariat class, which has emerged from global capitalism and austerity measures. The precariat endures insecure employment and debt as well as a lack of belonging, and is diverse and divided. The precariat is the migrant worker, the single mother, the teenager in the internet café, the backpacker, the environmental activist, for example, and what they all have in common is that 'labour is instrumental (to live), opportunistic (taking what comes) and precarious (insecure)'.[8]

One of the problems with the contemporary discourse of social class is that the term 'class' is often eradicated. Sheppard and Biddle note, 'researchers now commonly talk about intergenerational mobility, social cohesion, social capital, and entrenched disadvantage: each an important concept on its own. However, … objective and subjective measures of social class are still very much present in Australian society'.[9] Media scholars Tony Moore, Mark Gibson and Catharine Lumby also note the absence of class in Australian policy discourse, in politics and in academic scholarship and advocate for class to be viewed as culture and not merely as 'socio-economic categories' that negatively stigmatise low-income communities by labelling them as 'disadvantaged'.[10] The Australian Government's Department for Education, Skills and Employment includes 'low socioeconomic status' in its equity groups as part of its higher education policy but this is addressed in the absence of the terminology of class.[11] David Fleming in his chapter in this volume also notes that the UK's occupation-based National Statistics Socio-economic Classification superficially serves a 'society [that] continues to strive to classify people for marketing purposes'.

Current discussions emphasising the discourse of class is also evident beyond English-speaking countries. The Association of Indian Labour Historians was founded in New Delhi in 1996. Since the late-1970s, the History Workshop movement throughout South Africa reveals a strong emphasis on labour history and the working classes. The 'Mundos do Trabalho' (Worlds of Labour) was established as part of Brazil's Associação Nacional de História in 2000. There is also the Pakistan Institute for Labour Education and Research (PILER). These are responses by labour historians who know that the working classes are growing[12] and not 'extinct' at all. But, of course, discussions concerning the working and poverty classes are not confined to the discipline of history, and in relation to museology, the discourse of class has implications for *all* genres of museums, beyond social history to natural history, science, technology and industry.

A broad social justice framework

This volume does not position the discourse of class as an isolated issue for museums. Paying attention to class need not, and should not, be at the expense of other predicaments that have implications for the museum sector such as climate change, threats to democracy, (de)colonisation, displacement and social disconnection.[13] In 2009, Robert R. Janes noted that museums were rarely mentioned in the literature that warned about climate change, which exemplified for him how museums had become irrelevant as 'social institutions'.[14] In 2017, Newell et al. asked 'how can museums collaborate in building communities able to engage with and respond to climate change?'[15] They also note how, recently, museums have exhibited climate change and the emergence of museums devoted to climate change.[16]

Attention has been drawn to an epistemic crisis, exemplified by the work of the RAND Corporation, a US not-for-profit research organisation, that applies the term 'truth decay' to its identification of 'heightened disagreement about facts' and the 'blurred line between opinion and fact' as threats to democracy.[17] This global democracy recession is also characterised by 'a steep rise in far-right nationalism'[18] and power-sharing democracies being replaced by governments comprising leaders who are 'masters of deception and seduction'.[19] Some political scholars may debate the existence of this democratic recession[20] while its ramifications echo through the museum and heritage sectors. American sociologist Norman K. Denzin asks in relation to the failure of the United States' Bush administration to stop the destruction of museums in Iraq, 'Is this what American democracy stands for?... With the death of culture in Iraq comes violence and a new American enemy, one of our making'.[21] In relation to knowledge, museums aim to be more participatory and this in turn means that 'visitors are more and more able to question the curators' truths'.[22] However, this does not relinquish the museum's role in providing necessary information: 'Simply inviting the visitor to state opinions based on the same knowledge as entering the museum makes no one smarter'.[23] Arts sector commentators Janet Marstine and Svetlana Mintcheva draw attention to the 'tightening of cultural controls in authoritarian regimes' to support their assertion that 'developing curatorial agency to negotiate self-censorship has particular urgency'.[24]

Our society is also experiencing a critical loneliness epidemic, which has serious, negative impacts on physical and mental health.[25] Research has indicated that, whether intended or not, museums have an important function in facilitating social interaction.[26] Given the social role of museums, there is a clear mandate for the sector to be positively address severe community disconnection. The heritage and museum sectors have also sought to understand and reveal the significance of LGBTQ+ narratives, exemplified by the *Prejudice and Pride* which explores this living history in places owned by the National Trust (UK).[27] Museums have also extended their attention to the needs of disabled people beyond a dominant, conventional preoccupation with visitor access or as exhibited 'objects of curiosity' to a meaningful exhibited representation of their narratives, informed by the experiences of the disabled themselves.[28] Attention to human remains in museum collections throughout the world is a social justice imperative demanding respectful and consultative repatriation to Indigenous communities[29] or as a means to challenge 'reductive stereotypes' of disabled people.[30] Communities have made claims from museums for the repatriation or restitution of objects pertaining to their cultural heritage.[31]

Museum Detox, the UK network of Black, Asian and Minority Ethnic (BAME) museum workers, formed in 2014, confronts racism in museum employment and aims to decolonise museum practice.[32] Museum Hue in the United States was founded in 2015 to support and advocate for 'Black, Indigenous and other People of Color'.[33] Museums have also represented the impact of displacement in Holocaust and memory museums, for example.[34] However, the cultural sector has also been responsible for the displacement of people. When culture is used to transform sites, the 'effect of regeneration may be to squeeze out poorer residents of communities'.[35] The term 'heritage dispossession' is also used to refer to the process of eviction of underprivileged people when certain areas are redeveloped in order to support heritage tourism.[36] The intersectional stance of this book[37] argues that the understanding and support of diversity and democracy through practice does not excuse the issue of class being ignored or placed on the backburner of the work of any museum or heritage site.

This volume affirms the necessary push for museums to be at the forefront of an activist and socially relevant practice and argues for the working and poverty classes to be granted visible agency in museums. The intersection between class and the cultural sector has been the subject of scholarship evident in Tony Bennett et al.'s *Culture, Class, Distinction* (2009) and the work of Dave O'Brien et al. (2014). In 2003, Bobbie Oliver and Andrew Reeves co-edited a special thematic edition of the international journal *Labor History*, which examined ways in which working life was represented, or not, throughout Australian museums and galleries. This edition includes courageous and substantiated accounts from a range of scholars on examples of exhibited labour history throughout Australia, including descriptions of associated controversies. *Museums and the Working Class* extends this discussion both internationally and beyond the bounds of exhibited representation. Laurajane Smith et al.'s *Heritage, Labour and the Working Classes* (2011) examines how working-class communities and labour organisations use heritage and also identifies where working-class heritage is excluded. This volume includes the heritage sector and expands this discussion to include museums, archives and libraries. Nina Simon's *The Art of Relevance* (2016) and C. A. Scott's (ed.) *Museums and Public Value: Creating Sustainable Futures* (2016) exemplify the international push to make museums relevant to the public. This volume argues the case for the perspectives of the working and poverty classes to be central to this ambition. *Museums and the Working Class* is also inspired by Tony Bennett's research in *The Birth of the Museum* (1995) concerning the emergence of the public museum as a means to reform the behaviour of the working class. How museums still respond to the working classes is central to the purpose of this volume.

While there is extensive literature in which scholars and practitioners from the museum sector observe the imperative quest for diversity, such declarations co-exist with current sociological commentary. For example, Owen Jones' *Chavs* (2011) and Matt Wray's *Not Quite White: White Trash and the Boundaries of Whiteness* (2006) note the contempt for certain constructed sub-groups within the working class. Richard Sandell and Eithne Nightingale's co-edited volume *Museums, Equality and Social Justice* (2012) includes a chapter by British journalist and academic Gary Younge, 'The Margins and the Mainstream', in which he draws attention to the importance of nuancing in identity politics. For example, he notes:

> One of the problems with diversity, as currently understood, is that it can often take precious little account of economic difference – an omission that leaves the white working class stranded without a sponsor. In the world of multi-culturalism, as it is often portrayed, they are assumed to have no culture. They are told their whiteness is a mark of power they have never felt and a signifier for potential bigotry they may not harbour. Caught in a pincer between the battle for scarce resources and the battle for equality, the white working class might then feel concerned – forced to argue not for more resources but against 'others' getting their cut. Under those conditions they experience their race and class not as interlocking identities but as a besieged grievance which the Right are only too happy to leverage for political gain.[38]

Museums and the Working Class continues, applies and extends discussions concerning the cultural sector to serve to ensure that the working class and the diversity throughout are not left behind.

Class-based prejudice

Any quest to extend museum inclusion to the working and poverty classes is, to put it euphemistically, a 'challenge'. This push is positioned against a wider societal backdrop characterised by elitist identity trends that are driving a wedge through the working and poverty classes, dividing them into deserving and undeserving sub-groups. The construction and demonisation of a white working class is an apt example. It denotes a false class because the working and poverty classes are culturally diverse and yet derogatory terms such as 'chavs', 'scum', 'chav scum', 'white trash', 'trailer trash' or 'bogans', in everyday conversation, are unlikely to be challenged and serve to reinforce elitism and associated privileged notions of good taste.[39] Television programming includes 'poverty porn', unsympathetic voyeuristic television portraits of those cast as the undeserving poor,[40] evident in *Skint* and *Benefits Street* on Channel 4 in the UK[41] and *Struggle Street* in Australia. The abuse of those living in poverty is acceptable in ways that would not be tolerated for other marginalised groups.[42] Lynsey Hanley notes, '"Chavscum.co.uk", a website hosting reams of virulent abuse against the "undeserving poor", would be shut down immediately if the same dehumanizing language were to be directed at people of another colour or different religion. But because its targets are merely of another class, we can log on and have a good laugh'.[43] Constructing a white working class as separate from their diverse colleagues and then insulting them is justified on the basis that it is a defence against bigotry and racism[44] but it may be argued that such validation is an attempt at disguising snobbery. British journalist Johann Hari states, 'It's one of the ways people have made their snobbery socially acceptable… by acting as though they are defending immigrants from the "ignorant" white working class'.[45]

In Australia, it wasn't all that long ago that working-class culture was celebrated. In the 1980s, former rigger Paul Hogan as Crocodile Dundee as well as the bands AC/DC and Cold Chisel were not only applauded but identified as crucial cultural contributions. Now, the notion of class is largely absent in Australian policy discourse, politics and academic scholarship.[46] The Hawke and Keating Governments in Australia addressed ethnic and cultural diversity in their social policies but none of the categories were based on income.[47] Academic scholarship, too, turned away from the discourse of class at the end of the 1980s, fuelled by the need to address inequity in the areas of 'gender, sexuality, ethnicity, indigeneity and disability' and informed by a refocus in cultural studies. This pluralism in understanding diversity was an imperative in Australia. Moore et al. note 'the urgency of political questions around multiculturalism, indigeneity and postcolonialism, and because of the way in which new intellectual formations of the 1970s and 1980s [that] came to be associated with a distinctive "Australian" style of work… Australian cultural studies never had a "class moment"'.[48] This constellation of diversity resulted in the marginalisation of class from academic discourse[49] and in turn, from the work of the Australian museum sector. This book argues for diversity in the museum and heritage sectors to include attention to the poverty and working classes as a conscious discourse and meaningful approach.

It is too easy for museums to romanticise the working class through limiting their representation in the past – those sepia-toned images, as Michelle McGrath describes in Chapter 12, 'of men up north [UK] in the 1960s with their flat caps doing heavy labour in the mining industry'. Such exhibited photographs can be a means to disengage visitors from current struggles. While traipsing through a house museum, we may also catch sight of a cornered mannequin, inanimate beneath a mop cap, apron and vacant stare. Displays of trade union banners are an apt reminder of past struggle. Yet, too, these faded icons with unravelling tassels seemingly symbolise the loosening of a tight fist that previously gripped them. A glass display case both imposes a restrained stillness that negates the movement of the march that once impelled it and reduces the mise-en-scene to that of a constructed mausoleum for passers-by to mourn as if a proud working-class movement is dead.

Paying meaningful, multi-discursive attention to class with contemporary relevance is far from inconceivable. The HumanKind project at Calke Abbey, National Trust (UK), for example, comprises a series of installations that link site-based historical narratives with the current loneliness and includes the story of Harriet Phillip, a domestic servant and unwed mother who could not read or write.[50] This volume shares other examples and, conversely, where opportunities to pay attention to the working and poverty classes are ignored, or more regrettably, where the working class is disparaged. It is not unusual for the working or poverty classes to be attacked.[51]

Working class habits are scrutinised through a range of responses, including the subtlety of the 'inspecting gaze',[52] commonly understood as 'looking down their nose'. In order to draw attention to such disapproval, the titles of each section of this book reference the language and associated contempt. Part I of this volume, 'Shut out', concerns challenges to those museums and archives whose practices prevent access to the working class. Part II, 'Shut up', addresses the exclusion of class-based narratives and policies in museums. Part III, 'Know your place', considers the responses at heritage sites. Part IV, 'Answering back', illustrates how the experiences of the working and poverty classes can enhance the work of the museum and, in turn, the wider community.

Class matters arising

Classless multiculturalism

This volume identifies key areas in which class matters require attention. Through its intersectional stance, it refutes any classless multiculturalism that may dominate the methodology of museum and heritage sectors in their attempt to be diverse and inclusive. In Chapter 10, I acknowledge, as part of my overall analysis of the $18 million refurbishment of the Hyde Park Barracks Museum in Sydney, Australia, the commitment by senior museum staff to promote reconciliation with the First Peoples of Australia. This obligation is realised in the Museum's exhibition module concerning the Myall Creek Massacre in 1838, interpreted through a superficial binary of race relations, without consideration of class analysis. As a result, the necessary condemnation of the perpetrators was confined to 'white' convicts, excluding the privileged free settler who was the ringleader and a British Jamaican convict who were also responsible for the mass murder.[53]

In Chapter 6, Paolo Magagnoli presents a comparative analysis of two photographic exhibitions at the State Library of Queensland, Australia, including *Plantation Voices*, which told 'the story of the South Sea Islanders who were forcefully brought to Queensland in the mid-nineteenth century to work as indentured labour for cotton and sugar cane plantations' through 'a "culturalist" notion of recognition'. Magagnoli reasons that this limiting interpretative lens disavowed the economic struggles of this group that endure in the present. The much-needed representation of this crucial analysis, Magagnoli explains, could have been fulfilled if 'the exhibition's conceptual framework had included the notion of class'.

In Chapter 15, anthropologist Diana James analyses the controversy in 2014 of the *Ngintaka Exhibition* fuelled by the powerful Murdoch Press resulting in Pitjantjatjara Yankunytjatjara traditional owners gathering outside the South Australian Museum in Adelaide to protest the proposed closure of the exhibition. James makes the case for the discourse of class, as well as race, to be brought to the understanding of the dynamics of privilege that dominate the commodification of modern Aboriginal art in the western fine art market and in the positioning of 'experts' who influence 'the national cultural narratives of museums, universities, literature and the media'. Further, James challenges white, western- dominated notions of 'work' through her emphasis on the importance of 'Aboriginal traditional work that is generated by and sustains living on country'.[54]

Absent presence

The notion of 'absent presence' is a recurring motif in this volume: an application of Derrida's discussion that nothing exists beyond the text.[55] In the museum and heritage sectors, the text exists in the representation of displays, exhibitions, collections, conservation – what is kept, exhibited, conserved, refurbished and who visits these sites and who is employed to work in them. There is meaning in the omissions of curatorial and heritage work because these gaps contain the traces of the missing. In Chapter 11, in their analysis of the SEKA Paper Museum in Izmit, Turkey, authors Meral Akbaş and Özge Kelekçi note the absence of factory workers and the cacophony of machines that have all been rendered silent. Rabia Nadir, in Chapter 8, draws attention to the Walled City of Lahore in Pakistan, which is being redeveloped for the purposes of global tourism. This heritage policy threatens the rights of poor residents to inhabit 'prime, urban land' and, in turn, their means to livelihood.

This volume pays attention to working-class narratives that have been overlooked. In Chapter 4, Philip Payton writes a compelling case for the need for the museum sector to recognise South Australia's Labor movement, led by the emigrant Cornish mining community. While this history has been acknowledged by UNESCO World Heritage, this international recognition has not been mirrored by the National Museum of Australia or in any of the museums operated by the History Trust of South Australia. Such visibility should not confine working-class struggle to the past. In Chapter 9, Wesley R. Bishop evaluates the collegial action of academics, labour leaders and other members of the community that saved the family home of US socialist politician Eugene Victor Debs from demolition in 1962. Bishop argues that the public history associated with Debs should be confrontative, where past struggles are connected with the present. This volume also echoes the observation of Amy K. Levin in her discussion concerning museums, sexuality and gender, that 'the recognition of women in museums is not old news'.[56] In Chapter 7, José Manuel Vázquez Lijó, director of the Marea Museum, which opened in 2012 in Porto do Son in the northwest of Spain, discusses his work in redressing the invisibility of women workers in the history of Galicia's maritime industry.

Hands on

The notion of absence in this volume does not only concern exhibited representation museums or redevelopment within the heritage sector. Paying attention to class means not only acknowledging content and narratives but also aesthetics and the mode of representation itself. Here, the volume contributes to critical discussions concerning museums and the attention economy. The latter term refers to human attention being cast as a 'quantifiable commodity', the cornerstone of operations for the marketplace of art and objects.[57] This mode of consumption is central to the conventional museum. Alternatively, there have been considerations concerning how museums may be places of useful activity – not places of mere participatory events but as a source of essential contribution to everyday life.[58] There is criticism of the prescription of Ritalin to children who are not suited to the passive pedagogy of the bourgeois classroom.[59] In a working-class livelihood, characterised by making and repairing, lies a rich source of instruction for any museum or heritage site that wishes to revise its privileged emphasis on the commodified gaze.

The quest for the useful museum can be traced back to the birth of the public museum itself, which was developed in the late eighteenth and early nineteenth centuries in order to reform and civilise the behaviour of the 'working-class man'.[60] In Chapter 1, Alexander Scott relates the challenge from new museum visitors to the bourgeois expectation of passive observation. In 1870, the curator of Liverpool's new public museum reported to the museum committee the 'inconvenience' caused by 'young people' who used evening visits to socialise instead of viewing objects. Scott also recounts a poignant and successful plea by an Irish family against the prohibition on touching objects.

Public museums were established and opened their doors in the hope that, as Tony Bennett notes, 'the rough and raucous might learn to civilize themselves'.[61] Their status as 'instruments of state power' (to borrow Alexander Scott's phrase from his chapter) prevented the middle class from learning about alternative modes of interactions with visitors and artefacts. In Chapter 2, David Fleming elucidates this ongoing dynamic with his scrutiny of a range of cultural forms which he casts as created from the 'vantage point' of privilege, a position characterised by both fear and ignorance of the working class. Fleming dedicated his leadership in museums to redress this elitism, through dogged dedication amidst a complex policy landscape. The legacy of his commitment to social justice is exemplified in Chapter 14. Here, Kerry Wilson evaluates *House of Memories*, the 'multiple award-winning dementia awareness programme led by National Museums Liverpool (NML) in the UK' and substantiates its success as the result of 'the active process of co-design and production in collaboration with people with dementia and their carers from traditional working-class communities in the city of Liverpool'. Further, Wilson emphasises the power of museum objects 'to stimulate and inspire enhanced communication and connection between carers and people with dementia'. This volume, then, brings a class discourse to current discussions concerning the therapeutic value of museum objects.[62]

In Chapter 13, Martin Hughes, the manager of the Boatbuilding School at the Scottish Maritime Museum, also notes the capacity of museum-based interaction with objects to change the lives of young people who bear the brunt of intergenerational unemployment and/or struggle with addiction. Here, however, it is these trainee boatbuilders that *create* large seaworthy 'objects' from the ground up. Both Martin Hughes' work and Rabia Nadir's ethnographic analysis of local artisans in Lahore (Chapter 8) corroborate similar contemporary discussions, which note that while capitalism has resulted in manufacturing jobs being outsourced offshore, localised manual labour is still relevant.[63] Moreover, Hughes' and Nadir's contributions to this volume locate this imperative as central to the policies of the museum and heritage sectors. An understanding of the importance of trades is not a mere exercise in nostalgia and, conversely, a disregard for the same is not only an act of snobbery.[64] Philosopher and mechanic Matthew Crawford states, 'Grime under the fingernails, bodily involvement with the machines we use entails a kind of agency'.[65]

Ethics

This volume also makes the case for extending critical attention to human remains in museum collections so that the remains of those from the working-class deceased are also considered. In Chapter 5, Jamie Jelinski's research reveals the practice of medical practitioners and criminologists who have collected the remains of deceased perpetrators and victims of crime, including tattooed skin from working-class people, which have been collected and displayed by museums. Jelinski exemplifies museum ethical guidelines that include standards for the handling of the human remains from Indigenous communities but excludes principles for the treatment of human remains of other groups such as non-Indigenous, working-class people.

Museums and the Working Class also has implications for how museums conduct 'stakeholder engagement', or, to use a less corporate term: genuine community collaboration. Contributors to this volume reveal their frustrations in their interactions with museums while undertaking their work. Museums may publicly espouse their commitment to research, public engagement, access and inclusion, but in this volume there are personal accounts of museums instituting barriers to scholarly inquiry. Jelinski reports in his chapter that a museum's response to his request for more information about displayed human remains was 'obstructive' and was followed by the Museum's removal of the items from public display only days after his inquiry. In Chapter 3, Silvio Tamaso D'Onofrio recounts his efforts to find a cultural institution to accept his researched and curated collection of material that belonged to Brazilian working-class writer Edgard Cavalheiro. He notes that the governing body of one archival organisation lied to him by saying that they had no space, only later accepting a much larger collection of an internationally famous musician. His autoethnographic analysis prompts his associated hypotheses concerning ubiquity of this elitism throughout the wider archival sector. There is a call through this volume for museums to understand that ethical behaviour is not served by avoidance of issues that may be deemed controversial or challenging but instead may start with honest and authentic interactions with the public.

Employment

Museums are being challenged to critically examine their power relationships and how these are played out in what they collect, whose stories they exhibit and who is made to feel welcome in their halls,[66] including who is employed. Sociologists Orian Brook, Dave O'Brien and Mark Taylor have found that the cultural sector is highly inequitable, as evident in who produces and consumes artforms (a minor segment of the population) as well as its precarious and elite workforce. They observe, 'creative jobs are thus highly exclusive. Culture has a class problem. This class problem sits alongside the other, well-known, problems of gender and racial exclusions in cultural and creative occupations'.[67] David Fleming, in Chapter 2, applies his term 'pattern of privilege' to his analysis of the significant absence of working-class people in British museums, a privilege that is also perpetuated throughout museum governance. In Chapter 12, Michelle McGrath, who describes her origins as 'benefits class', undertook extensive volunteer work in museums, despite her relevant qualifications, before being offered paid employment. Through her establishment of *Museum as Muck*, the UK network of working-class museum professionals, she and her 'Mucker' colleagues collectively apply their lived experience to affect change in the museum sector through running workshops, staging interventions and collecting data to address the disparity inherent in museums' working populations.

This volume does not suggest that *all* museums do not pay *any* meaningful attention to class. There are case studies throughout the following pages that exemplify life-changing engagement. Beyond this text, it is important to note, for example, the extensive work of people's and workers' museums throughout the world, the push from communities to gain a voice in the cultural sector and the organisations that listen. But there are contributors here whose research and lived experience denote struggle of virtually life-denying proportions, relentless toil veiled by invisible prejudice. Such case studies should not be dismissed with platitudinal references to unsubstantiated 'what abouts'. Paying meaningful attention to class involves taking notice of existing research and undertaking more.

The authors have come together through the pages of this volume, in some cases, through an international call for papers. For others, their contributions followed opportune and enriched meetings, through places of work, at international conferences or through social media. One author came to this book following family association through his research. Such networks while vast and relevant are not internationally or culturally even. It is hoped, then, that *Museums and the Working Class* marks an opening for further discussions from countries that are absent in this volume.

'Will you be a lousy scab or...?'

Museums and the Working Class is a manifesto for change through the voices of the working class in exhibitions, collections, conservation policy, community collaboration, programmes, visitor engagement, employment and governance. Florence Reece's father was killed while working in a coal mine in Tennessee. Later, with her husband Sam, also a coal miner, she helped organise miners. The song that Florence wrote, 'Which Side Are You On?' became the anthem of the coal miner's strike of 1931 in Harlan County, Kentucky.[68] The song was revived as part of the radical folk song movement in the United States after the Second World War.[69]

The lyrics make it quite clear that there is no neutral position amidst strike action. Anyone who crosses the picket line is, as the song states, a 'scab for the bosses'. Anyone who doesn't support a union's work to organise is a scab. In recent years, we have also been appropriately reminded that throughout the museum sector, there is no neutrality there either.[70] This volume extends the scab label to those cultural organisations that accept public funds (albeit reduced in many countries), to which workers have contributed through their hard-earned taxes, and yet refuse to pay meaningful attention to their living history. Public museums, since their inception, have promoted their role as the driver of social transformation while perpetuating inequality.[71] Too often, museums drive a divisive wedge between marginalised groups, refuting that class matters and ignoring those who are deemed to have no culture. *Museums and the Working Class* is a manifesto that stands in opposition to such snobbery.

We, the contributors, stand together to ask all museums, archival organisations, libraries and heritage sites throughout the world, that when it comes to class matters:

Which side are you on?

Notes

1 Sheppard and Biddle, "Class, Capital, and Identity in Australian Society," 501.
2 Sheppard and Biddle, "Class, Capital, and Identity in Australian Society," 502.
3 Bennett, "Introduction to the Routledge Classics Edition," xvii.
4 • Elite: 'absurdly rich global citizens'
• Salariats: in 'stable full-time employment'
• Proficians: a combination of the terms 'professional' and 'technician', referring to those who can market their skills on well-paid contracts.
• 'Old' working class: industrial labourers
• Precariat: the unemployed or insecurely employed who distrust the state (Standing, *The Precariat*, 7–9).
5 • Elite
• Established middle class
• Technical middle class
• New affluent workers
• Traditional working class
• Emergent service workers
• Precariat (Savage et al., "A New Model of Social Class?," 230).
6 Sheppard and Biddle, "Class, Capital, and Identity in Australian Society," 500.
7 • Precariat
• Ageing workers
• New workers
• Established middle
• Emerging affluent
• Established affluent (Sheppard and Biddle, "Class, Capital, and Identity in Australian Society," 506, 513).
8 Standing, *The Precariat*, 15.
9 Sheppard and Biddle, "Class, Capital, and Identity in Australian Society," 513.

10 Moore et al., "Recovering the Australian Working Class," 218.
11 These equity groups comprise non-English-speaking backgrounds (NESB), students with a disability, women in non-traditional areas, those who identify as Indigenous, from low SES (socio-economic status) locations based on postcode of permanent home residence and those from regional and remote locations based on postcode of permanent home residence (Australian Government Department for Education, Skills and Employment, *2017 Section 11 – Equity Groups*).
12 van der Linden, "Speaking Globally," 184, 185, 186.
13 I am indebted to Richard Hil for several of the following observations, provided in his analytical inventory of the socio-political crises emerging from neoliberalism in his lecture as part of the National Tertiary Education Union's Australian Capital Territory Division Seminar Series 'Matters of Concern', 27 September 2019, The Australian National University.
14 Janes, *Museums in a Troubled World*, 26.
15 Newell et al., "Introduction," 32.
16 Newell et al., "Introduction," 36–37.
17 RAND, "Truth Decay."
18 Wajid and Minott, "Detoxing and Decolonising Museums," 27.
19 Keane, *The New Despotism*, 14.
20 For example, Diamond, "Facing Up to the Democratic Recession"; Levitsky and Way, "The Myth of Democratic Recession."
21 Denzin, "The War on Culture," 138–39.
22 Rekdal, "Why a Book on Museums and Truth?" xxiii.
23 Rekdal, "Why a Book on Museums and Truth?" xxiv.
24 Marstine and Mintcheva, "Introduction."
25 In 2018, a survey conducted by the Australian Psychological Society and Swinburne University of Technology found that one in four Australians feel lonely and 'nearly 30% of Australians rarely or never feel part of a group of friends' and that loneliness is associated with a suite of physical symptoms (*Australian Loneliness Report*, 7, 9, 15). In the UK, the Jo Cox Commission was established in 2017 in order to combat loneliness (Jo Cox Foundation, *Combating Loneliness One Conversation at a Time: A Call to Action*).
26 Katifori et al, "Cultivating Mobile-Mediated Social Interaction in the Museum"; Falk and Dierking, *The Museum Experience Revisited*, 171.
27 For example, Sandell et al., *Prejudice and Pride*.
28 Sandell and Dodd, *Activist Practice*.
29 Fforde and Hubert, "Indigenous Human Remains and Changing Museum Ideology," 83–96.
30 Sandell et al., "Beggars, Freaks and Heroes?," 17.
31 Duthie, "The British Museum"; Whitby-Last, "Legal Impediments to the Repatriation of Cultural Objects to Indigenous Peoples."
32 Wajid and Minott, "Detoxing and Decolonising Museums," 27.
33 Museum Hue, "About the Founders."
34 Lleras et al., "Memory Exercises"; Bernard-Donals, *Figures of Memory*.
35 Brook et al., *Culture is Bad for You*, 35.
36 Janoschka and Sequera, "Gentrification in Latin America," 1182.
37 Kimberlé Crenshaw's notion of intersectionality (1989) aims to assist the acknowledgement of multiple forms of inequality such as race and gender.
38 Younge, "The Margins and the Mainstream," 109.
39 See Jones, *Chavs*; Newitz and Wray, *White Trash*. The term 'bogan' emerged in the 1980s, considered to have originated in the Western suburbs of Melbourne, Australia (Gibson, "Welcome to Bogan-ville," 63).
40 The notion of the 'undeserving poor' dates back to Elizabethan law which served to classify poor people in order to determine 'the limits of our social obligations' (Katz, *The Undeserving Poor*, 4).
41 Jones, *Chavs*, xiv–xv.

42 Jones, *Chavs*, 1.
43 Hanley, *Estates*, 176.
44 Jones, *Chavs*, 8.
45 Jones, *Chavs*, 116.
46 Moore et al., "Recovering the Australian Working Class," 218.
47 Moore et al., "Recovering the Australian Working Class," 221.
48 Moore et al., "Recovering the Australian Working Class," 225.
49 There were exceptions to this as seen in the scholarship throughout the 1980s and 1990s of Ann Curthoys, Anne Game, Rosemary Pringle, R. W. Connell et al., Marcia Langton, Andrew Jacubowicz, Stephen Castles, Mary Kalantzis et al. and Ghassan Hage who examined how class interacted with 'gendered, ethnic and other identities' (Moore et al., "Recovering the Australian Working Class," 225–26).
50 RCMG and National Trust "HumanKind."
51 Michell et al., "Introduction," vii.
52 Hanley citing Foucault, "Respectable," 45.
53 This scapegoating of white, working class people for race-based genocide can be elucidated by philosopher Shannon Sullivan:

'[T]he white desire for innocence is implicated in the middle-class dumping of responsibility for racism on lower- and working-class white people, who are posited as the true source of ongoing racial injustice. Lower-class white people allegedly are the bad white people who are too unintelligent or unenlightened to know that people of color aren't inferior to white people. With their disdain, scorn, and even hatred of lower-class white people, good white liberals often use their guilt and shame to exploit class differences among whites, which allows them to efface their own complicity in white racism and white domination' (Shannon, *Good White People*, 6).

54 'Living on country' refers to the 'deep responsibilities' of Aboriginal peoples 'developed over 40,000 years, to live on and care for their traditional Countries. Land connects Aboriginal peoples to their sense of self and wellbeing, and represents part of their identity that has carried through generations' (Mohamed, "'Living on Country Represents More than a 'Lifestyle Choice'.")
55 Derrida, *Of Grammatology*, 158.
56 Levin, "Introduction," 17.
57 Crogan and Kingsley, "Paying Attention," 1.
58 Hudson, "Building a User-Generated Museum."
59 Crawford, *Shop Class as Soulcraft*, 73.
60 Bennett, *The Birth of the Museum*, 19, 31.
61 Bennett, *The Birth of the Museum*, 28.
62 Exemplified by Cowan et al., *Museum Objects, Health and Healing*.
63 Crawford, *Shop Class as Soulcraft*, 3.
64 Crawford, *Shop Class as Soulcraft*, 8, 32.
65 Crawford, *Shop Class as Soulcraft*, 63.
66 For example, Sandell, "Museums as Agents of Social Inclusion"; Sandell, *Museums, Society, Inequality*; Sandell and Nightingale (eds), *Museums, Equality and Social Justice*.
67 Brook et al., *Culture is Bad for You*, 63.
68 Ackley, "In the Footsteps of Mother Jones," 234.
69 Weissman, *Which Side Are You On?* 7.
70 Autry, "Museums Are Not Neutral"; Fleming, "Do Museums Change Lives?," 74.
71 Brook et al., *Culture is Bad for You*, 30.

Bibliography

Ackley, H. Adam. "In the Footsteps of Mother Jones, Mothers of the Miners – Florence Reece, Molly Jackson, and Sarah Ogan Gunning." In *Women of the Mountain South:*

Identity, Work, and Activism, edited by Connie Park Rice and Marie Tedesco, 226–241. Athens (Ohio): Ohio University Press, 2015.

Australian Government Department for Education, Skills and Employment. "2017 Section 11 – Equity Groups." Accessed 14 June 2020. https://docs.education.gov.au/documents/2017-section-11-equity-groups.

Australian Psychological Society and Swinburne University of Technology. *Australian Loneliness Report: A Survey Exploring the Loneliness Levels of Australians and the Impact of Their Health and Wellbeing*. Accessed 22 November 2020. https://psychweek.org.au/wp/wp-content/uploads/2018/11/Psychology-Week-2018-Australian-Loneliness-Report.pdf.

Autry, La Tanya S. "Museums Are Not Neutral." Artstuffmatters. Accessed 20 December 2020. https://artstuffmatters.wordpress.com/museums-are-not-neutral/.

Bennett, Tony. "Introduction to the Routledge Classics Edition." In *Distinction: A Social Critique of the Judgement of Taste* by Pierre Bourdieu (translated by Richard Nice), xvii–xxiii. London and New York: Routledge, 2010.

Bennett, Tony. *The Birth of the Museum: History, Theory, Politics*. Abingdon and New York: Routledge, 1995.

Bennett, Tony, Mike Savage, Elizabeth Bortolaia Silva, Alan Warde, Modesto Gayo-Cal, and David Wright. *Culture, Class, Distinction*. London and New York: Routledge, 2009.

Bernard-Donals, Michael. *Figures of Memory: The Rhetoric of Displacement at the United States Holocaust Memorial Museum*. Albany: State University of New York Press, 2016.

Brook, Orian, Dave O'Brien, and Mark Taylor. *Culture is Bad for You: Inequality in the Cultural and Creative Industries*. Manchester: Manchester University Press, 2021.

Cowan, Brenda, Ross Laird, and Jason McKeown. *Museum Objects, Health and Healing: The Relationship between Exhibitions and Wellness*. London and New York: Routledge, 2020.

Crawford, Matthew B. *Shop Class as Soulcraft: An Inquiry into the Value of Work*. New York: Penguin, 2010.

Crenshaw, Kimberlé. "Demarginalizing the Intersection of Race and Sex: A Black Feminist Critique of Antidiscrimination Doctrine, Feminist Theory and Antiracist Politics." *University of Chicago Legal Forum* (1989): 139–167.

Crogan, Patrick, and Samuel Kingsley. "Paying Attention: Towards a Critique of the Attention Economy." *Culture Machine* 13 (2012): 1–29. Accessed 30 December 2020. https://culturemachine.net/wp-content/uploads/2019/01/463-1025-1-PB.pdf.

Denzin, Norman K. "The War on Culture, The War on Truth." *Cultural Studies - Critical Methodologies* 4, no. 2 (2004): 137–142.

Derrida, Jacques. *Of Grammatology*. Translated by Gayatri Spivak. Maryland: Johns Hopkins University Press, 1997.

Diamond, Larry. "Facing up to the Democratic Recession." *Journal of Democracy* 26, no. 1 (2015): 151–155.

Duthie, Emily. "The British Museum: An Imperial Museum in a Post-Imperial World." *Public History Review* 18 (2011): 12–25.

Falk, John H., and Lynn D. Dierking. *The Museum Experience Revisited*. London and New York: Routledge, 2013.

Fforde, Cressida, and Jane Hubert. "Indigenous Human Remains and Changing Museum Ideology." In *A Future for Archaeology: The Past in the Present*, edited by Robert Layton, Stephen Shennan, and Peter Stone, 83–96. London: UCL Press, 2006.

Fleming, David. "Do Museums Change Lives? Ninth Stephen Weil Memorial Lecture." *Curator: The Museum Journal* 59, no. 2 (2016): 73–79.

Gibson, Chris. "Welcome to Bogan-ville: Reframing Class and Place through Humour." *Journal of Australian Studies* 37, no. 1 (2013): 62–75.

Hanley, Lynsey. *Estates: An Intimate History*. London: Granta, 2017.

Hanley, Lynsey. *Respectable: Crossing the Class Divide*. London: Penguin, 2017.

Hudson, Alistair. "Building a User-Generated Museum: A Conversation with Alistair Hudson." *Civil Society Futures: The Independent Inquiry*. Accessed 30 December 2020. https://civilsocietyfutures.org/building-a-user-generated-museum-a-conversation-with-alistair-hudson/.

Janes, Robert R. *Museums in a Troubled World: Renewal, Irrelevance or Collapse?* London and New York: Routledge, 2009.

Janoschka, Michael, and Jorge Sequera. "Gentrification in Latin America: Addressing the Politics and Geographies of Displacement." *Urban Geography* 37, no. 8 (2016): 1175–1194.

Jo Cox Foundation. *Combating Loneliness One Conversation at a Time: A Call to Action*. London: Jo Cox Foundation, 2017.

Jones, Owen. *Chavs: The Demonization of the Working Class*. New York and London: Verso, 2016.

Katifori, Akrivi, Sara Perry, Maria Vayanou, Laia Pujol, Angeliki Chrysan, Vassilis Kourtis, and Yannis Ioannidis. "Cultivating Mobile-Mediated Social Interaction in the Museum: Towards Group-Based Digital Storytelling Experiences." In *Annual Conference of Museums and the Web: MW2016*, Los Angeles, CA, USA, 6–9 April 2016. Accessed 20 November 2020. https://eprints.gla.ac.uk/143241/.

Katz, Michael B. *The Undeserving Poor: America's Enduring Confrontation with Poverty*, 2nd ed. Oxford and New York: Oxford University Press, 2013.

Keane, John. *The New Despotism*. Cambridge (Mass) and London: Harvard University Press, 2020.

Levin, Amy K. "Introduction." In *Museums, Sexuality and Gender Activism*, edited by Joshua G.Adair and Amy K.Levin, 5–20. London and New York: Routledge, 2020.

Levitsky, Steven, and Lucas Way. "The Myth of Democratic Recession." *Journal of Democracy* 26, no. 1 (2015): 45–58.

Lleras, Cristina, Michael Andrés Forero Parra, Lina María Díaz, and Jennifer Carter. "Memory Exercises: Activism, Symbolic Reparation, and Non-Repetition in Colombia's National Museum of Memory." In *Museum Activism*, edited by Robert R. Janes and Richard Sandell, 139–151. London and New York: Routledge, 2019.

Marstine, Janet, and Svetlana Mintcheva. "Introduction." In *Curating Under Pressure: International Perspectives on Negotiating Conflict and Upholding Integrity*, edited by Janet Marstine and Svetlana Mintcheva, xviii–xxiv. London and New York: Routledge, 2021.

Michell, Dee, Jacqueline Z. Wilson, and Verity Archer. "Introduction: A Working-Class World-View in an Academic Environment." In *Bread and Roses: Voices of Australian Academics from the Working Class*, edited by Dee Michell, Jacqueline Z. Wilson, and Verity Archer, vii–xvi. Rotterdam: Sense Publishers, 2015.

Mohamed, Justin. "Living on Country Represents More Than a 'Lifestyle Choice'." 12 March 2015, Reconciliation Australia. Accessed 31 December 2020. www.reconciliation.org.au/living-on-country-represents-more-than-a-lifestyle-choice/.

Moore, Tony, Mark Gibson, and Catharine Lumby. "Recovering the Australian Working Class." In *Considering Class: Theory, Culture and the Media in the 21st Century*, edited by Deidre O'Neill and Mike Wayne, 217–234. Leiden and Boston: Brill, 2017.

Museum Hue. "About the Founders." Accessed 21 February 2021. www.museumhue.com/the-founders.

Newell, Jennifer, Libby Robin, and Kirsten Wehner. "Introduction: Curating Connections in a Climate-Changed World." In *Curating the Future: Museums, Communities and Climate Change*, edited by Jennifer Newell, LibbyRobin, and Kirsten Wehner, 30–40. London and New York: Routledge, 2017.

Newitz, Annalee, and Matt Wray, eds. *White Trash: Race and Class in America*. London and New York, Routledge, 1997.

Oliver, Bobbie, and Andrew Reeves. "Crossing Disciplinary Boundaries: Labour History and Museum Studies." *Labor History* 85 (2003): 1–7.

RAND. "Truth Decay: A Threat to Policymaking." Accessed 11 October 2020. www.rand.org/pubs/research_briefs/RB10002.html.

Rekdal, Per B. "Why a Book on Museums and Truth?" In *Museums and Truth*, edited by Annette B. Fromm, Per B. Rekdal, and Viv Golding, xix–xxv. Newcastle upon Tyne: Cambridge Scholars Publisher, 2014.

Research Centre for Museums and Galleries, University of Leicester and National Trust. "HumanKind." Accessed 22 November 2020. https://humankind.le.ac.uk.

Sandell, Richard. *Museums, Society, Inequality*. London and New York: Routledge, 2003.

Sandell, Richard. "Museums as Agents of Social Inclusion." *Museum Management and Curatorship* 17, no. 4 (1998): 401–418.

Sandell, Richard, and Eithne Nightingale, eds. *Museums, Equality and Social Justice*. London and New York: Routledge, 2012.

Sandell, Richard, and Jocelyn Dodd. "Activist Practice." In *Representing Disability: Activism and Agency in the Museum*, edited by Richard Sandell, Jocelyn Dodd, and Rosemarie Garland-Thomson, 3–22. London and New York: Routledge, 2010.

Sandell, Richard, Rachael Lennon, and Matt Smith (eds). *Prejudice and Pride*. Leicester: Research Centre for Museums and Galleries (RCMG), School of Museum Studies, University of Leicester, 2018.

Sandell, Richard, Annie Delin, Jocelyn Dodd, and Jackie Gay. "Beggars, Freaks and Heroes? Museum Collections and the Hidden History of Disability." *Museum Management and Curatorship* 20, no. 1 (2005): 5–19.

Savage, Mike, Fiona Devine, Niall Cunningham, Mark Taylor, Yaojun Li, Johs Hjellbrekke, Brigitte Le Roux, Sam Friedman, and Andrew Miles. "A New Model of Social Class? Findings from the BBC's Great British Class Survey Experiment." *Sociology* 47, no. 2 (2013): 219–250.

Scott, Carol A. (ed.). *Museums and Public Value: Creating Sustainable Futures*. London and New York: Routledge, 2017.

Sheppard, Jill, and Nicholas Biddle. "Class, Capital, and Identity in Australian Society." *Australian Journal of Political Science* 52, no. 4 (2017): 500–516.

Simon, Nina. *The Art of Relevance*. Museum 2.0, 2016. Accessed 27 June 2021 www.artofrelevance.org/read-online/

Smith, Laurajane, Paul Shackel, and Gary Campbell, eds. *Heritage, Labour and the Working Classes*. London and New York: Routledge, 2011.

Standing, Guy. *The Precariat: The New Dangerous Class*. London and New York: Bloomsbury Academic, 2016.

Sullivan, Shannon. *Good White People: The Problem with Middle Class White Anti-Racism*. New York: State University of New York Press, 2014.

van der Linden, Marcel. "Speaking Globally." *International Labor and Working Class History* 75 (2009): 184–188.

Wajid, Sara, and Rachael Minott. "Detoxing and Decolonising Museums." In *Museum Activism*, edited by Robert R.Janes and Richard Sandell, 25–35. London and New York: Routledge, 2019.

Weissman, Dick. *Which Side Are You On? An Inside History of the Folk Music Revival in America*. New York and London: Continuum, 2006.

Whitby-Last, Kathryn. "Legal Impediments to the Repatriation of Cultural Objects to Indigenous Peoples." In *The Long Way Home: The Meaning and Values of Repatriation*, edited by Paul Turnbull and Michael Pickering, 35–47. New York and Oxford: Berghahn Books, 2010.

Wray, Matt. *Not Quite White: White Trash and the Boundaries of Whiteness*. Durham: Duke University Press, 2006.

Younge, Gary. "The Margins and the Mainstream." In *Museums, Equality and Social Justice*, edited by Richard Sandell and Eithne Nightingale, 105–113. London and New York: Routledge, 2012.

PART I

Shut out: Access and the working class

The contemporary museum is expected to be accessible to, and representative of, the wider society. It is ironic that, historically, the genre of the public museum was established for the benefit of the working classes in the absence of their objects and narratives. Instead, advocates for public museums and libraries assumed that exposing labourers to artefacts pertaining to bourgeois and ruling class culture in a public arena in which their behaviour would be observed would have a reforming influence. Current prescriptions of 'shhh' and 'don't touch' remain as hangovers of this nineteenth-century function of the museum as social apparatus.

Such observations do not necessarily imply changes to the conservation, display and security protocols of valuable artefacts but instead assist our understanding of the historical and sociological context for museum's prescriptions for their visitors. If the working classes are deemed by leaders and staff of cultural institutions as displaying behaviours that require modification, then any associated public claims of inclusion and diversity are disingenuous. In Part I, the notion of access is not confined to visitor numbers or demographic representation but is extended to inform analysis of the cultural and class signifiers that museums may value or, alternatively, frown upon. How leisure time is defined and spent is class-based and impacts museum attendance. How museum staff treat visitors, what museums collect and display are also class-based. Being 'shut out' (excluded) may permeate all levels of museum policy and practice.

Through historical research, references to literature, professional experience and action research, the following chapters analyse who and what is valued by the cultural sector. These chapters are linked by a discursive thread that challenges the belief that the working class is valued by museums and archival organisations.

DOI: 10.4324/9781003029519-2

1

'A PERMANENT CIVILISING EFFECT'?

The impact of reforming working-class museum visitors in Liverpool during the nineteenth century

Alexander Scott

On 18 October 1860, William Ewart MP (1798–1869) spoke at the opening of the new Liverpool public museum. Ewart was peculiarly well-positioned to commentate on the Museum's virtues: a native Liverpudlian, he had sponsored the 1845 Museums Act, which for the first time allowed town councils to levy taxation to fund municipal collections. Liverpool's new museum – which replaced a smaller venue in operation since 1852 – thus represented another step towards meeting Ewart's ambition that 'every large town' should possess 'a museum of such character as might give sound taste to the population… and enable them to apply the skill they obtain to manufactures'.[1] Ewart believed that the Liverpool Museum would 'extend the benefits of education amongst the people' and have 'a permanent civilising effect on the character of our population'.[2]

This chapter assesses the extent to which Ewart's 'civilising effect' was borne out by using archival material (newspapers, annual reports, minute books) to evaluate working-class visitors' experiences during the period from Liverpool Museum's foundation through to the First World War. The chapter begins by outlining the reforming intent which motivated the creation of civic museums in the mid-nineteenth century before questioning whether the reality matched the rhetoric. The second section demonstrates that in practice Liverpool Museum remained a bourgeois stronghold, remaining closed when working-class men had most free time available to attend.[3] Having outlined these points, the final section contends that barriers to entry did not go unnoticed or unopposed, and that working-class visitors occasionally found novel ways to defy the expectations of middle-class museum professionals.

The chapter revisits debates about Victorian museums' ideological functions. The opening section parallels Eilean Hooper-Greenhill and Tony Bennett's respective arguments regarding museums' status as instruments of state power. Developing Michel Foucault's analyses of prisons, Hooper-Greenhill's *Museums and*

DOI: 10.4324/9781003029519-3

the Shaping of Knowledge (1992) suggested that nineteenth-century museums were 'disciplinary technologies' which sought to produce a 'docile', governable citizenry through 'hierarchical observation, normalising judgement and examination'.[4]

In *The Birth of the Museum* (1995), Bennett nuanced Hooper-Greenhill's points by proposing that public museums and penitentiaries were the 'Janus face of power': where carceral institutions meted out punitive instruction and correction, museums sought to peaceably regulate and reform the working classes through (self-)surveillance and exposure to the 'educative and civilising' influence of middle-class morals, tastes and habits.[5] But while it shares common ground with Bennett and Hooper-Greenhill's analyses, the chapter ultimately sides with more recent scholarship in querying the extent that their theses stand up to archival scrutiny. As Kate Hill pointed out in *Culture and Class in English Public Museums, 1850–1914* (2005), a lack of sources authored by members of the working class makes it difficult to substantiate how they actually experienced museums, meaning visitors remain 'the great unknown' for historians 'despite the weight of speculation, assumptions and pedagogy targeted at them'.[6] Without disputing Hill's general conclusion, the chapter endeavours to make working-class museumgoers three-dimensional and 'knowable', in the process arguing that Victorian museums were more contested spaces than historiography sometimes allows.

The birth of Liverpool Museum

Campaigning for a public museum in Liverpool began in response to the 1845 Museum Act. *The Liverpool Mercury* newspaper published various stories in favour of founding a municipal collection, and in 1850 Liverpool town council agreed to establish a museum committee.[7] The plans gained momentum with the bequest of an extensive natural history collection by the deceased 13th Earl of Derby (Edward Smith Stanley, 1775–1851). Items from the Derby collection first went on show in October 1852, with bigger natural history galleries opening the following March. Construction of enlarged premises began in 1857, funded by Liverpool merchant banker William Brown (1784–1864). The new museum opened in October 1860 at a site renamed William Brown Street. This remains home to World Museum Liverpool (as the public museum has been known since 2005), the Walker Art Gallery (est. 1877) and the city's central library (built 1879).[8]

William Ewart was not alone in identifying Liverpool's Museum as an agent of moral uplift. The 1860 opening ceremony was accompanied by a 'Working Man's Meeting' at which a 'testimonial of the working men of Liverpool' was delivered by Daniel Guile, a trade unionist. Guile's speech related the Museum to wider efforts to educate workers. Whereas earlier generations had regarded tradesmen as 'mere beasts of burden', Guile reported that more recently 'spirits had arisen amidst this intellectual gloom … showing that in the masses there was mind'. Praising the engineering achievements of George Stephenson, James Watt and Isambard Kingdom Brunel – 'men … sprang from us, the masses' – Guile expressed hope that the Museum would inspire comparable excellence. To do so, Guile cautioned that 'the power of the mind' needed to win 'complete victory over sensual appetites' and that 'self-denial must be exercised'. He encouraged workers to devote their spare time to 'study, thought, perseverance and industry' at the Museum instead of indulging themselves inside 'the taproom, singing room [or] dancing room'.[9]

Commentary on workers' alcohol habits was a recurrent feature of museums discourse. For instance, the earliest parliamentary proposals for provincial museums came during a Select Committee on Drunkenness in 1834. The committee chair James Silk Buckingham (1786–1855) identified the 'prevalence of drunkenness among the labouring classes' as an 'evil' side effect of industrialisation and urbanisation, suggesting that 'humble museums and collections of works of nature and art' would offer a solution by affording 'opportunities for development of mental faculties and moral feelings'.[10] Arguments for temperance likewise factored into discussions of Liverpool's public museum. In December 1850, the *Mercury* reported that a meeting of people 'favourable to the establishment of a free museum and library' had resolved that 'nothing could be so desirable as to give the lower orders some better mode of spending their time than in the cursed dramhouse saw at the corner of every street'.[11] Another *Mercury* editorial recommended that museums might 'cleanse our cities of the moral and physical filth which abounds in them' by providing amusements to rival 'a street row, a dog fight or a quarrel between two men'.[12]

Allusions to 'cleaning the streets' intimate that maintaining law and order was one rationale for creating public museums. In 1850, the *Mercury* urged Liverpool town council to allocate funds to museum collections on the basis that, 'while a police officer is a serviceable person', institutions dedicated to 'self-improvement' were more 'powerful agents of order, morality and wellbeing'.[13] Reiterating museums' connections to the carceral system, Liverpool's chief magistrate, Thomas S Raffles, was among the invited speakers at the 1860 workers' meeting. Raffles wished the Museum 'every success' in helping 'diminish vice', predicting that if working men spent more time at the Museum 'the court will become comparatively empty and make me an idle man'.[14]

Reforming discourse also related museums to urban sanitation systems. In 1851, for example, the *Mercury* published an editorial on 'the water question' featuring a plea that Liverpool town council should fund museum and library collections alongside municipal reservoirs and bathhouses.[15] As Bennett has explicated, investment in public hygiene and cultural institutions was regarded as complementary: specifically, museum attendance and drinking fresh water were each reckoned wholesome alternatives to consuming alcohol inside public houses. Despite this, the utilitarian ethos of museum reformers did not seek to improve workers' physical and spiritual wellbeing as an end in itself. Rather, the ultimate goal was an 'inner or moral transformation' whereby working men actively *chose* to become industrious, economically productive citizens.[16]

Such realpolitik was another feature of discussions surrounding the creation of Liverpool's public museum. The *Mercury* reasoned the Museum might 'raise the intellectual standard of that class who contribute most largely to the production of the luxuries and necessities of life' by 'placing discoveries of great chemists, mechanists, naturalists and inventors ... before every artisan'.[17] Upskilling the working population was also deemed crucial for Britain's industrial competitiveness. At the opening of Liverpool Museum in 1860, Thomas Bazley (1797–1885), MP for Manchester, commented that the ongoing 'prosperity of Lancashire depends upon the increase of intelligence ... amongst all classes of the community', while William Brown stressed 'the importance of putting ... means of instruction within reach of the masses' because 'the more we are instructed, the more value we possess over every other nation'.[18] Patriotic sentiment likewise rationalised that working-class visitors would willingly align themselves with displays of national and civic power encountered at public museums. In 1851, the *Mercury* forecast that the creation of a municipal museum would eventuate a situation where 'the poorest as well as the richest can visit it at all times – look upon it with pride, and, as a member of this great community, call it *his own* [original emphasis]'.[19]

Social distinctions and barriers to entry

Liverpool Museum's presumed significance for the city's labouring classes is clear enough. However, we should be cautious about taking the ideology of Victorian museum reformers at face value. As Bennett conceded, although civic museums were typically founded in the name of the working class, they were 'appropriated by social elites' and in practice acted to 'differentiat[e] elite from popular social classes ... rather than functioning as instruments of homogenisation as reforming thought had envisaged'.[20] This was, I would argue, true from the outset. For all the talk about the humbler classes, the ceremonies which marked the different stages of Liverpool Museum's opening were highly exclusive occasions. Events were generally ticketed, and offered a forum for merchants, industrialists, MPs, lords, church ministers, judges, colonial officials and visiting emissaries to address members of the working class about their particular social and political interests. The visual record testifies to the power differentials enforced on such occasions: photographs of the Museum's 1857 ground-breaking ceremony show a top-hatted clique segregated from the watching crowd by terracing.

This is indicative of how museum administration acted to reinforce social hierarchies. Patronising cultural institutions like parks, libraries, art galleries and orchestras was a means of the industrial middle classes legitimating their newfound wealth and status.[21] As Kate Hill noted, a major benefaction like William Brown's left 'one's name attached to a grand and imposing civic building that was moreover a storehouse of knowledge'. More modestly, the middle classes 'proclaimed symbolic ownership' over Victorian cities by 'donating, getting on committees or working for the museum'.[22] Evidencing this, throughout the nineteenth century, Liverpool Museum committee was dominated by members of the city's 'Old Families' – consisting mainly of merchant capitalists such as the Rathbone dynasty, the Forwoods, Pictons and Holts but also landed aristocrats like the Earls of Derby.[23] Underlining the social cachet associated with museum connoisseurship, committee activities were given extensive coverage in the local press, including *The Liverpool Mercury* – the 'organ' of the city's Liberal merchant elite.[24]

Admittedly, Liverpool Museum's bourgeois status did not automatically preclude it from making a positive impact on the lower orders of society. The mechanics' institute movement, which had comparable roots in middle-class philanthropy, proved successful in attracting subscriptions from members of the working class as the nineteenth century progressed.[25] Likewise, Jonathan Rose has shown that grassroots 'mutual improvement' networks often conformed to values and sensibilities espoused by the Victorian middle class, especially regarding the latter's belief in the inherent improving influence of art, literature and culture.[26] The important distinction from these other forms of adult education, though, is that Liverpool Museum was not readily accessible to working men *at their own leisure*. Throughout the chronology covered in this chapter, the Museum was typically open only during working hours (10am till dusk) and remained closed on the day when labourers had most free time to frequent it (Sunday). Initially, it opened just three days a week, and even when workers' Saturday 'half-holiday' was added in 1857, the Museum remained closed to the public on Tuesdays and Fridays and completely shut on Sundays – the latter omission being noteworthy given that Sunday schools were central to the mutual improvement tradition.[27] The introduction of wintertime Monday evening openings marked a partial concession to workers' schedules – although even this proved sufficiently controversial that the practice was terminated between 1871 and 1888 (see the next section). Tuesday opening eventually began in 1890, with Sundays added following the First World War. A full seven-day week was finally implemented in 1922 – seven decades after the first museum exhibits went on show.[28]

Committee minutes attest that other rules and practices served to shore up unequal access to the Museum. A lengthy disquisition on the opening of new natural history galleries in March 1853 reveals that selective admission was instituted after the volume of visitors – 10,000 people in four days – rendered the exhibitions 'impassable'. The committee thus determined to 'restrict admission to persons presenting some attempts at decency of appearance', refusing entrance to those 'roughest' members of 'the labouring population' who 'flow in during the usual dinner hour 12 to 1'. Reinforcing the point, notice boards were erected bearing the inscription:

> It is requested that all parties visiting the museum come clean and in decent apparel to preserve an appearance of order and propriety. All smoking and spitting strictly prohibited. Children in arms not admitted nor children under 12 years of age unless accompanied by an adult.[29]

By contrast, individuals with the right credentials and connections were granted privileged access to museum collections. Entrance on closure days was extended to people who possessed a 'written order signed by a member of the [town] council', with students likewise permitted during cleaning hours – providing they obtained 'satisfactory references'.[30] Committee members also had liberty to use museum collections for private delectation. The Museum keeper, Reverend Henry Hugh

Higgins (1814–1893) and its curator, Thomas J Moore (1824–1892), each on occasion used specimens from the natural history galleries when delivering presentations to members-only associations such as Liverpool's Literary and Philosophical Society.[31]

These inequities did not go unnoticed, and the committee was periodically asked questions about admissions procedures at town council meetings.[32] During the 1880s, the Museum's policies were concertedly targeted by Liverpool Sunday Society, an organisation which campaigned for public institutions to open on the Sabbath. The Sunday Society's secretary Robert McMillan sent a series of letters to the *Mercury*, which were later collected in the pamphlet *Workmen and Museums* (1886). Protesting that 'thousands of people are debarred from museums on the only day they could possibly visit them', McMillan's letters sought to draw renewed attention to museums' educative potential.[33] Echoing pronouncements in favour of civic museums heard during the 1840s–1860s, McMillan estimated that every 'trade in our city' would 'be improved by the education of toilers', arguing that widening access to the types of instruction available through studying museum collections could prevent 'our working people losing their supremacy in the markets of the world'. Diversifying audiences was deemed of acute urgency because 'the average member of the Trades Congress has no more idea of the treasures in our museums than if they were in the mountains of the moon'.[34]

This verdict prompts re-evaluation of the rhetoric that surrounded Liverpool Museum's creation; had its 'civilising effect' been what it was cracked up to be, McMillan would not have needed to rehearse familiar arguments about museums' utility twenty-to-thirty years later. Nor did working-class habits become moderate in these intervening decades. Efforts to discourage alcohol consumption (always an unlikely goal) especially seem to have amounted to little. Committee minutes record that 'drink and signs of drink were occasionally noticed' among museumgoers, particularly on bank holidays.[35] This reflected wider phenomena. In 1874, *The Times* reported that 20,000 people were arrested for drinking-related offences annually in Liverpool, making it 'the most drunken town in England'. A follow-up editorial condemned Liverpool's 'leading citizens' as 'negligent of their duties' for 'not attempting to exercise proper influence over their fellow townsmen'.[36] By framing the matter in these terms, *The Times* pinpointed the absence of precisely the sort of corrective influence Liverpool Museum was supposed to offer.

Working-class agency inside the Museum

The archival record nevertheless attests that *some* working-class visitors managed to attend the Museum irrespective of the limitations and obstacles placed in their way. As noted, however, attempts to interpret visitor working-class behaviour and opinions face methodological constraints. Hill has explained that little effort was made to record visitors' views in comment books or suchlike, and that surviving sources were predominantly written by middle-class museum professionals and journalists.[37] Consequently, we have a fuller picture of how working-class visitors were *perceived* than of their own understandings of museum-going.

This broadly holds true for documents produced by Liverpool Museum, which contain numerical attendance data but sparing references to visitor's thoughts and actions. Occasional efforts to collate visitor feedback mark a partial exception to this rule. In a paper to the Literary and Philosophical Society in 1884, Henry Higgins discussed 'valuable information' he had obtained by observing and interviewing visitors. Making 'overtures inducing remarks on the objects exhibited', Higgins was able to piece together a general profile of Liverpool Museum's audience. He calculated that of every thousand visitors, 10 to 20 were 'students' 'who come with a definite purpose of improving their knowledge', with around two hundred mere 'loungers' and an overwhelming majority (about 780) of 'observers' 'not conscious of any purpose beyond a wish to see the museum'. Within these broad brushstrokes, Higgins noticed a high proportion of 'emigrants' (classed as 'observers') and children ('loungers'), adding that 'observers' were 'more numerously attracted by the birds than by the invertebrate animals' with the opposite true of 'students'. Higgins differentiated the 'direct' learning undertaken by 'men with a cultivated interest in science' from the 'indirect influence upon the mass of visitors ... hundreds of thousands of whom it was vain to hope were deriving much in the way of scientific instruction'. Tellingly, Higgins regarded the former as museums' core demographic, contending that 'the interests of ordinary observers' ought not 'lead the construction or arrangement' of exhibits. In any case, Higgins curtailed his surveys upon realising that 'conversationally approachable' visitors were 'scattered like flowers amidst the innumerable culms of grass in a meadow'.[38]

Higgins's comments betray wider reservations about working-class visitors. Befitting Hooper-Greenhill's theories about museums' disciplinary functions, museum professionals tended to view visitors as nuisances and threats that they needed to exert control over. The dress codes issued in 1853 (see above) were part of an attempt to 'organise a system of discipline and supervision so as to carry on the institution with order and regularity'. This involved employing attendants and policemen to monitor the public's behaviour plus the use of 'direction papers ... to keep visitors moving in the right direction'. The committee gauged these measures' success by inspecting exhibition cases and finding 'not a single square of glass in the slightest degree damaged ... the very best test of quiet and orderly conduct of spectators'. On the contrary, visitors' 'greatest fault' was their 'very free indulgence in an exportation' – i.e. spitting.[39]

Such squeamishness hints at the broader body politics which governed visitors' engagement with museum space – the most obvious example being prohibitions against touching exhibits. Besides enacting legitimate conservation concerns, regulations on handling objects reflected social prejudices about working-class bodies specifically. As Fiona Candlin has observed, banning touch only became commonplace when museums began freely admitting the general public in the nineteenth century. Prior to this, touch had been deemed congruent to eighteenth-century museums' Enlightenment ideals and remained so as long they maintained de facto exclusivity. Only once efforts were made to democratise museum audiences did it become expedient to determine who could handle artefacts, when and on what basis – typically using class distinctions.[40]

Classing of touch is discernible in Liverpudlian museums discourse. When, for example, Liverpool Royal Institution considered opening its national history galleries to non-members in 1826, an objection was raised about the 'mischief' likely to result from the 'too prevalent habit' of 'lower classes … examining objects of curiosity through the medium of their fingers'.[41] The cleanliness of working-class hands too represented a cause for concern. Liverpool Museum's first annual report, published in 1853, remarked on the 'slight degree of disorder and irregularity' arising from visitors arriving 'direct from their occupations with unwashed hands and negligent attire'. Lavatories were thus installed 'to leave no excuse for this conduct' – a contingency which was said to have improved the hygiene of the 'operative classes'.[42] This presents a vivid example of museums' civilising intent; here, visitors' bodies were literally *cleansed* inside the museum.

Yet the archive also contains instances where working-class visitors appear far less pliant to museum professionals' instructions. A striking example pertains to the Museum's experiments with evening openings. Beginning in 1863, the initiative – which provided extra visiting hours from 7pm on Mondays during the winter months – initially proceeded with little incident. This changed in January 1870, when Thomas Moore notified the Museum committee of 'the great inconvenience' generated by 'large and increasing numbers of young people' using evenings 'for promenading and conversation rather than for the inspection of objects'.[43] That December, youngsters again caused 'annoyance and crowding out [of] well-conducted persons' via a litany of 'irregularities' such as 'persons wandering about without any object', 'idlers … occup[ying] seats to the exclusion of others', and visitors 'spitting on the floors, lounging about and obstructing passages'.[44] After further instances of 'gross misconduct', the Museum committee discontinued evening openings in September 1871.[45]

Descriptions of the evening openings support Hill's suggestion that working-class visitors tended not to regard museums as 'different, quasi-spiritual spaces', instead adopting patterns of behaviour familiar to other recreation activities.[46] In 1888, the *Mercury* recalled the 'rough play' of 'rowdies' which characterised evening openings, noting that 'flirting' by 'young men and women' had been commonplace.[47] A reader's letter drew attention to the 'open and gross misconduct by a multitude of girls and boys – of course generally of the lowest classes' who 'flooded in such enormous numbers as to be practically unmanageable and uncontrollable'. Respectable museumgoers, the reader added, were put off by 'roughs of the same class as those who … at certain times make the boulevards, Newsham Park, and the landing-stage unfit for decent people to use'.[48]

By this time, however, evening openings were judged the lesser of two evils. In October 1888, the *Mercury* reported that the Museum committee had agreed to temporarily reintroduce evening hours as 'a counterblast to the effort being made to open the place to the masses on Sunday'.[49] Addressing visitors at the first of the resumed evening openings, committee member GH Ball refuted allegations that 'the working classes had no opportunities of seeing the museum under present circumstances', and challenged visitors to adopt appropriate 'conduct … to show how much they appreciated the place'.[50] Not leaving this to chance, Henry Higgins reminded attendees of their duty to 'aid staff in protecting against all unnecessary interruption', while the *Mercury* advised that 'all rate-paying adult visitors constitute a vigilance committee to keep in order the young savages who frequent every place warm, light and free during the winter nights'.[51] Such precautions made a satisfactory impact. Confirming the absence of 'disorderly conduct … levity and boisterousness', the committee agreed to permanently reinstitute evening openings during winter months – a policy which remained in place throughout this chapter's timespan.[52]

The debates about evening openings exaggerate the gap between rhetoric and reality which characterised Victorian museums. Testament to this, the *Mercury* reports featured an aside lamenting the high price of museum catalogues – something which had not been a problem 'so long as the museum was reserved for genteel visitors … but should be looked into now an attempt is being made to induce the poor'.[53] This statement amounts to tacit admission that the Museum contravened the principles espoused at its inception, which ought to have translated into attempts to 'induce the poor' from the get-go. Indeed, exhibitions becoming *too popular* was a somewhat perverse bugbear for committee members. After an influx of '6730 excursionists' in August 1863, Thomas Moore was empowered to 'close the doors' whenever the 'pressure' of visitor numbers 'jeopardise[d] the safety of the property under his care'.[54] Worries about visitor volume too had factored into the committee's decision to suspend evening openings. Explaining the ban, Ball cited statistics that showed that where the average nightly attendance was 'only 954' during the winter of 1864, it 'had been 2000' in 1870–1871.[55]

Discussions of evening openings also provide a rare glimpse of Liverpool's working classes *speaking back* to the discourses surrounding museum attendance. The *Mercury* recorded that Ball and Higgins's speeches on the resumption of evening openings provoked 'two working men' to make 'very strong remarks as to the foolishness of expecting artisans to come to such a place after a hard day's work'.[56] One of the (unnamed) men objected that he was 'too tired to appreciate the beauties of the place', highlighting various impracticalities associated with evening attendance:

> As most working men live a mile or two from their work, it was impossible for them to get home after a hard day's work, get cleaned and get tea, then go to the museum with his wife and children, especially as he had to go to bed early in order to rise at five in the morning.

The second man clarified that he sacrificed a day's work in order to bring his family to the Museum, drawing applause when affirming a preference for opening on Sundays, 'our only leisure day'.[57]

These snatches of dialogue reiterate that members of the working class took an active interest in museums, while also hinting they were wise to some of the vacuities associated with Victorian reforming ideology. Furthermore, working-class Liverpudlians do not appear to have accepted the Museum's rules and regulations as non-negotiable. One remarkable incidence of this is found in the 1897 *Bulletin of the Liverpool Museum*. An article headlined '"Medicine" at the Museum' recounted how:

> A few days ago, an Irish lad suffering badly from scrofulous sores was brought to the museum by his parents, who earnestly besought that they be allowed to touch the child's neck with an Irish Stone Celt exhibited in one of the cases. It was unavailing to try and persuade the deluded and superstitious couple that no possible good could follow such an application. [But] as their faith in the efficacy of the Stone could not be shaken, and they were loath to go away without being allowed to try this, in their behalf, unfailing remedy, opposition was finally, and not without some hesitation, withdrawn, and the ancient implement placed in their hands. After the operation, the parents departed happy, grateful, and in the most perfect confidence that their child would be healed, and not without expressions of surprise that so great a boon had been conferred without fee.[58]

This anecdote is rich in detail about how museumgoers and curators cohabited. On the face of it, the power resided with the 'authorities' who were able to guard access to the Stone Celt. The *Bulletin* likewise retained the capacity to name and frame the visitors' experience, with the choice of language ('deluded', 'suspicious') affecting disdain towards the visitors and their apparent mysticism. Yet, far from being cowed into obedience, the Irish family ultimately emerged triumphant. Acting despite themselves, the curators acquiesced to the 'deluded couple' and allowed them to handle the Celt – thus breaking the taboo on visitors touching exhibits. Moreover, the family then proceeded to use the Celt to administer an act – one of religious devotion or rudimentary medicine – that went totally against the grain of a publication produced by a purportedly modern and scientifically rational institution.

Conclusion

The Stone Celt incident provides a singular example of visitors' propensity to confound museum committee edicts and expectations. It also conveys the sense of mutual unintelligibility which characterised working-class museumgoers' interactions with middle-class museum professionals. Henry Higgins conceded this in an 1892 speech which affirmed that Victorian society was 'divided into various classes each of which has its own habits and modes of life, and between them exists a good deal of the spirit of Oriental cast'. For Higgins, this lack of common comprehension presented museums with a dilemma 'now we are supposed to be bidding for visitors from all classes'.[59]

Higgins's statement exposes the fallacy behind sentiments originally expressed in favour of civic museums: had the lofty ideals of Ewart et al. materialised, museums like Liverpool's would have been bidding for working-class visitors from their very inception. The reality, as we have seen, was that numerous obstacles and practicalities inhibited working-class attendance at the Museum, and the kneejerk response to 'misconduct' tended to restrict access rather than trying to correct or re-educate. Nevertheless, as also demonstrated, working-class Liverpudlians showed enthusiasm for the educational opportunities offered by the Museum, and proved adept at circumnavigating barriers to accessing its collections. Restrictive opening hours were contested, and, once inside the Museum, working-class visitors often acted in ways which challenged middle-class etiquette. This, I would argue, allows us to recover a fuller appreciation of working-class *agency* than is provided by Hooper-Greenhill and Bennett's interpretations of public museums. In sum, we should neither *overestimate* the ingenuousness of museum reformers nor *underestimate* working-class visitors' potential to resist museums' 'civilising effect'.

Notes

1 HC Deb, 6 March 1845. Accessed 4 April 2020. http://hansard.millbanksystems.com/commons/1845/mar/06/museums-of-art.
2 *Liverpool Mercury*, 19 October 1860, 5–7.
3 Museum audiences were conceptualised in highly gendered ways. Because civic museums were (in theory) geared towards the 'working man', female visitors initially received relatively little attention in museums discourse. This held true even though femininity itself was considered an auxiliary of museums' 'civilising' influence (Bennett, *The Birth of the Museum*, 28–33). Women increasingly challenged these norms as the nineteenth century progressed (Hill, "Women and Museums 1850–1914").
4 Hooper-Greenhill, *Museums and the Shaping of Knowledge*, 168–90.
5 Bennett, *Birth of the Museum*, 5–66, 86–88.
6 Hill, *Culture and Class in English Public Museums*, 125.
7 See: *Supplement to the Liverpool Mercury*, 28 November 1845, 1;12 December 1845, 1; *Liverpool Mercury*, 16 January 1846, 12; 6 July 1846, 6; 29 February 1848, 5, 7 December 1847, 6; 5 April 1850, 3.
8 A word on nomenclature. Although for simplicity this chapter refers to 'Liverpool Museum' or 'Liverpool's Museum', various titles (Derby Museum, Brown Library and Museum) denoted different sections of the Museum during in the nineteenth century. Note also: the library, museum and art gallery were part of the same institution before the 1870s.
9 *Mercury*, 18 October 1860, 3.
10 HC Deb, 3 June 1834
11 *Mercury*, 13 December 1850, 3.
12 *Mercury*, 30 April 1850, 4. On alcohol and street entertainments in Victorian Liverpool, see Macilwee, *The Liverpool Underworld*,103–17, 272–86.
13 *Mercury*, 30 April 1850, 4.
14 *Mercury*, 18 October 1860, 5.
15 *Mercury*, 12 September 1851, 6.

16 Bennett, 'The Multiplication of Culture's Utility' in *Museums, Power, Knowledge*, 68–71.
17 *Mercury*, 8 October 1852, 6.
18 *Mercury*, 19 October 1860, 5.
19 *Mercury*, 19 August 1851, 4.
20 Bennett, *Birth of the Museum,* 28.
21 See Joyce, *The Rule of Freedom*, Gunn, *The Public Culture of the Victorian Middle Class.*
22 Hill, *Culture and Class*, 50–60.
23 Lane, *Liverpool*, 53–84.
24 *Mercury*, 1 January 1850, 8. On museums and newspapers see Flanders, "Early Museums and Nineteenth-Century Media," 72–81.
25 Walker, *The Development of the Mechanics' Institute Movement in Britain and Beyond*, 40–81.
26 Rose, *The Intellectual Life of the British Working Class*, 38–48, 58–91.
27 Rose, *Intellectual Life of the Working Class*, 62, 64.
28 Millard, *Liverpool's Museum*, 2, 114–20, 31, 46. Liverpool's libraries and art gallery enacted Sunday opening earlier than the city Museum. See: Woodson-Boulton, *Transformative Beauty*, 69–73.
29 Liverpool Record Office [LRO] 352 MIN LIB 1/2 Library and Museum Committee Minutes, 17 March 1853, 84–86.
30 LRO 352 MIN LIB 1/5, 10 September 1863, 371; 19 January 1871, LRO MIN LIB 1/8, 192.
31 See for example the Higgins paper cited below and Moore's contributions to *Proceedings of the Literary and Philosophical Society of Liverpool Vol. 16: 1861–1862*, 10, 26–27, 45.
32 LRO 352 MIN/LIB/1/4, 21 April 1859, pp. 105–6; 352 MIN/LIB/1/7, 21 October 1869, 405–6.
33 Robert McMillan letter, *Mercury*, 9 June 1886, 7.
34 McMillan, *Workmen and Museums: Being Selections from a Series of Letters Contributed to the Liverpool Mercury*, 2–7.
35 LRO 352 MIN LIB 1/19, 29 March 1888, 159.
36 *The Times*, 25 December 1874, 9; 26 December 1874, 7.
37 Hill, *Culture and Class*, 125–53.
38 Henry H. Higgins, "Museums of Natural History," *Proceedings of the Literary and Philosophical Society of Liverpool, Vol. 38: 1883–1884*, 183–89.
39 LRO 352 MIN LIB 1/2, 17 March 1853, 84–86.
40 Candlin, "Art, Museums and Touch," 58–90, 110–11.
41 *Mercury*, 17 February 1826, 3.
42 *Report of the Library and Museum Committee of the Town Council of the Borough of Liverpool*, 6–7.
43 LRO 352 MIN/LIB/1/7, 20 January 1870, 448.
44 LRO 352 MIN/LIB/1/8, 10 March 1870, 474.
45 LRO 352 MIN LIB 1/11, 23 February 1871,14 September 1871, 214, 331.
46 Hill, *Culture and Class*, 125–42.
47 *Mercury*, 30 March 1888, 5; 27 September 1888, 7.
48 *Mercury*, 31 March 1888, 3. The letter refers to a public park, opened 1868, and the shipping depot at Liverpool's Pier Head.
49 *Mercury*, 4 October 1888, 7.
50 *Mercury*, 2 October 1888, 5.
51 *Mercury*, 27 September 1888, 7.
52 *Thirty-Sixth Annual Report of the Committee of the Free Public Library, Museum and Walker Art Gallery the Borough of Liverpool*, 3–4.
53 *Mercury*, 15 November 1888, 7.
54 LRO 352 MIN/LIB/1/5, 20 August 1863, 363.
55 *Mercury*, 2 October 1888, 5.
56 *Mercury*, 4 October 1888, 7.
57 *Mercury*, 2 October 1888, 5.
58 *Bulletin of the Liverpool Museums*, 1:1 (1897), 28.
59 Higgins, "On the Cultivation of Special Features in Museums," *Report of Proceedings with Papers Read at the Third Annual General Meeting Held in Manchester*, 39.

Bibliography

Printed primary sources

Literary and Philosophical Society of Liverpool. *Proceedings of the Literary and Philosophical Society of Liverpool, Vol. 38: 1883–1884*. Liverpool: D Marples & Co, 1884.

Literary and Philosophical Society of Liverpool. *Proceedings of the Literary and Philosophical Society of Liverpool, Vol. 16: 1861–1862*. Liverpool: Thomas Brackell, 1862.

Liverpool Town Council. *Thirty-Sixth Report of the Committee of the Free Public Library, Museum and Walker Art Gallery of the Borough of Liverpool*. Liverpool: JR Williams & Co, 1889.

Liverpool Town Council. *Report of the Library and Museum Committee of the Town Council of the Borough of Liverpool*. Liverpool: Robert H Fraser, 1853.

McMillan, Robert. *Workmen and Museums: Being Selections from a Series of Letters Contributed to the Liverpool Mercury*. Liverpool: Egerton Smith, 1886.

Museums Association. *Report of Proceedings with Papers Read at the Third Annual General Meeting Held in Manchester*. Sheffield: Museums Association, 1892.

Printed secondary sources

Bennett, Tony. *Museums, Power, Knowledge: Selected Essays*. Abingdon: Routledge, 2018.

Bennett, Tony. *The Birth of the Museum: History, Theory, Politics*. London: Routledge, 1995.

Candlin, Fiona. *Art, Museums and Touch*. Manchester: Manchester University Press, 2010.

Flanders, Rosemary. "Early Museums and Nineteenth-Century Media." In *Museum, Media, Message*, edited by Eilean Hooper-Greenhill, 72–81. London: Routledge, 1995.

Gunn, Simon. *The Public Culture of the Victorian Middle Class: Ritual and Authority in the English City*. Manchester: Manchester University Press, 2000.

Hill, Kate. *Women and Museums 1850–1914: Modernity and the Gendering of Knowledge*. Manchester: Manchester University Press, 2016.

Hill, Kate. *Culture and Class in English Public Museums, 1850–1914*. Aldershot: Ashgate, 2005.

Hooper-Greenhill, Eilean. *Museums and the Shaping of Knowledge*. London: Routledge, 1992.

Joyce, Patrick. *The Rule of Freedom: Liberalism and the Modern City*. London, Verso2003.

Lane, Tony. *Liverpool: Gateway of Empire*. London: Lawrence & Wishart, 1987.

Macilwee, Michael. *The Liverpool Underworld: Crime in the City, 1750–1900*. Liverpool: Liverpool University Press, 2011.

Millard, John. *Liverpool's Museum: The First Hundred Years*. Liverpool: National Museums Liverpool, 2010.

Rose, Jonathan. *The Intellectual Life of the British Working Class*. London: Yale University Press, 2001.

Walker, Martyn. *The Development of the Mechanics' Institute Movement in Britain and Beyond: Supporting Further Education for Adult Working Classes*. Abingdon: Routledge, 2017.

Woodson-Boulton, Amy. *Transformative Beauty: Art Museums in Industrial Britain*. Stanford: University of California Press, 2012.

Unprinted primary sources

Liverpool Record Office, Town Council Library and Museum Committee minute books, LRO 352 MIN LIB.

Newspapers

The *Liverpool Mercury*.
The Times.

House of Commons debates

HC Deb, 6 March 1845, Accessed 4 April 2020. http://hansard.millbanksystems.com/commons/1845/mar/06/museums-of-art.

HC Deb, 3 June 1834, Accessed 4 April 2020. http://hansard.millbanksystems.com/commons/1834/jun/03/drunkennes.

2

HOW BRITISH MUSEUMS HAVE FAILED THE WORKING CLASS

David Fleming[1]

> ...But you're still fucking peasants as far as I can see...
>
> *(Lennon 1970)*

Introduction

This chapter aims to explore the myth that British museums have done other than neglect large swathes of British society, in concentrating their attentions on the machinations of a minority of the British population – that which holds most of the resources and which has dominated the politics of this nation. British museums have long betrayed working-class audiences by displaying little or no interest at all in working-class history. There have been few exceptions to this. British museums have been places where the exceptional and the exotic have been shown as a tribute to British White imperial and colonial maleness, and to the exclusion of lots of potential content relating, for example, to the roles of women, to LGBTQ+ issues, to Black histories, as well as to the place in British society of people from a working-class background. Privilege has been championed by British museums and only in recent times has there been any serious challenge to the traditional approach.[2] This situation is improving as the museum workforce becomes more diverse, but anyone who underestimates the capacity of museums, especially those museums that are funded by the British Government to continue to do their own thing, pretending that their ability to attract tourists is synonymous with opening up access, is likely to be confounded. The pattern of privilege is engrained in British cultural life. There are many examples of this – anyone in any doubt should read any of the 'art' reviews in *The Sunday Times* 'Culture' magazine, or in *The Times* itself.

The notion of museums being interested in the business of fighting inequalities in society has often been challenged, and the frequent equation of this with

DOI: 10.4324/9781003029519-4

reducing the care and scholarship accorded to object collections has had the impact of misleading some museum people, and others, into continuing their support for traditional approaches to interpretation.[3]

Influences

The grip of privilege on museums is echoed throughout the British cultural sector. Rare, just to take one example, were writings by working-class people during the twentieth century. People from a working-class background tended not to have access to the kind of education required in the creation of literary works. Robert Tressel's *The Ragged Trousered Philanthropists* is the exception that proves the rule, because it was hardly part of a movement. The famous War Poets, Siegfried Sassoon and Rupert Brooke, came from very privileged backgrounds. D.H. Lawrence perhaps represented working-class literature, though he was widely reviled by the Establishment as a pornographer (Prosecutor Mervyn Griffiths-Jones spoke eloquently for a nation dominated by privilege when he asked at the trial of Penguin Books, prosecuted under the Obscene Publications Act 1959, whether *Lady Chatterley's Lover* was a book 'you would wish your wife or servants to read'). Not until the 1950s can we see signs of working-class novelists and playwrights in some numbers, with the advent of writers such as Alan Sillitoe, whose books were frequently adapted into films: *Saturday Night and Sunday Morning, The Loneliness of the Long Distance Runner*, for example; there was also *Room at the Top, Billy Liar* and *A Taste of Honey*; but compare these pickings with the massive output of, among others, Arthur Conan Doyle, William Golding, Graham Greene, Aldous Huxley (in whose *Eyeless in Gaza* he refers to 'slum children'); he says they would have been called 'scadgers' at the public school attended by the narrator, Anthony Beavis, and that their existence would have been:

> offensively ignored... he was secretly afraid of these stunted and horribly mature little boys... he feared and therefore disliked them. They seemed immeasurably foreign. Their patched, stained clothes, their shapeless boots, were like a differently coloured skin... The mere appearance of them made him feel guiltily self-conscious.[4]

There was some sympathy here, as would be expected from an undoubtedly intelligent man, but fear is expressed, at least on the part of Beavis. We may also cite E.M. Forster (whose novel *Where Angels Fear to Tread* shows throughout a disdain for the working classes from those who had led privileged lives), Somerset Maugham, George Orwell, Anthony Powell, C.P. Snow, Evelyn Waugh, Angus Wilson, P.G. Wodehouse, Virginia Woolf – there are so many. Even Ian Fleming's James Bond was a 'toff'.

In *Eyeless in Gaza*, Huxley writes of:

> a country where a quarter of the population's genuinely bourgeois and another quarter passionately longs to be... What does the Labour Party poll at

> an election? A third of the votes. I'm generously assuming it might some day poll half of them. The rest's bourgeois. Either naturally bourgeois by interest and fear, or else artificially, by snobbery and imagination.[5]

In *The Moon and Sixpence*, meanwhile, Maugham wrote of what the privileged classes saw as normality:

> There were photographs in the drawing-room of her son and daughter. The son – his name was Robert – was a boy of sixteen at Rugby; and you saw him in flannels and a cricket cap, and again in a tail-coat and a stand-up collar. He had his mother's candid brow and fine, reflective eyes. He looked clean, healthy and normal.[6]

Later in *The Moon and Sixpence*, Maugham writes of the abandoned Mrs Strickland, 'she could not get over the idea that to earn her living was somewhat undignified', and when Mrs Strickland speaks of her daughter, 'just out' she says that 'I shouldn't like her to mix with all sorts of people'.[7]

In his dystopian novel *Nineteen Eighty-Four*, Orwell wrote:

> There was a whole chain of separate departments dealing with proletarian literature, music, drama, and entertainment generally. Here were produced rubbishy newspapers containing almost nothing except sport, crime and astrology, sensational five-cent novelettes, films oozing with sex, and sentimental songs which were composed entirely by mechanical means...[8]

Orwell also wrote, positioning the elite carefully:

> ...the proles were natural inferiors who must be kept in subjection... In reality very little was known about the proles. It was not necessary to know much. So long as they continued to work and breed, their other activities were without importance.[9]

In the words of Emmanuel Goldstein, leader of the opposition to the ruling Party:

> ...if leisure and security were enjoyed by all alike, the great mass of human beings who are normally stupefied by poverty would become literate and would learn to think for themselves; and when once they had done this, they would sooner or later realize that the privileged minority had no function, and they would sweep it away. In the long run, a hierarchical society was only possible on a basis of poverty and ignorance.[10]

While I have dwelled upon writers, the same point could be made about many cultural forms, such as classical music, opera, or theatre: during the twentieth century, almost all output has been created by people, mostly men, from a particular vantage point. And that vantage point has not been one of knowledge of people from a working-class background. Moreover, this output demonstrates not just ignorance of the working class, but fear, and the need to keep members of the working class quiescent and 'in their place'.

An honourable exception to this has been television soap and other dramas and comedies, where issues of importance to working-class people have been explored, notably in *Coronation Street*, in *EastEnders* and in *Brookside*. Other influential television shows include *Cathy Come Home* and *Up the Junction*; the latter was based on the writing of Nell Dunn. Working-class dramas are now far more common on television than they used to be, but it is hard to avoid the nagging suspicion that a great deal of television output is made because of its tendency to deflect the attention of poorer people away from the fact that they are being kept spoon-fed and 'in their place'.

Another cultural exception has been popular music. The Beatles, for example, were from working-class backgrounds (John Lennon probably had the wealthiest background among the four Beatles, in that he grew up in a privately owned house, but to claim him as middle class would be a gross distortion of the truth). As part of the track *Working Class Hero*, in which he sang 'But you're still fucking peasants as far as I can see', John Lennon captured the sense of contempt with which the privileged view the working classes – fit for acting as cannon fodder in their own imperial adventures, but unfit for admission to their world of privilege. Both before and after The Beatles, there have been popular musicians from working-class backgrounds, though there have also been plenty with more privileged origins.[11]

We do not need to blame everyone, only those who knowingly subscribe to innate British superiority, viz: 'I should have thought that a pack of British boys – you're all British aren't you? – would have been able to put up a better show…'[12] None of the writers cited above is to blame for his or her beliefs; indeed, many of the writers appear to be acutely aware of what it means to be privileged; but there is a discernible discomfort with privilege to be seen in much of the writing. None of this discomfort has, however, been manifest in museums, and it is because of engrained biases, rooted in ignorance and fear, that working-class people have long been largely absent from British museums. While statistics are hard to come by (it has not been in the interests of those responsible for this absence to publicise their failings), there is evidence that, with a little effort, museums are more than capable of attracting a diverse range of users.[13]

The pattern of privilege

In this chapter, I intend to analyse in what ways the 'pattern of privilege' can be overcome.[14] First we need to understand what the 'pattern of privilege' looks like.

Privilege comes in many forms, and it varies according to circumstances: to be White is to be privileged; to be male is to be privileged; to be educated well is to be privileged; to be wealthy is to be privileged; not to be deaf or blind, for example, is to be privileged; to be heterosexual is to be privileged; to have two parents throughout childhood is to be privileged; there are many ways people may be privileged, and even although there are times when privilege may turn into disadvantage, the norm is that privilege wins preferment, and nowhere is this more true than in the world of museums.

Governance

Governance is supposed to provide protection from privilege by overseeing efficient and effective operations, but in fact governance systems have helped perpetuate traditional approaches, especially in being dominated by White males who have enjoyed various privileges, notably access to private education. Governing Boards are meant to provide bridges to the 'community', but in reality they do the exact opposite. Boards suffer from weak recruitment (many attempts to build Boards which are representative of society at large have failed because of the inbuilt nature of privilege) and the nominating process is fatally flawed – it is far too reliant upon familiarity with potential candidates among people who themselves represent privilege: Boards continue to be dominated by the same privileged people, some of them more concerned with career advancement than with effecting good governance, many from wealthy backgrounds (often appointed in the hope that their wealth will translate into more money for their museum). Few Board members of the bigger British museums are not from the privileged classes.[15]

As museums become ever more reliant upon private funding, and as governance systems fail so constantly to keep up with change in society, this situation will likely continue. Economic, political and cultural systems represent the old imperial and colonial approach – many museums were created under the auspices of these systems, and while ever the systems persist then so will the museums created by them.

The self-styled *Philistines for Labour* (the UK's Labour Party has, since its creation in 1900, traditionally been the political party of the working classes. The Party has provided the main opposition to the UK's Conservative Party since the 1920s) in Newcastle upon Tyne of the early 1990s were suspicious of the entire cultural world, and these suspicions (held by many Left-wing politicians) were deeply lodged. Those who suspected that privileged access to culture is real were not wrong – they articulated a real situation that was hardly deniable. As it happens, the Newcastle *Philistines for Labour* were eventually persuaded that museums *could be* of relevance to everybody through the performance especially of the Newcastle Discovery Museum, sited in Newcastle's deprived West End and used extensively by the people who lived there. Between 1989 and 1997, the proportion of C2DE (who could in those days roughly be equated to 'working class'; today we are likely to call them NS-SEC Groups 5–8, which is an occupation-based classification, as society continues to strive to classify people for marketing purposes. We are referring to people with relatively low disposable incomes) visits to Newcastle's Discovery Museum rose from 28 per cent to 53 per cent. In Newcastle Residents' Survey of 1998, museums were voted the most popular council service. Even more spectacular, the Survey revealed that museums were used by 74 per cent of

Newcastle residents (compared with a national figure of 35 per cent). These statistics were consistent across all Newcastle wards, rich and poor.[16] As a result, enabling museum accessibility was cited in the election manifestos of the Newcastle Labour Party in local government elections in the late 1990s.

The growth of the working-class museum audience in Newcastle was achieved because of four factors: firstly, there was a *desire* to achieve this, through policy and culture and through staff commitment; secondly, there were *long-term*, consistent approaches – there were no quick fixes, and exhibitions, activities and publicity, plus an air of liveliness, all made major contributions, for example in the building of otherwise disadvantaged audiences for Discovery's People's Gallery (we said to our politicians at the time that it could take a whole generation to effect lasting change. This time period was way longer than the normal political life expectancy): thirdly, at Tyne and Wear Museums we *structured* ourselves for inclusion, with more education and marketing staff, for example; and fourthly, TWM staff had consistent *political support* and funding.[17]

So if governance is a big issue, what about attitudes among museum staff? These are very much coloured by the fact that many museum staff, and nearly all directors, have come from the very privileged class that was brought up to regard scholarship as the be all and end all qualification needed to operate successfully in museums. The notion of working-class stories having any significance in the museum world has often been seen as an absurdity,[18] despite well-founded claims that Britain is 'addicted to inequality'.[19]

Is there such a thing as 'working class' anyway?

What we really mean is *low-income*, though it is true that there is much more to 'class' than purely economic factors. The notion of 'working class' largely lost relevance in the UK during the twentieth century, with the loss of 'traditional' industries, the expansion of travel opportunities, the loss of political focus on the Labour Party and the rise in home ownership.[20] John Holden tried to summarise the changes thus:

> Class divisions are no longer between fairly homogenous groups of upper, middle and working class. Instead, there are financial divisions between the super-rich… the prosperous middle class; the aspirant middle class; the working class; and the non-working poor, sometimes referred to as 'the underclass'.[21]

Holden pointed out that many politicians, up to and including Tony Blair, have claimed that the UK is no longer a class-based society, but that the discussion of class 'is firmly back on the agenda'.[22] Holden makes the point that the rich 'know very little about the poor'[23] and this is a common theme in the literature cited above. Indeed, it may be that it is the very ignorance of working-class life and motivation on the part of those who have had the benefit of privileged upbringings that really explains why the working classes have been so absent in so many British museums. Holden went on to say that:

> The era of different classes having easily identifiable and separate cultures is long gone. Working class culture, as understood in the twentieth century, arose from a particular combination of circumstances: towns where there was one dominant industry and a football team with players taken from the backstreets, a mutual building society bearing the town's name, a local brewery, bakery and newspaper owned by prominent families whom everyone knew. Even the bus colours adopted by local authorities gave a sense of distinctiveness, pride and solidarity. All of these have gone.[24]

But redefining the working class, and redefining the 'high culture' to which the working classes did not have access, do not make the absence of many people from museums go away. It remains a mystery why statistics on how many (or how few) people from lower-income groups actually visited the national museums funded by the British Government disappeared from public view on the Department for Digital, Culture, Media and Sport (DCMS) website in the early years of the twenty-first century. I have always assumed that such revelations were embarrassing to DCMS, but I acknowledge that I may be wrong – I would love to know the real reason.

It would, however, be true to say that Government nervousness about the exclusion of many people from museums peaked at the beginning of the twenty-first century, and in May 2000 the DCMS published a document entitled *Centres for Social Change: Museums, Galleries and Archives for All*, to act as a guide to policy for the museums, galleries and archives funded by DCMS and for those run by local authorities. In his Foreword to this document, the then Secretary of State for Culture, Media and Sport, Chris Smith, wrote that:

> combatting social exclusion is one of the Government's highest priorities, and I believe that museums, galleries and archives have a significant role to play in helping us to do this... I am enormously impressed by the good practice already taking place... I recognise that this change will not be easy, and will take time.[25]

Smith won few friends among those who were content with the maintenance of the status traditional quo and *Centres for Social Change* fell largely upon deaf ears.

The Group for Large Local Authority Museums published a report in October 2000 entitled *Museums and Social Inclusion*. This report described work which was being undertaken in the larger local authority-funded museum sector to combat the type of social exclusion that had led to a betrayal of working classes in museums for many years, and in some ways it could be seen as a response to the DCMS Policy Guidance that had been issued in May of that year. The report saw as the main obstacle to socially inclusive museum work the provision of funding.[26]

Since that time Government has, arguably, become more interested in reducing the cost of museums to the public purse than it has been worried about the exclusion of so many people from what museums do. The Mendoza Review of

November 2017 takes a very positive view of English museums, citing funding problems as the main issue confronting them.[27] The Mendoza Review was an opportunity to create a strategy for English museums, which was not taken, and its references to the need to diversify audiences seemed to be token ones. In particular, the London-based national museums were given a very easy time.

It was the two great open-air museums that were created in England that began to ask new questions in museums about the condition of the working classes. Beamish and Ironbridge museums were both created in order to ensure that industrial life in their respective regions – the North East and the West Midlands of England – was recorded and not forgotten. In this, these two museums were forerunners of the social history movement that finally gained traction in museums in general in the 1980s. This movement got under way because of a variety of factors,[28] which combined to change the nature of many local museums; though not, I have to note, the nationally funded ones (with the exception of those among the Tyne & Wear Museums group in the 1990s). It was a characteristic of this movement that stories, especially those of working-class people, began to gain prominence and that the importance of object collections, so representative of privilege and so unrepresentative of society at large, began to wane. This pattern of change has led to various supporters of privilege to bemoan the loss of the prominence of collections, as though some kind of sacrilege was being committed, rather than the addressing of a gross imbalance.[29] Indeed, the whole attempt to address working-class history in museums has been condemned as 'dumbing down'.[30] Right-wing polemicist James Delingpole wrote of '...glib pacifism, woolly cod-sociological gobbledegook, cultural relativism and political correctness'.[31]

Notwithstanding such bleats from privileged people that modern museums are at risk of deviating from their core functions of research, preservation and display, through their attempts to 'democratise' access to their holdings, there is definitely change discernible, especially in the local authority sector, where much of the innovation in museum techniques takes place. It has taken the Black Lives Matter movement to shine a global spotlight on the complacencies and inadequacies of many British museums, museums having been forced onto centre stage with regard to the desirability of 'decolonising' them through the repatriation of items (and other measures) that they hold that were acquired during eras of White dominance of many peoples of colour, and with regard to the future role of museums in 'saving' the statuary which memorialises characters such as slave traders and White supremacists.

But British museums' complicity in evoking the so-called 'greatness' of our imperial and colonial forebears is just one of the failings of the British museum sector, and its failure to address the needs of poorer people by excluding them from the sector, in terms of collecting, staffing and governance, as well as in terms of use, has been of criminal dimensions. The stench emanating from many British museums is that of privilege.

Notes

1 The author was brought up in rented, back-to-back housing in Armley and Burmantofts, Leeds, UK, before moving, aged 11, to a rented house on the Swarcliffe Council Estate, in east Leeds. His father was a joiner (veneer preparer); his mother, when in work, was variously a school dinner lady and a school and hospital cleaner; she also worked in the textiles industry and finally as a nursing auxiliary. The author attended state schools in Leeds, and he studied at three British universities. He worked in museums in York, Leeds, Hull and Tyne & Wear before becoming Director of Museums at National Museums Liverpool in 2001. He went into the museum profession in the 1980s because he (mistakenly) believed that museums were places which welcomed people from the working classes, and where working-class people could continue their (often-truncated) education. Only belatedly did he realise that museums were run by people from privileged backgrounds who, largely, did not care that museums had their own values system, based upon a White, male and colonialist mentality. This realisation fired his own efforts to address these issues when he was in a position to do so. One of the opponents of change, among many, was the British Government, which tended to back privilege when able to do so – hence Government's repeated efforts to reduce the costs of publicly funded museums and to make museums more 'resilient'.

2 *Museum as Muck* is a British group made up of people from working-class backgrounds who work in the museum and gallery sector; *Museum Detox* is a British network for Black, Asian and Minority ethnic heritage professionals. Both of these networks are challenging the traditional, privileged museum; and both have the support of the British Museums Association.

3 Janes and Sandell, *Museum Activism*; Delingpole, *What Are Museums For?*; Appleton, *Museums for 'The People'?*

4 Huxley, *Eyeless in Gaza*, 71. Page references in this chapter to works by Huxley, Forster, Golding and Orwell are to the Penguin editions.

5 Huxley, *Eyeless in Gaza*, 149–50.

6 Maugham, *The Moon and Sixpence*, 23.

7 Maugham, *The Moon and Sixpence*, 86.

8 Orwell, *Nineteen Eighty-Four*, 38.

9 Orwell, *Nineteen Eighty-Four*, 60.

10 Orwell, *Nineteen Eighty-Four*, 154

11 Many famous bands, such as Pink Floyd, Genesis, Blur and Coldplay, have had their origins in privilege. Many others have not!

12 Golding, *Lord of the Flies*, 192.

13 Arts Council England, "Taking Part Survey." According to Arts Council England: '... adults from the upper socio-economic group are significantly more likely to visit a museum or gallery compared with adults from the lower socio-economic group... The gap in engagement between the two socio-economic groups has remained large...'

14 See Fleming, "Positioning the Museum for Social Inclusion."

15 As a museum Director, the author has known good, indifferent and outright bad Board members. Some have done the job of understanding and agreeing institutional priorities, forging mutually acceptable working relationships with staff, establishing and following good management practices within the Board and focusing their energies in productive ways; others have not done any of these things, instead allowing the elevation of individual interest over institutional interest. The author learned a great deal about Board management from the late Stephen Weil, whose lectures to the MMI class of 1996 have since provided much food for thought. Assembling effective Boards is far from easy, but Boards must not become agents of privilege first and foremost.

16 Fleming, "A Question of Perception."

17 It should be noted that one of the leading figures in the *Philistines for Labour*, Heaton Councillor Don Price, a former member of the Trotskyist Militant Tendency, was 'banished' to the TWM Committee by Newcastle City Council though he was, for a

time, the Committee Chair. He became Deputy Leader of Newcastle City Council and made an ultimately abortive bid for the Council Leadership. The author is in possession of a letter from Westerhope Councillor Gina Tiller, signed 'Past President – Philistines for Labour – currently reformed!' It was Councillor Price and Walkergate Councillor Barney Rice (the latter also Chaired the TWM Committee) who between them ensured that the museum service enjoyed constant political support from Newcastle City Council.
18 Fleming, David, "Positioning the Museum for Social Inclusion"; Delingpole, *What Are Museums For?*
19 Holden, *Culture and Class*, 19.
20 Hopkins, *The Rise and Decline of the English Working Classes*, 265–79.
21 Holden, *Culture and Class*, 17–18.
22 Holden, *Culture and Class*, 17.
23 Holden, *Culture and Class*, 18.
24 Holden, *Culture and Class*, 27.
25 Department for Culture, Media and Sport, *Centres for Social Change*, 3.
26 GLLAM, *Museums and Social Inclusion.*
27 Mendoza, *The Mendoza Review.*
28 Fleming, "Social History in Museums."
29 Fleming, "Positioning the Museum for Social Inclusion."
30 Appleton, *Museums for 'The People'?*, 8.
31 Delingpole, *What Are Museums For?*

Bibliography

Appleton, Josie. *Museums for 'The People'?* London: Institute of Ideas, 2001.

Arts Council England. "Taking Part Survey: Engagement with Museums and Galleries." Accessed 20 September 2020. www.artscouncil.org.uk/taking-part-survey.

Bennett, Tony, Mike Savage, Elizabeth Silva, Alan Warde, Modesto Gayo-Cal, and David Wright. *Culture, Class, Distinction*: Abingdon and New York: Routledge, 2009.

Delingpole, James. "What Are Museums For? (Charles Douglas-Home Memorial Trust Award 2005)." The Times online, 2005.

Department for Culture, Media and Sport. *Centres for Social Change: Museums, Galleries and Archives for All.* London: DCMS, 2000.

Fiske, John. *Understanding Popular Culture.* Winchester, Mass.: Unwin Hyman, 1989.

Fleming, David. "Social History in Museums; 35 Years of Progress?" *Social History in Museums* 34 (2010): 39–40.

Fleming, David. "Positioning the Museum for Social Inclusion." In *Museums, Society, Inequality*, edited by Richard Sandell, 213–224. Abingdon and New York: Routledge, 2002.

Fleming, David. "A Question of Perception." *Museums Journal* (April 1999): 29–31.

Forster, E.M. *Where Angels Fear to Tread.* London: Penguin, 1959, 1905.

Golding, William. *Lord of the Flies.* Harmondsworth: Penguin1960, 1954.

Group for Large Local Authority Museums. *Museums and Social Inclusion.* Leicester: GLLAM, 2000.

Holden, John. *Culture and Class.* London: Counterpoint, 2010.

Hopkins, Eric. *The Rise and Decline of the English Working Classes 1918–1990: A Social History.* London: Weidenfeld & Nicolson, 1991.

Huxley, Aldous. *Eyeless in Gaza.* Harmondsworth: Penguin, in association with Chatto and Windus, 1955.

Janes, Robert R., and Richard Sandell, eds. *Museum Activism.* Abingdon and New York: Routledge, 2019.

Lennon, John. *Working Class Hero.* John Lennon/Plastic Ono Band recording, 1970.

Maugham, W. Somerset. *The Moon and Sixpence* (Collected Edition). London: William Heinemann Ltd., 1935.

McGuigan, Jim. *Cultural Populism*. London: Routledge, 1992.

Mendoza, Neil. *The Mendoza Review: An Independent Review of Museums in England*. London: DCMS, 2017.

Orwell, George. *Nineteen Eighty-Four*. London: Penguin in association with Secker and Warburg, 1954.

Tressell, Robert. *The Ragged Trousered Philanthropists*. London: Grant Richards, 1914.

3

'SEAT OF THE MUSES OR THE MOOLAH?'

New working-class demands on elitist archival practices

Silvio Tamaso D'Onofrio

In 2008, in São Paulo, Brazil's overarching trade union organisation Central Única dos Trabalhadores hosted a conference 'The Workers' World and its Archives'.[1] The autoethnographic study that forms the basis of this chapter raises questions as to whether such fora have resulted in any noteworthy influence on current policy and practices of archival organisations in Brazil (and perhaps beyond), in relation to the working class. Here, I discuss the response of the archival sector in Brazil to a collection by a noteworthy working-class writer. Will Brazilian archival organisations understand the worth of working-class culture and, if so, how might this be reflected in their collecting policies? Unexpectedly, these questions gained importance when I decided to donate a collection of documents to an institution with the necessary resources for the maintenance of the material. This chapter, then, is a call for further attention on this issue, fuelled, I hope, by this case study concerning the intellectual contribution through an archival collection of Brazilian writer Edgard Cavalheiro (1911–1958).

My research enabled me to gather together an important set of his documents that had been dispersed. There was a parcel in possession of his daughter in one city, another parcel with his granddaughter in another city, and two more parts with two nephews of Edgard Cavalheiro in a third city. In addition, as many of the books written by Edgard Cavalheiro were not part of this family collection, I needed to source additional data, such as the year of publication of these books, their reissues and reprints. It was necessary to have access to these publications that were often not even found in public libraries. The solution was to acquire copies from second-hand stores. Further, there was secondary source material: biographies, autobiographies, historical studies of the press and Brazil's publication history, which referred to the work of Edgard Cavalheiro. And when I couldn't find these works in libraries, I bought them. My research also sought to locate documents of handwritten correspondence. I acquired books that included this, in

DOI: 10.4324/9781003029519-5

addition to correspondence between Cavalheiro and the Portuguese novelist José Rodrigues Miguéis, which was located at Brown University,[2] in the United States. Having completed my research, I then wanted to donate to an archival collection my personal collection along with the additional material that had belonged to Edgard Cavalheiro and was now with his family.

Who was Edgard Cavalheiro?

Grandson of a paternal Italian, his mother having been born in Bologna, Edgard Cavalheiro was a journalist, biographer, literary critic and editor of his time, in Brazil. His body of work records five biographies, three works of literary criticism and an additional contribution to 51 works of collective authorship. In addition to his separate articles, he was responsible for 12 journalistic columns in the mainstream Brazilian press of his day, mainly exploring the subjects of his profession: biographical writing and literary criticism. In total, almost a thousand articles from journals came from his pen[3] in addition to his being the founder of a fortnightly cultural journal.[4] He also wrote translations and worked with intellectual groups in a variety of ways, driven by his work as an author as well as editor for some of the main publishers in the country. As a member of the first associations of writers in Brazil, he worked in the company of those who favoured the recognition of this working class, in addition to the defence of intellectual property, which was hardly respected then, resulting in writers suffering financial loss. His intellectual trajectory is also distinguished by his activism to support democracy. Cavalheiro was a participant of the First Brazilian Congress of Writers,[5] an event promoted by the Brazilian Writers Association of which Cavalheiro was one of the founders. This Congress is recognised as the main social movement against the dictatorship of President Getúlio Vargas,[6] a political regime that was extinguished in that same year – 1945.

To give an idea of Edgard Cavalheiro's activity, when he died at the age of 46, the author had nine books submitted to publishers, in preparation for release. On this occasion, the translator and literary critic Paulo Rónai submitted an obituary in the press. In his writings, Rónai reveals, between the lines, a sense of Cavalheiro's influence:

> Large, also, are Cavalheiro's dispersed work in newspapers, magazines, prefaces by others' books [...] Only after this heritage was catalogued and the part ready for printing was published, will it be possible to evaluate exactly the production of this fertile spirit, one of the great disseminators of culture among us.[7]

Edgard Cavalheiro was a person from the working classes and there he remained during his life. It is known that a famous writer once visited Cavalheiro at his home, a small rented house in downtown São Paulo where Edgard lived with wife and four children, and said when he entered the space, 'This is a can of sardines!' Only at the end of his life did Cavalheiro buy his own house to live with his wife

and children. Soon after that, facing the premature death of her husband and having just a small house as her patrimony, Cavalheiro's widow was forced to seek extra work outside the home. This reveals the financial status of the family. So Edgard Cavalheiro did not infiltrate the ruling classes or the so-called elite. He also did not have prestigious relatives and, for this, he could be characterised as a 'poor cousin', according to the definition of the Brazilian sociologist Sergio Miceli in his effort to comprehend the intricacies among intellectuals and dominant classes in Brazil.[8] Like the other 'poor cousins', Edgard Cavalheiro was also born in the interior of the state and went to the capital at the end of his adolescence. Subsequently, isolated in the state capital, the poor cousin would not access any financial and social help from uncles and other family members because they lived further away and were also of modest means. Besides that, the poor cousin could not expediently improve his circumstances because of his humble formal education.

Family poverty emphasised the importance of a source of auxiliary income, either by washing or sewing the clothes of others, or by cooking, for example. These activities were predominantly performed by women, often due to a lack of choice of work opportunities outside the family, and also due to a lack of affinity with men's work, in terms of external expectations of physical prowess. According to Miceli, many of these poor cousins initiated feminisation of their work, dedicating themselves to house duties initially identified as reserved for women. As an alternative, the poor cousin would enter into the priesthood or, perhaps, become a writer. It was through this process that the first professional writers appeared in Brazil.[9]

Cavalheiro's father had a small grocery trade in the interior of the state of São Paulo and, due to the consequences from the crisis of the New York stock market crash in 1929, his family moved to the capital and went to live, father, mother and seven children, in a house with two rooms. His father passed away in 1936 and, with that, at the age of 25, Cavalheiro, as the eldest male sibling, was faced with new family responsibilities, 'work to eat, eat to work ... Joys parallel to fatigue. Sensitive joys. Eat, rest ... But not the money' – what could be the mystique of work, perfectly applicable here, in the words of Simone Weil, when the sole purpose of daily toil comes down to the basic maintenance of existence?[10]

Despite almost no formal education, Edgard Cavalheiro managed to print his name in the canon of Brazilian literary criticism and biography, counting on the help of none other than his great dedication and persistence, fulfilling the role of efficient bureaucrat by day, and engaging in intellectual work through the night and on weekends.[11] His first job was at the São Paulo Railway offices, where he worked for two and a half years. Then he became a junior accountant at the Bank of the State of São Paulo for about ten years. From the age of 28 onwards, Edgard Cavalheiro begin to work in the publishing sector. There he remained until his final days.

The Edgard Cavalheiro Fund and the Edgard Cavalheiro Collection

The estate that was once owned by Edgard Cavalheiro, comprising books, journal articles, handwritten notebooks, correspondence, photographs, documents and

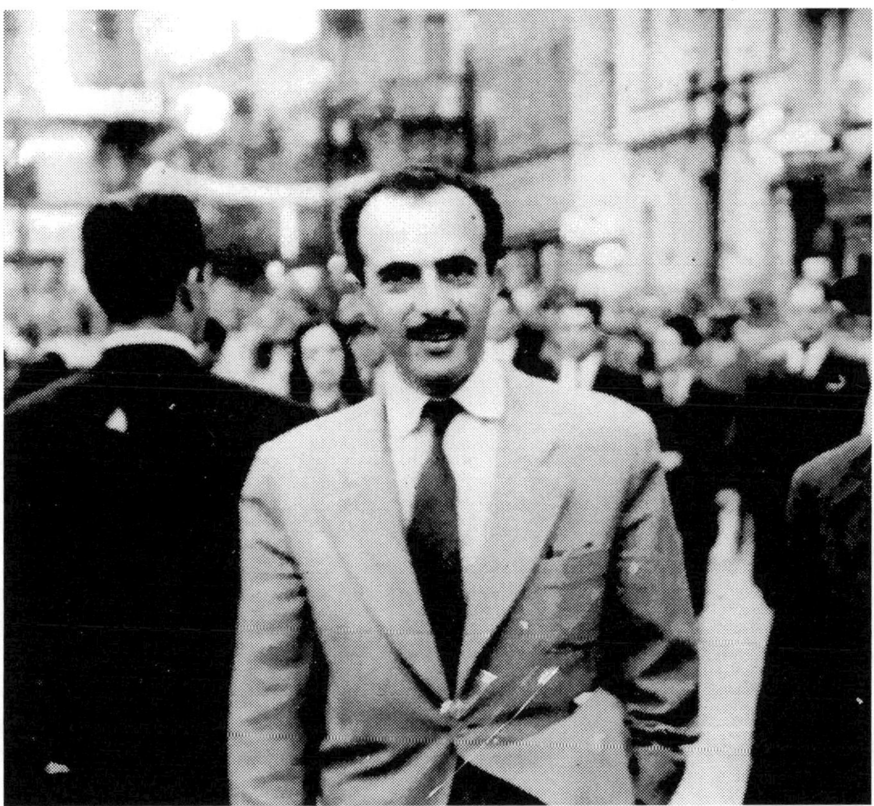

FIGURE 3.1 Edgard Cavalheiro in downtown São Paulo, late 1930s. Photographer unknown.

three-dimensional objects,[12] portrays an important part of the cultural life of Brazil from the 1930s to the 1950s, and undocumented material that was forgotten in time, unacknowledged and at risk of deterioration as a result of the lack of financial resources of Edgard Cavalheiro's heirs. This material, composed of works that he wrote, in addition to works written by third parties, collected by Edgard himself, comprises the Edgard Cavalheiro Fund. This collection was augmented by my aforementioned research: the Edgard Cavalheiro Collection. Thus, as a result of these two collections, with a clear distinction between the primary and secondary source material, the Edgard Cavalheiro Archive was created. Together, the owners of this material started to look for an institution that would be interested in maintaining, conserving, publicising and enabling access to the material.

The first action we took was the creation of an accessions proposal to document the material. This approach was informed by the principles of archivist Bernardine Dodge, who advocates that 'documents speak' instead of family members and researchers. According to Dodge, 'both archivists and researchers are storytellers',[13] who impose their own meanings. In addition, we followed the advice of Angelika Menne-Haritz, who asserts that archives involve the 'science of contexts and relationships'.[14] Therefore, instead of separating each component within the collection, we attempted to maintain the connections, based on documents, photographs and testimonies, between the original owners of the archive, the eldest daughter of Edgard Cavalheiro, Maria Helena, her daughter Maria Christina and their cousins, the brothers Roberto Dante and Luís Carlos. And following the suggestions of Camargo and Goulart, we also sought to value those documents that were not characterised by any external value, like intimate diaries.[15] Such documents are usually overlooked by archivists due to their negative, emotional aspects. Personal diaries, for example, are intended to be private, and so do not possess, in the words of Luciana Duranti, an 'archival bond'.[16] For this scholar, this 'is what transforms a document into a record', and also, for her, 'documents that are expressions of a transaction are not records until they are put into relation with other records'. At the same time, some would argue that the aspect of 'collected' material, instead of 'accumulated' (by the original owner, for example), would hinder the acceptance of our donation.

In terms of scale, the Edgard Cavalheiro Archive comprises approximately 500 volumes. However, among these volumes are 19 multi-paged bindings containing articles torn from journals, and some of these bindings are very bulky. It is estimated that the total number of individual items in the Edgard Cavalheiro Archive is something around 10,000 – from material that belonged to the author as well as the collection that was compiled by subsequent research.

Searching for a location

As anticipated, having concluded the research in 2012, the Edgard Cavalheiro family and I began to search for an institution that could be interested in the material we had gathered. It was our intention, from the outset, to send the material to a public institution, preferably a university, because that would support research and development, thereby optimising the documentary and testimonial value of this rich material. Also, from the beginning, our interest was in donating the material; in spite of its esteemed historical and documentary value, we believed that if we tried to sell it, we could find it harder to locate the material.

We started to contact some institutions, initially those whose affinity with the material seemed to be greater, for example, the university where the postgraduate research which gave rise to all of this was developed. In total, we contacted less than a dozen institutions and prioritised, at first, those that were geographically closest to the collection, in the southeastern region of Brazil. This would facilitate logistics for eventual technical visits and/or the transportation of material, in addition to the fact that the collection holder's own life writer Edgard Cavalheiro had definite ties with the region of São Paulo, in southeastern Brazil. We received, from these contacts, some responses. Some just confirmed the receipt of our contact; others claimed injunctions of all kinds to postpone a clearer position on our offer.

During our pilgrimage in search of an institution that could house the material that we had in hand, we perceived that some of the negative responses that we received were skewed and selective. One of these museum-documentation centres, a member of a public university, refused our donation proposal on the grounds that there was no useful space available in its infrastructure. The explanation came in an email from a representative of the Technical-Administrative Council of that unit, explaining the recent decision of the governing body that discussed our donation offer. A few weeks later, however, the same documentation centre accepted the donation of an infinitely larger collection than ours. Apparently the only difference between the two cases was that the accepted collection was of a person more famous than Edgard Cavalheiro: an internationally known musician and composer, with several prized awards throughout his career. Possibly the negotiations for the incorporation of the great musician's collection were in progress when the institution refused our offer, alleging lack of space. So their position would be perfectly understandable: they would be saving space for the imminent request. However, the process of incorporating new collections continued in the following months and years, without the physical storage structure having changed and therefore without increasing space. So we started asking ourselves, how?

It is clear that the institution was not obliged to accept our proposal, but the argument used for the refusal, in contrast to the subsequent facts and procedures, led us to reflect. Was our offer, or our collection, outside the terms of reference of their archival policy? The institution, in its published guidelines, emphasises the need to expand its collections, starting with the statement that they value well-known collections.[17] Then we continued asking ourselves: how does a familiar, disparate archive which has never been united, a collection that has never been seen before except in fragments and only by a few family members, a collection never before seen or studied in the so-called 'public sphere' – how could an archive like that be known, or have earned fame? So, in valuing only famous archives, the Museum shows it only has room for one part of society, and this could be deemed dysfunctional on the basis of the absence of inclusion and what is seemingly desirable: covering the culture of a wider society. This kind of museum seems, at least in part, unhelpful. It seemed to us that this would be a contradiction, and if true of our collection, then probably likely for other collections too, from different people, of diverse origins, or even in different countries. Sadly, it was easy to draw an overseas parallel, which suggests a more widespread phenomenon, not one that is local or which is nationally restricted to Brazil: scholar of museum studies Adele Chynoweth wrote something that fits perfectly here, even though she is talking about Australia: 'Does this observation apply to the ethos of other museums? While austerity measures, efficiency dividends and right-wing populism pose real threats to the fight against inequity, might they also be used to feed a culture of well-disguised excuse-mongering throughout the unhelpful museum?'[18] As a federative member of the Brazilian republic, the state of São Paulo, where some of these public cultural institutions are located, has been politically governed by the same party since 1998. The right-wing-oriented Brazilian Social Democracy Party

(PSDB, in Portuguese) won nothing less than seven consecutive elections. The keywords are the same: austerity, efficiency, numbers. This elicited a sense of disquiet in our minds.

As for the other items in the guidelines for the accession of collections, our archive seemed to fit perfectly. It was related to:

1. (proximity to) one of the constitutive areas of the institution (to be clear, our archive was related to four of them: Language, Literature, History and Music).
2. to the generic denomination of 'Brazilian Studies'.
3. the institution's existing and/or emerging research areas, research projects and study groups.
4. interdisciplinarity, no doubt, because there were specific collections entered in our catalogue: on music; about the so-called Constitutionalist Revolution of 1932, an armed uprising which occurred between the state of São Paulo and the Brazilian federation, among other collections.
5. the material was in its integrity (we understood this to refer to the conservation state of the material, without pests, for example). Alternatively, if we define integrity as the total amount of documents, in our case all living family members had been contacted and 100 per cent of the original material that had been located was integrated into our collection in a closely supervised process by Edgard Cavalheiro's daughter, Mrs. Maria Helena Cavalheiro Neves, currently a sweet great-grandmother, 74 years old.

Reflections on the twenty-first-century museum

Maybe all of this is just another case of an institution that behaves as a person – and not a very well-balanced person. Through the lens of social psychology, it is common to attempt to understand the escape mechanisms of the individual, and one of these very common methods occurs when the individual stops acting according to his or her own will and starts to adopt a posture offered by external cultural standards.

> ...the individual ceases to be himself; he adopts entirely the kind of personality offered to him by cultural patterns; and he therefore becomes exactly as all others are and as they expect him to be. The discrepancy between 'I' and the world disappears and with it the conscious fear of aloneness and powerlessness.[19]

It could be that the institution in its refusal of the collection does not understand its meaning or significance. Or should we think of it as a matter of social class? If so, again we may be facing a case of anthropomorphising, because if the institution pursues famous people, and it is perhaps fair to take it for granted that most famous people are from middle and ruling classes – except in exceptional cases – the institution, perhaps, has some kind of prejudice against the working class. Is this also reflected in the employment of its staff, its human resources? In terms of its collection, however, the situation seems more complicated when the institution itself becomes a gatekeeper from the outset, through its public guidelines, that a collection must be 'well-connected' or possessing a renowned status. Except for one or another sporadic case of a working-class person who managed to form a well-known collection, all other notable collections seem to come from famous people. Perhaps the institution believes in the stereotypes so commonly associated with people from the working classes, such as bad taste, insufficient intellectual resources, reactionary political tendencies, weak work ethics and dysfunctional family values.[20] So, in the view of the institution, if this is the case, with so many subjective obstacles, how could someone build a well-known archive?

After this, we arrived at the simple and obvious conclusion that even today's museums – and I include the archival sector here – seem to have surrendered to the logic of the market when it comes to the accession of materials into their particular collection. Apparently the historical and documentary value of the material they select becomes less important each day compared to materials that are more easily capitalised upon, in some way more superficial, more visible, as if they had greater sales appeal, with greater potential for marketing and exposure in the media, with greater chances of receiving likes, re-tweets and shares. In addition, it perhaps affords a more palatable content – because it is derived from celebrity, capable of reaching a larger number of people, possibly culturally less demanding and 'uninitiated'. Is the museum becoming a new window for mass consumption? Following this path, in a short time the museum will be competing with the large networks of popular commerce stores that sell low-quality products to the low-income population. For popular commerce, this is not a problem at all: to adapt itself to the demands of the people, prices always lower and lower. But maybe it is not the same reasoning when we are talking about an institution responsible for guarding and promoting culture: art, objects, documents, knowledge, tradition, customs, habits, practices, ceremonies, rituals, dance, music, legends, tales, plays, instruments, accounts, rituals, places and so on. And with archives from celebrities originated in showbiz, preferably people who are easily identifiable because they are frequently seen on mainstream media, the attached content, exposed with all pomp and circumstance, seems not to matter as long as the museum grabs the attention of the public and sell more tickets, more t-shirts, mugs of coffee, gains more views, likes and becomes an internet trending topic. If it is the image that sells, as the adage tells us, Guy Debord, for his part, in one of his sharp observations, reflects about the power of image to promote consumption:

> Consumable pseudo-cyclical time is spectacular time, both in the narrow sense as time spent consuming images and in the broader sense as image of the consumption of time. The time spent consuming images (images which in turn serve to publicize all the other commodities) is both the particular terrain where the spectacle's mechanisms are most fully implemented and the general goal that those mechanisms present, the focus and epitome of all particular consumptions.[21]

In the midst of the concerns raised, the underlying issue seems to revolve around ideas of cultural value and, more specifically, the public value of some museum item, a collection/archive or its own symbolic representation, for example, in terms of its ideology, or even the cultural equipment, the building, responsible for hosting this. Dave O'Brien, a scholar in the field of cultural and creative industries, dedicated an entire chapter to historicise, analyse and reflect upon theories of 'public value' and cultural organisations, and his findings seem to be valid not only to his local context, but also globally.[22]

According to O'Brien, the development of urban cultural facilities is currently mediated by 'narratives of success and the social science providing the evidence for such claims'[23] (something that illustrates and encourages reflections about the process of elaborating public policies as a whole, and not just those pertaining to culture).[24] The author defines the United Kingdom as the starting point of his analysis, investigating in detail the peculiarities of cultural policies promoted in the last decades, either under the command of New Labour, or under the tutelage of Conservative governments. He then expands the discussion to include North America and Australia,[25] pointing to the specificities of public and private cultural institutions, emphasising the need for the correct distinction between the two spheres as the associated cultural infrastructure plays a large part in determining the mode of relationships that these institutions created with its public or other stakeholders.[26] Still in the process of approaching the core of the issue of public value, O'Brien claims that this is a difficult concept to define. Reading the definition proposed by Alford and O'Flynn, Dave O'Brien states that these authors identified:

> Several meanings and uses of the term, ranging from an overarching policy paradigm responding to new public management, a rhetorical strategy for under-fire bureaucracies and public managers, a narrative or ethnographic account of the world and practices of public managers and as a framework for measuring the performance of organisations and staff that moves beyond the narrowly managerialist focus of much new public management.[27]

As seen, that disquieting headache of what denotes 'public value' is reverberating throughout the world, affecting many people, a matter that deserves prompt resolution. On the other hand, and at the same time, investing and valuing more up-to-date collections, with multimedia resources instead of the yellowed and predictable paper sheet, museums give the impression of also giving in to popular longings of 'novelty', which cannot exist without a providential 'erasure' of the past – be that in the form, be that in the content; after all, there is no room for everything at the same time. There are numerous findings and publications related to our current 'culture of forgetfulness', 'in a world that paints its wrinkles quickly, in the media that educates and pampers us in a culture of "the instant"',[28] covering everything with the veneer of a supposed modernity.[29] There was a Brazilian poet, a composer and singer, with the artistic name of Cazuza, who in a song from 1998, 'Time Doesn't Stop', reflects about life and time. Some of these verses seem prophetical about what we were about to see in the museum of the twenty-first century, a place where culture is sometimes confused with entertainment: 'I see the future repeating the past / I see a museum of big novelties / Time doesn't stop'.

Valuing only famous figures, thus taking up the cult of celebrity, the twenty-first-century museum runs the risk of disavowing an observation that Jacques Le Goff had made years ago and which continues to be pondered: 'The interest of collective memory and history is no longer crystallised exclusively about great men, events, fast-moving history, political, diplomatic, military history. It is interested in all men, it raises a new hierarchy'.[30] If Le Goff is correct, a brand-new world is emerging, with a new understanding that says history has many sides, and not just one as used to be assumed. If, in fact, history is constructed by the history of the winners – the so-called official history, but also by the history of the anonymous voices (the object of the so-called microhistory) who also shared the same experience lived by the winners – and if the museum proceeds in this way, here we get the ideal situation when the House of the Muses works to really empower people by expanding their cultural horizons, as pointed to by the classical statement by Pierre Bourdieu in which the power of someone is made up of a combination of economic capital, social capital and cultural capital.[31] On the other hand, if the museum has only space for the famous guy and his assets, how can people improve their cultural capital knowing only one side of history? And what about minorities and their culture? What about Indigenous peoples and other subjugated groups; how long will we continue to tell their story through the lens of the winners, instead of letting them tell their own story? And if the governing bodies of museums consistently insist on this practice, that is, that of just opening up space for the notable person, this may be a deliberate attempt to invent a tradition, in the terms proposed by Hobsbawm,[32] or even to continue it. It is necessary to reflect on the process because, as this English historian has pointed out, the 'invented tradition', besides having as its main characteristic invariability, establishes itself as a procedural reference and, worse: its occurrence demonstrates a loss of adaptability and flexibility of the museological institution, two characteristics that we can only hope to increase, instead of decreasing, in cultural equipment.

At least in part, a happy ending

Finally, in October 2017, five years after the search for a suitable place for the Edgard Cavalheiro Archive began, a private contract was signed, featuring as donors myself and the Edgard Cavalheiro heirs. The material was then transferred to the receiver: the Cultural Documentation Center 'Alexandre Eulalio' (CEDAE), at the Institute of Language Studies (IEL) of the State University of Campinas (UNICAMP), located in the interior of the state of São Paulo, about 100km from the capital.[33] Until today, we didn't contemplate where, in its collecting policies, CEDAE-UNICAMP differs from the other archive centres and museums that we tried to access.

The overall conclusion from our experience is that, at worst, it seems that what matters is profit: the museum of the twenty-first century needs to sell products: mugs, pens, posters, t-shirts, etcetera, to assist in its maintenance. The museum itself now seems to have the need to pose as profitable in an urge to increase its number of followers on social media, as if this legitimises its importance, or the importance of the material it stores. Who knows whether with this strategy a museum can get more supporters, donors, investors and investments? It's a very logical equation, but we may have to observe if these goals will benefit the majority of those interested and affected: the public, the community. We must remain firm and united to fight if these new and modern museum policies, that is, those that which say there is only space for celebrities, are reflected in greater distancing between people, genders, ethnicities and social classes. The world does not need this. By following this path, it is possible that the old 'mouseion', 'seat of the Muses', from Greek through Latin, will be known, in the near future, as the 'seat of the Moolah'.

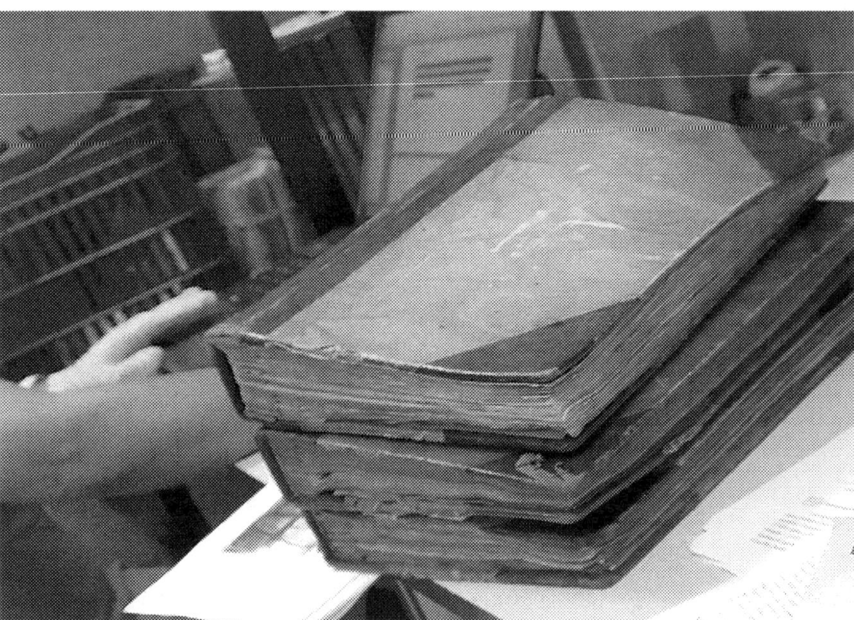

FIGURE 3.2 Bound volumes, letters and books: in 2017, the Edgard Cavalheiro Archive became part of the UNICAMP collection. Photograph: Silvio Tamaso D'Onofrio.

Notes

1 van der Linden, "Speaking Globally," 186.
2 Ref. Ms. 89.7 box 3, Manuscripts Division, John Hay Library, Brown University, Providence, Rhode Island, USA.
3 For more about Edgard Cavalheiro and his production, see: D'Onofrio, "Fontes," 4.

4 D'Onofrio, "Grupo da Baruel," 11.
5 *Atas*, 11.
6 Mota, *Ideologia*, 157.
7 Rónai, "Edgard." All translations from Portuguese to English in this chapter were done by me.
8 Miceli, *Intelectuais*, 105.
9 Miceli, *Intelectuais*, 176–78.
10 Weil, *Simone*, 89.
11 And he (Cavalheiro, my note) then said to me: '– You can't imagine the effort I make to write this book, because I have to work hard all week at Globo and still write things for the newspaper, all of that. I work on Sundays'. (Candido, interview).
12 For more detailed information about the Edgard Cavalheiro Collection, consult: D'Onofrio, "Estudo de caso."
13 Dodge, *Across*, 26.
14 Menne-Haritz, "What," 11.
15 Camargo and Goulart, *Tempo*, 40.
16 Duranti, "Archival," 216.
17 It is not a case of my pointing my finger at anyone here, or revealing which institutions I am referring to, even though this renders my text incomplete, because I cannot give exact references such as the document with the guidelines for the expanding of collections from one of these institutions, for example, material that is on the internet.
18 Chynoweth, "A Call," 174.
19 Fromm, *Fear*, 159.
20 Alper and Leistyna, *Class Dismissed.*
21 Debord, *Society*, 88–89.
22 O'Brien, *Cultural Policy*.
23 O'Brien, *Cultural Policy*, 112,
24 O'Brien, *Cultural Policy*, 113.
25 O'Brien, *Cultural Policy,* 116–17,
26 O'Brien, *Cultural Policy*, 119.
27 O'Brien, *Cultural Policy*, 17.
28 Saliba, "Mentalidades," 28.
29 To better understand the issue of forgetfulness, it is recommended to consult the following: Lebrun, *Amenagement*, 528; Plumb, *Death*, 2004.
30 Le Goff, *História*, 531.
31 Bourdieu, "Forms," 243.
32 Hobsbawm, *Introdução*, 9–10.
33 Rónai, "Edgard."

Bibliography

Alford, John, and Janine O'Flynn. "Making Sense of Public Value: Concepts, Critiques and Emergent Meanings." *International Journal of Public Administration* 32, no. 3–4 (2009): 171–191.

Alper, Loretta, and Pepi Leistyna. *Class Dismissed: How TV Frames the Working Class* (Film). Northampton, Mass.: Media Education Foundation, 2005.

Arendt, Hannah. *Between Past and Future: Six Exercises in Political Thought*. New York: The Viking Press, 1961.

Atas do I Congresso Brasileiro de Escritores. São Paulo: Associação Brasileira de Escritores, 1945.

Bourdieu, Pierre. "The Forms of Capital." In *Handbook of Theory and Research for the Sociology of Education*, edited by John Richardson, 241–258. New York: Greenwood, 1986.

Camargo, Ana Maria de Almeida, and Silvana Goulart. *Tempo e circunstância: A abordagem contextual dos arquivos pessoais: procedimentos adotados na organização dos documentos de Fernando Henrique Cardoso*. São Paulo: Instituto Fernando Henrique Cardoso, 2007.

Candido, Antonio. "Edgard Cavalheiro." Interview by Silvio D'Onofrio. Unpublished. São Paulo, 24 June 2009. Audio, 17:15.

Chynoweth, Adele. "A Call to Justice at the National Museum of Australia." In *Museums and Social Change: Challenging the Unhelpful Museum*, edited by Adele Chynoweth, Bernadette Lynch, Klaus Petersen, and Sarah Smed, 173–185. London and New York: Routledge, 2020.

D'Onofrio, Silvio CesarTamaso. "Estudo de caso: O acervo Edgard Cavalheiro na UNICAMP." *Conference Proceedings of IX National Seminar of the Memory Center of State University of Campinas* (July 2019). Accessed 15 October 2020. www.ixseminarionacionalcmu.com.br/resources/anais/8/1565409467_ARQUIVO_DONOFRIO,Silvio_9o.Sem.Nac.do.CEME-UNICAMP_final.pdf.

D'Onofrio, Silvio Cesar Tamaso. "*O Grupo da Baruel e a intelectualidade paulista nos anos 1940*." DSc diss., Universidade de São Paulo, 2017.

D'Onofrio, Silvio CesarTamaso. "Fontes para uma biografia intelectual de Edgard Cavalheiro (1911–1958)." MPhil diss., Universidade de São Paulo, 2012.

Debord, Guy. *Society of the Spectacle*. Translated by Ken Knaubb. London: Rebel Press, 2005.

Dodge, Bernardine. "Across the Great Divide: Archival Discourse and the (re)Presentations of the Past in Late-Modern Society." *Archivaria: The Journal of the Association of Canadian Archivists* 53 (Spring 2002). Accessed 15 October 2020. https://archivaria.ca/index.php/archivaria/article/view/12834/14050.

Duranti, Luciana. "The Archival Bond." *Archives and Museum Informatics* 11 (1997): 213–218.

"Edgar Cavalheiro's Personal Archive is part of the CEDAE Collection." Accessed 1 June 2020. www3.iel.unicamp.br/cedae/noticia.php?view=details&article=286.

Hobsbawm, Eric. "Introdução." In *A invenção das tradições*, edited by Eric Hobsbawm and Terence Ranger. Translated by Celina C.Cavalvanti. 16th ed. São Paulo: Paz e Terra, 2008.

Fromm, Erich. *The Fear of Freedom*. London and New York: Routledge, 2001.

Le Goff, Jacques. *História e memória*. 5th ed. Translated by Bernardo Leitão et. al. Campinas: UNICAMP, 2003.

Lebrun, Jean. *Amenagement du territoire de l'historien*. Paris: Center de Recherche et d'Action Sociale, 1978.

Menne-Haritz, Angelika. "What Can Be Achieved with Archives?" In *The Concept of Record: Report from the Second Stockholm Conference on Archival Science and the Concept of Record, May 1996*. Stockholm: Riksarkivet, 1998.

Miceli, Sergio. *Intelectuais à brasileira*. São Paulo: Companhia das Letras, 2001.

Mota, Carlos Guilherme. *Ideologia da Cultura Brasileira (1933–1974): Pontos de partida para uma revisão histórica*. 3rd ed. São Paulo: Editora 34, 2008.

O'Brien, Dave. *Cultural Policy: Management, Value and Modernity in the Creative Industries*. London and New York: Routledge, 2014.

Plumb, John H. *The Death of Past*. 2nd ed. London: Palgrave Schol, 2004.

Rónai, Paulo. "Edgard Cavalheiro." *O Estado de S. Paulo*, São Paulo, 13 July 1958.

Saliba, Elias Thomé. "Mentalidades ou história sociocultural: A busca de um eixo teórico para o conhecimento histórico." *Margem* no. 1 (March 1992): 119–130.

Sodré, Nelson Werneck. *Em defesa da cultura*. Rio de Janeiro: Bertrand Brasil, 1988.

van der Linden, Marcel. "Speaking Globally." *International Labor and Working-Class History* 75 (2009): 184–188.

Weil, Simone. *Simone Weil: La condition ouvrière: oppression et liberté*. 2nd ed. Translated by Therezinha Langlada. Rio de Janeiro: Paz & Terra, 1996.

PART II

Shut up: The struggle to end the silence

Museums are being challenged to: be more collaborative; refuse claims of neutrality; be more representative of the wider population; support research and debate; decolonise; and, critically reflect on their sources of corporate sponsorship. Amidst this culture of justified complaint, museums are also highly valued given their resources and technical prowess in registering, conserving, storing and exhibiting objects. Museums are both contested and respected by communities. Museums continue to be approached by interest groups with offers of material to donate to collections and suggestions of subjects for public display.

It is against this backdrop of expectations that case studies emerge concerning exemptions, gaps, invisibility, silence and even deliberate cover-up. There is as much meaning and power in absence as there is in tangible representation. And even when certain narratives are exhibited, there may be exclusions of crucial nuancing that impact on meaning or there may be preferences for particular modes of representation or sites at the expense of others. Why does one historical narrative inform a heritage listing but is ignored by the museum sector? Why is labour history exhibited without the discourse of class informing the curator's interpretation? Conversely, in the case of a museum that is committed to exposing a hidden working-class history, how and where does it source tangible material for display?

Collectively, the chapters in Part II not only encourage museums to pay attention to how, and if, working-class narratives are represented, but also demand that museums be transparent about the logistics and principles that inform the acquisition and display of those objects, sourced from labourers and the poor.

DOI: 10.4324/9781003029519-6

4

'ONE AND ALL'?

Retrieving South Australia's forgotten Labor history

Philip Payton

On 9 May 2017, the Australian Cornish Mining Sites – Burra and Moonta (Mines) – were included in the prestigious National Heritage List of 'natural, historic and indigenous places of outstanding significance to the nation'.[1] Hailed at the time as a landmark achievement, the preparation of the case for inclusion and the attendant lobbying of the Commonwealth government had been a decade-long process, spearheaded by the South Australian State Government Heritage Unit and the South Australian Heritage Council.[2]

Prompted initially by an approach from Cornwall in the United Kingdom, which in 2006 had been awarded UNESCO World Heritage Site status for the mining landscapes of Cornwall and West Devon, the quest for National Heritage listing was seen as a potential first step towards achieving World Heritage Site status for the South Australian sites, possibly as part of a transnational network of Cornish mining sites linking Cornwall, South Australia, South Africa, Mexico and Spain. Earning their place on the National Heritage List, the twin Australian Cornish Mining Sites, Burra and Moonta (Mines), were designated 109th and 110th, respectively, out of a total in 2017 of 119 sites nationally, of which only eight were located in South Australia.

The ambitious scope of the Australian Cornish Mining Sites project, with its proposed international dimension, was a reflection of the extent of Cornwall's nineteenth-century 'Great Emigration', when in the period 1815 to 1914, from the end of the Napoleonic Wars to the eve of the Great War, some 250,000 Cornish people emigrated overseas.[3] Many of these emigrants were miners and their families, escaping hard times at home but also taking advantage of new opportunities abroad, particularly on the rapidly expanding international mining frontier. The Cornish, with their expertise in deep hard-rock mining and associated steam engineering, formed a significant element of the newly emergent mobile labour force that responded to the demands of the new frontier. Employing separate identity as

DOI: 10.4324/9781003029519-7

an economic device, the Cornish argued that they were innately qualified as hard-rock miners, especially when compared to potentially competing ethnic groups. This 'myth of Cousin Jack', as it has been called (a Cousin Jack was an emigrant Cornish miner), played a major role in securing preferential treatment for the Cornish in mining districts across the globe, and became a central plank of a vibrant Cornish transnational identity. There was also a parallel 'myth of Cousin Jenny', an assertion that emigrant Cornish women were innately attuned to the rigours of the frontier, triumphing over hardships where lesser women might fail.[4]

In mining districts across the world, the Cornish cultivated their separate identity, speaking a rich dialect of English (including words and mining terms inherited from the recently defunct Celtic language of Cornwall), importing foodways (not least the far-famed Cornish pasty), participating in Cornish sports (notably wrestling), making music – especially brass bands and Cornish carols – and worshipping in the Nonconformist chapels of the Bible Christians, Primitive Methodists and Wesleyans. They considered themselves 'Ancient Britons', more British than the English, and spoke habitually of 'Cornwall, near England'.[5]

An important element of this Cornish transnational identity was 'the Cornish radical tradition', which in Cornwall had emerged in the years before the Great Reform Act of 1832, when Nonconformists had led the demand for reform and opposed the authority of the established Church of England, especially the requirement to pay tithes to the Church. Later, in the 'Hungry' 1840s, food riots erupted across Cornwall, and many Nonconformists (including those implicated in the riots) were attracted to the Chartist movement, with its agitation for universal male suffrage, secret ballots, abolition of property qualifications for Members of Parliament, payment for MPs, equal-size electoral districts (to ensure one-man, one-vote, one value), and annual elections. In the heady atmosphere of the 1830s and 1840s, many of those in Cornwall seeking civil and religious freedom, economic opportunity and social mobility were drawn to the United States of America. But others were enticed to South Australia's so-called 'Paradise of Dissent', following the colony's foundation in 1836, where they formed a sizeable part of the province's early population.[6]

On the mining fields in the 'New World', Cornish radicalism, with its strong Nonconformist flavour, turned to trade unionism and Labor politics. In the United States, for example, the Cornish became, as Richard E. Lingenfelter put it, 'the leaders of the mining labor movement of the West', forming unions in places such as Grass Valley in California, Virginia City in Nevada, and Butte, Montana.[7] In South Africa, the Cornish miners were likewise prominent in the mining labour movement, leading the demand for improved health and safety conditions in the deep and dangerous mines of the Rand, which resulted among other things in two milestone Miners' Phthisis Acts being passed by the Transvaal Parliament.[8]

But it was in South Australia that the Cornish influence was most noticeable. The discovery of copper in the mid-1840s, first at Kapunda and then, and more importantly, at Burra, drew the Cornish to South Australia in their thousands in the 1840s and 1850s. Then, in 1859–61, came the even more spectacular copper finds at Moonta and Wallaroo on northern Yorke Peninsula, attracting many more

Cornish from elsewhere in Australia and Cornwall itself, a migration stream that ran strong until the mid-1880s. From the start, the mines of South Australia were run on Cornish principles, which ranged from technology and architecture to terminology and the managerial organisation and practices of the industry.[9]

Prominent among the latter was the 'tribute' and 'tutwork' system of employment, where part of the entrepreneurial function was performed by the miners themselves, in contracts that related to the value of ore won ('tributing') or the amount of ground excavated ('tutwork'). The latter was usually reserved for the sinking of shafts or the driving of underground tunnels. In 'tributing', individual sections of the mine ('pitches') were contracted out to individual miners or – more usually – small groups of miners ('pares') as a result of open bidding on 'survey day'. Prior to this bidding, each pitch was inspected by an experienced mine agent ('captain') who would estimate the value of the ore that it contained. Each pitch would then be offered at 'captain's prices'. For a rich section of ground, the captain's price might be as low as a few shillings in the pound, so that for each pounds-worth of ore raised the individual tributer or pare received only a couple of shillings. For lower-grade pitches, however, the captain's price might be considerably higher, an incentive for a tributer or pare to work indifferent ground. It was unusual, in fact, for tribute pitches to be let at captain's prices. More often, there was considerable competitive downward-bidding between rival tributers or pares, especially for attractive sections of ground. A pitch was awarded to the lowest bidder, often at a figure well below captain's prices, and the tributers – being in a sense self-employed – were required to provide their own tools, candles, blasting powder, timber and other equipment.[10]

Initially, Cornish miners in South Australia welcomed the introduction of tributing and tutwork, with which they had been familiar in Cornwall, and which allowed them to benefit from their own skill and enterprise. However, shortcomings in the system soon became apparent, first of all at the Burra mine in 1848 where there was a dispute over the value of ore won, discrepancies between the miners' own estimates and the results of the mining company's assayer, provoking a major strike. The authorities in distant Adelaide feared an insurrection at the Burra, recalling darkly that 1848 had become a year of European revolution, but the strike was peaceful enough, moderated and managed by Nonconformist local preachers drawn from the ranks of the miners themselves. By January 1849, the strike had been resolved, the company shaken by the solidarity of the Cornish miners.[11]

The Burra strike did not lead to the emergence of a permanent trade union movement but those who later moved on to Moonta and Wallaroo took their experience of strike action with them. In 1864, for example, a strike broke out at both the Moonta and Wallaroo mines, a protest against the oppressive style of the two mine managers. The 'two tyrants' were duly removed, a victory for the striking miners, and as before at the Burra mine, the miners' leaders and spokesmen were Nonconformist local preachers. These men provided the kernel of what would become a more enduring trade union movement, leading to the formation of the Moonta Miners' and Mechanics' Association in November 1872. In urging solidarity, the Association's founders made frequent recourse to the time-honoured Cornish motto, 'One and All?':

> We invite the young and old
> To join our miners' band;
> Come and have your name enrolled,
> And join us heart and hand.
> Cornwall was never conquered yet,
> By men of mighty powers;
> And shall we in silence sit
> And show ourselves like cowards?
> We have the motto 'one and all';
> This coat of arms is ours;
> Then let us rise both great and small
> To carry out our endeavours.[12]

By April 1874, a further strike had broken out. A major feature of this action was the role performed by the women. Unlike Cornwall, where women had been employed at surface as 'bal-maidens', breaking and sorting the ore, in South Australia they had been prevented from working at the mines, and were firmly confined to the domestic sphere. Nonetheless, in the 1874 strike at Moonta and Wallaroo, the miners' wives and other women were encouraged to participate in the industrial action, sweeping the blacklegs from the pump engine-houses and thus threatening to flood the underground workings. 'There is a rumour', John Prisk (one of the Association leaders, also a local preacher) was reputed to have told a meeting of local women, 'that you're going to sweep all the nuisances out of their engine-houses'.[13] Suitably enthused, the women promised 'to do their best with their mallee poles' – brooms and mops made from sticks of mallee scrub – and, as Prisk had urged, swept the blacklegs from the engine-houses, bringing the pump engines to an abrupt halt.[14] As the *Yorke's Peninsula Advertiser* explained:

> [the] women went vigorously to work with their brooms, charging in all directions. The females attached to the sweeping regiment numbered about a hundred strong … carrying, many of them, their brooms, poles and pine branches. Never before, perhaps, was such an extraordinary spectacle witnessed as here presented itself. The space between Bower's and Ryan's [shafts, at Moonta], an area covering acres of ground, was alive with people of all classes, miners, mechanics, tradesmen and travellers, boys and girls, women (some with children in arms) excitedly talking, shouting, laughing and hurrying towards the engine house.[15]

Thereafter, the strike was swiftly resolved, the company alarmed at the prospect of underground inundation. The women's exploits duly passed into local lore, and in subsequent industrial unrest the threat of similar action was made routinely. By now, criticism of tribute and tutwork had become more focused, the miners seeing it increasingly as a device to set worker against workers and to keep wages down. There was, for example, a brief strike over the matter in 1884, and trouble again in 1886 and 1889, with a major strike from September 1891 until February 1892. This time, the miners were defeated but agitation and negotiation continued, winning various concessions, the most significant being in 1903 when 'captain's prices' were at last replaced by a 'sliding scale' – based on movement in the price of copper – in which tribute and tutwork contractors participated directly in the company's profits.[16]

The local Association had become part of the Amalgamated Miners' Association, an Australia-wide trade union, and this consolidation was mirrored in the emergence of a political Labor movement at Moonta and on northern Yorke Peninsula. Richard 'Dicky' Hooper, a Moonta miner born in Cornwall, became South Australia's first Labor Member of Parliament in May 1891, heralding the foundation and growth of the state's United Labor Party. In 1902, John Verran, another Cornish miner from Moonta (and a local preacher to boot), was elected to the State Parliament, and in the election of 1910 became Premier and thus the leader of the world's first majority Labor government.[17] Verran returned to his home town in triumph, as the *People's Weekly* recorded:

> There could be no doubt as to the warmth of the welcome which the Cornish miners sought to give to their [trade union] President on being raised to place and power, and the gathering will be mark an epoch in the history of Moonta. Bunting was flying all over the town, and all Moonta and his wife were out to take part in the gathering. At Kadina and at Wallaroo hundreds of workers joined the train, and the scene at Moonta was an animated one. The Wallaroo town band and the combined Commonwealth and Model brass bands discoursed music as the train drew up in the platform.[18]

Verran's government was short-lived (it was defeated in the state election of 1912) but the influence of the Cornish radical tradition lived on in the state's Labor Party, surviving even the closure of the Moonta and Wallaroo mines in 1923 and exemplified in the political career of Robert Stanley Richards, another Moonta miner and local preacher of Cornish descent, who became Premier of South Australia in 1933.[19]

As historian Frank Bongiorno has observed, pondering the story sketched above, the 'South Australian Labor Party [was] shaped powerfully by migration, Methodism and mining … a political organisation that has exercised a remarkable and surprising influence over the making of modern Australia'.[20] Yet, as Bongiorno suggests, until very recently at least, this impact has been routinely underestimated or ignored, not least in South Australia's own museums. This omission may, perhaps, reflect a certain level of curatorial ignorance but it might also result from a deep-seated reluctance to interpret the past in a way that emphasises strife, discord and community tensions. As Margaret Anderson has commented: 'Generally the past presented in heritage building is a nostalgic past, wholesome, healthy and conflict free. The people who inhabit it are virtuous, hard-working, thrifty and usually successful'.[21] Likewise, Lucy Taska has shown how banal interpretation can serve to write out radical and uncomfortable history.[22] Graeme Davison, for example, in an early critique of the recreated gold-mining township of Sovereign Hill in Victoria, complained that it presented a 'necessarily quieter, cleaner and more orderly place' than the boisterous character of nineteenth-century Ballarat. In this recreated version, there were more 'middle-class matrons in crinolines and bonnets' and fewer young male miners and no prostitutes.[23] It was, as Michael Evans added, an attempt to 'distort the past and sentimentalise history'. Yet, as Evans added, this 'early mythologizing phase was, arguably, an unconscious interpretive intent', with later developments at Sovereign Hill evidencing a more thoughtful, reflective approach to the historiography of the goldfields and to heritage studies, public history and museology more generally.[24]

Although there was nothing in South Australia to compare (or even compete) with Sovereign Hill, there were early attempts to interpret the state's Cornish past. Both Burra and Moonta Mines had been designated State Heritage Sites some years before the drive for National Heritage listing, with the former in particular receiving significant interpretive and restorative work through the state government's Department of Mines and Energy. K.R. Johns, the Department's director-general, had made a comparative study tour of Cornwall in the mid-1980s, resulting in the Department's booklet *Cornish Mining Heritage*, published in 1986. Here Johns observed that derelict mine engine-houses and other physical remains in South Australia were more than redolent of Cornwall. But he also asked: 'What is their significance?' Answering the question himself, he went on to 'consider how [these] relevant archaeological relics might be recognised, interpreted and preserved for educational, historical and tourist purposes'. Johns had already approved the work and helped secured the funding for the restoration of one of the remaining Cornish engine-houses at the Burra mine site. As he explained, 'in the State's 150th year [1986] and in anticipation of the Australian bicentenary [1988], concerted effort is being given to the restoration of Morphett's Engine-house and appurtenances at Burra in association with a local committee concerned with planning, development and funding'. Johns added that his Department had also fostered 'awareness of South Australian mining heritage through publications, lectures and field activities, interpretation and identification of mining relics, conducting excursions for school parties and other interested groups … [we are] on the right track with regard to catering for [the] tourist'.[25]

Subsequently, G.J. Drew described the restoration project in his booklet *Morphetts Enginehouse and the Cornish Beam Engine, Burra Mine, South Australia. A Guide to the Museum and Interpretive Display*. The museum in question, it turned out, was the restored engine-house itself, with its three storeys or 'chambers' and protruding 'bob plat' (an external platform from which the rocking beam-engine would have been inspected for maintenance purposes). Interpretation boards were erected in each of the three storeys. As Drew explained, much of this interpretative work was of a technological nature, indicating the construction and functioning of a typical

Cornish steam beam-engine, and showing how such an engine had once been installed in Morphett's engine-house and other locations at the Burra mine site and across South Australia. There was considerable reliance on diagrams and scale drawings, including the visual reproduction of contemporary nineteenth-century documents. This was also reflected in Drew's publication itself, where the technical information dominated the text and illustrations. A biographical sketch of John Morphett, after whom the engine-house was named, was included in both the booklet and on interpretation boards in the Museum, and likewise there was brief discussion in both media of aspects of social life, including a note on Cornish emigration. Yet the overwhelming focus was technological, emphasising nineteenth-century technological transfer from Cornwall, with little room for social or cultural history, and nothing at all on the nationally significant 1848 strike at Burra.[26]

Meanwhile, at Moonta Mines the locality – which included both the remains of the mines themselves and the surrounding settlement of cottages and Methodist chapels – had been the subject of considerable conservation work by the Moonta Branch of the National Trust for South Australia. Prompted by Oswald Pryor's well-known book *Australia's Little Cornwall*, published as early as 1962, Moonta had projected itself as the historical heart of the northern Yorke Peninsula former copper-mining district, in particular emphasising the significance of the adjoining Moonta Mines heritage site.

Following its closure in 1968, the Moonta Mines Model School (first erected in 1878) had been acquired by the Moonta National Trust branch and developed as a museum devoted to the locality. In many ways typical of the eclectic, crowded, artefact-led country museums encountered across Australia, the Moonta Mines Model School nonetheless attempted some ambitious interpretation work, although the results were patchy. The mining exhibits were especially well done, making use of interpretation boards featuring historic mining scenes and the characteristic 'Cousin Jack' cartoons produced by Oswald Pryor in the 1940s and 1950s.[27] Working models of mining machinery, made by amateur craftsmen in the early twentieth century, were particularly effective. As the Moonta National Trust explained, overall the Museum's 14 rooms were devoted principally to 'thematic displays of the Cornish miners' lifestyles – mining, lodges and friendly societies, sports and pastimes, death and hardship, extensive displays of costumes, silverware, photographs and memorabilia and a classroom furnished c.1900'.[28] Additionally, Moonta National Trust had also acquired the former Moonta School of Mines (originally a Baptist chapel), situated just outside the Moonta Mines heritage site, developing it as part museum and part resource centre for family historians, especially those tracing their Cornish forbears. Historic mining photographs were again to the fore but, somewhat curiously, there was also 'a large display of medical and apothecary equipment', dating apparently from the late nineteenth and early twentieth centuries.[29] Although perhaps typical of an Australian country general practice in earlier times, the medical equipment was given a prominence that seemed excessive, even eccentric, given the (missed) opportunities for addressing other aspects of the locality's economic, social and cultural life.

One striking omission at both Moonta locations was the labour movement. The School of Mines displays were silent of the subject, while even the more sophisticated interpretive material at Moonta Mines Model School made mention only in passing, with a short reference to industrial action and a nod in the direction of John Verran. None of the Museum's 14 rooms was devoted to the labour movement, despite its local, state, national and international significance, an oversight, moreover, that had not been corrected in the Museum's periodic updates. For the casual visitor, the Museum appeared to suggest that industrial action and radical politics were but brief deviations or distractions within the dominant narrative of a harmonious and homogeneous community.

Local and regional museums are sometimes criticised for their 'antiquarian' approaches to interpreting the past. Yet in metropolitan Adelaide, the omissions evident at Burra and Moonta were also apparent. The Migration Museum, opened in 1986, like other museums across Australia formed at much the same time, was a valiant attempt by 'historians ... to undermine what they saw as the dominant and consensual models of Australian history'. Indeed, 'in Adelaide nervous administrators awaited the public opening of the Migration Museum with obvious trepidation'. However, fears were soon allayed by the approving comments of the Museum's visitors who were not averse, it turned out, to being 'challenged [in] their cosy perceptions of the past'.[30] A book published by the Museum in 1995 to complement its displays described the contributions to the South Australian multi-cultural way of life of no fewer than 97 different ethnic or national groups, from 'Aboriginal' to 'Zimbabwean'. Among these were the 'Cornish', who were afforded a substantial and well-researched chapter of their own.[31] Strangely, however, despite the Museum's avowed intention of showing a more confronting approach to history, there was no mention in the Cornish chapter of strikes, trade unions, Labor politicians, or even the first majority Labor government in the world, led by a Cornish miner.

A later initiative, the Centre for Democracy, opened in May 2017 as a permanent exhibition gallery in the Institute Building at the State Library of South Australia, offered a kaleidoscopic approach to the subject of 'democracy' in the state and in Australia as a whole. Here there were few inhibitions about discussing conflict and discord but, although there was acknowledgement that 'John Verran became leader of South Australia's first all-Labor government', there was no systematic coverage of the state's Cornish radical tradition.[32]

However, there was by this time a glimmer of light. In marked contrast to the meagre treatment at local and state museum level, there was at least some reference to the Labor movement in the documents prepared by D. A. Lenton and C. J. Frieman at the Australian National University at the request of the Commonwealth Government to assess the potential of the Australian Cornish Mining Sites for inclusion in the National Heritage List. In the first of these documents, a report on the Burra State Heritage Area prepared in December 2014, the authors observed briefly that 'The first industrial strike in Australian freesettler history was at the Burra Mines in 1848; therefore, the site comprises one of the first known incidents of organised mass resistance to authority in the history of Australian unionised industrial labour relations'.[33] This insight was expanded on in the second of the documents produced in December 2014, a report on Moonta and the Copper Triangle, which argued that the 'Copper Triangle's organised labour approach to industrial relations … laid the foundations of the trade unionist movement in Australia. The unionised miners, who included Richard Hooper, Robert Stanley Richards and John Verran went on to form the earliest Labor parties and first Labor governments in Australia'.[34] Thumb-nail sketches of Hooper, Richards and Verran were also provided, indicating their local importance but also their significance on the state and national stages.

The Lenton and Frieman reports played a major role in securing National Heritage listing for Burra and Moonta Mines (although their recommendation that the wider Copper Triangle of Moonta, Wallaroo and Kadina should also be included in its entirety alongside Moonta Mines was not accepted). Much of the discussion in the two documents focused on archaeological, architectural and technological matters, as the National Heritage criteria demanded, but it was significant that in the reports' consideration of the social and cultural environment, the early salience of the labour movement had been given at least some attention. Although the treatment remained cursory, it highlighted the importance of the labour dimension in a way that had not been achieved thus far at the several museums at the sites themselves, or indeed elsewhere.

Given the attention afforded the subject in the influential Lenton and Frieman reports, observers were entitled to expect that accession to the National Heritage List would provide new opportunities for the inclusion and interpretation of the labour movement at local, state and national levels. However, early indications proved disappointing. To begin with, the Australian Government's National Heritage List website, designed to elucidate key features of each place on the List, displayed an at best sketchy understanding of the characteristics of the labour movement in South Australia's historic mining communities. Although unable to adequately explain the Cornish 'labour system', it asserted nonetheless that 'Miners brought this labour system with them to South Australia. Later, at Moonta, miners advocated for improvements in mining conditions like a minimum wage applied to "down times"'. This surprisingly inaccurate assessment was repeated elsewhere on the website, with the further insistence that 'At Moonta the Cornish mining system was able to be repeated and applied at a larger scale. Improvement to the system was progressed in areas of labour organisation [and] labour relations (advocacy of a minimum wage through the "down times")'.[35] In fact, there had been no advocacy of a 'minimum wage' as such, at Moonta or indeed elsewhere in South Australia's Cornish mining towns, and such assertion was at best a gross over-simplification of the critiques of the time-honoured tribute and tutwork system of employment made increasingly by trade unionists in the closing decades of the nineteenth century.

There was worse. In an irrelevant but nonetheless irritating aside, the same National Heritage List website claimed mystifyingly that 'Popular legend has it that women workers or wives would call out "Oggie, Oggie, Oggie" and wait for the reply "Oi, Oi, Oi", before dropping the pasty down [the shaft]'. But there was no such 'popular legend' in South Australia! 'Oggie' (or Oggy) is indeed a Cornish dialect word for a pasty, but the fabricated story presented on the National Heritage List website has no basis in historical reality or community folklore and is the product of recent banter between Cornish, Welsh and other sporting enthusiasts who have co-opted the Oggie chant, typically at Rugby Union matches. The Welsh folksinger and comedian, Max Boyce, who did much to popularise the Oggie chant in Wales in the 1970s, conceded that the cry 'Oggie! Oggie! Oggie!', along with the response 'Oi! Oi!, Oi!', had its origins in early twentieth-century Rugby circles in Cornwall.[36] Additionally, the suggestion that women might drop their pasties down a shaft ignored the fact that the mines at Moonta and environs were extremely deep, and that in any case most of the men were employed in extractive areas of the mines ('stopes') far removed from the bottom of shafts. More importantly, perhaps, the reference to 'women workers' was itself erroneous, as no women were employed at the Moonta and northern Yorke Peninsula mines, although, paradoxically, as we have seen, they did play a significant role in the locality's labour movement.

The National Heritage List website, then, proved disappointingly ill-informed, a surprise to those who might have expected an authoritative statement of the sites' historical significance. More promising was the report *Moonta Mines Heritage Area: Site Development Plan*, published by the consultancies TRC Tourism and Locales in April 2018 for the Moonta Branch of the National Trust of South Australia and the District Council of the Copper Coast. This report acknowledged the attempts at 'interpretative display' in two of the rooms of the Moonta Mines Model School museum but considered the displays 'dated and in need of focus, repair and refreshing'. It also noted the 'thousands of items' on show in the Museum, and opined that 'the sheer volume of objects is overwhelming, and it is difficult for the visitors to understand the relevance of the collections in the story of the site … The collections are confusing and many of the artefacts do not relate to the heritage significance of the place'.[37] In calling for a major rationalisation of the museum collection and an upgrading of its displays, the consultants argued that there should be two main emphases in explaining the significance of the locality. The first was to promote understanding of the physical fabric of the mine site today, and to explain its former function. The second, importantly, was to tell 'the stories of people and the social structures. This will enable visitors to appreciate the important contribution made through innovative social organisations and to empathise with the stories and struggles of individuals'.[38]

Dioramas, scale models, map models and a theatrette with digital screens would help the Museum to tell these stories, it was argued, the consultants noting that they had used the theatrette device to good effect when 'we created the story of a Miners Strike in 1911 in Waihi, New Zealand, told through a groom on his wedding day, with talking portraits of his friends, his mother and fiancé. It tells the story of a major social event through a personal story'.[39] Although they did not say so explicitly, the TRC Tourism and Locales consultants had identified a method that could be used in like manner to illuminate key events in the labour history of Moonta and environs, or indeed in similar museum development work at Burra. It was, moreover, a method that might profitably be part of a yet more ambitious project to tell at last the hitherto 'forgotten' story of South Australia's labour movement and its Cornish origins, not only at state level but nationally too, perhaps earning a belated space in the National Museum of Australia itself.

Notes

1 Australian Government, "Australia's National Heritage List."
2 *Advertiser* (Adelaide), 8 May 2007.
3 Payton, *Cornish Overseas*, 24.
4 Payton, "Bal-maidens," 216–19.
5 Payton, "Cousin Jacks," 54–64.
6 Payton, *One and All*, 3–51.
7 Lingenfelter, *Hardrock*, 6.
8 Dawe, *Cornish Pioneers*, 255.
9 Payton, *Making Moonta.*
10 Payton, *One and All*, 39–41.
11 Davies, "Collective Action," 7–32.
12 *Yorke's Peninsula Advertiser*, 13 May 1973.
13 Pryor, *Little Cornwall*, 37.
14 *Yorke's Peninsula Advertiser*, 10 April 1874.
15 *Yorke's Peninsula Advertiser*, 10 April 1874; see also *South Australian Register*, 8 April 1874.
16 Payton, *One and All*, 97–117.
17 Payton, *One and All*, 132–33, 161–86.
18 *People's Weekly*, 25 June 1910.
19 Payton, *One and All*, 247–48.
20 Bongiorno, "Cover Notes."
21 Anderson, "Material Culture," 14.
22 Taska, "Remembering," 81–105.
23 Davison, "The Use," 72.
24 Evans, "Historical," 142, 152.
25 Johns, *Cornish Mining*, 5, 48.
26 Drew, *Morphetts.*
27 Pryor, *Cornish Pasty.*
28 National Trust SA, "Moonta Mines Museum."
29 National Trust SA, "School of Mines/Resource Centre."
30 Anderson, "History," 133–34.
31 Migration Museum, *Many Places*, 96–101.
32 Centre for Democracy, "Democracy Timeline."
33 Lenton and Frieman, *Burra*, 21
34 Lenton and Frieman, *Moonta*, 18.
35 Australian Government, "National Heritage Places – Australian Cornish Mining Sites."
36 Wales On-line, 14 November 2006.
37 TRC Tourism, *Moonta Mines*, 12, 16.
38 TRC Tourism, *Moonta Mines*, 21.
39 TRC Tourism, *Moonta Mines*, 28.

Bibliography

Advertiser (Adelaide).

Anderson, Margaret. "Material Culture and Australian Cultural Politics." *Museums Australia Journal* 2–3 (1991–1992): 3–19.

Anderson, Margaret. "Selling the Past: History in Museums in the 1990s." In *Packaging the Past? Public Histories*, edited by John Rickard and Peter Spearritt, 130–141. Melbourne: Melbourne University Press, 1991.

Australian Government. "Australia's National Heritage List." Accessed 22 May 2020. http://environment.gov.au/heritage/places/national-heritage-list.

Australian Government. "National Heritage Places – Australian Cornish Mining Sites." Accessed 22 May 2020. http://environment.gov.au/heritage/places/national/Australian-cornish-mining-sites.

Bongiorno, Frank. "Cover Notes." In *One and All: Labor and the Radical Tradition in South Australia*, edited by Philip Payton. Adelaide: Wakefield Press, 2016.

Centre for Democracy. "Democracy Timeline." Accessed 16 June 2020. http://centreofdemocracy.sa.gov.au/explore/timeline/.

Davies, Mel. "Collective Action and the Cornish Miner in Australia: An Early Repudiation of the 'Individualistic' Thesis." In *Cornish Studies: Three*, edited by Philip Payton, 7–32, Exeter: University of Exeter Press, 1995.

Davison, Graeme. "The Use and Abuse of Australian History." *Australian Historical Studies* 23, no. 91 (October1988): 55–76.

Dawe, Richard D. *Cornish Pioneers in South Africa: "Gold and Diamonds, Copper and Blood"*. St Austell: Cornish Hillside Publications, 1998.

Drew, G.J. *Morphetts Enginehouse and the Cornish Beam Engine, Burra Mine, South Australia: A Guide to the Museum and Interpretative Display*. Adelaide: South Australian Government of Mines and Energy, 1987.

Evans, Michael. "Historical Interpretation at Sovereign Hill." In *Packaging the Past? Public History*, edited by John Rickard and Peter Spearritt, 142–152, Melbourne: Melbourne University Press, 1991.

Johns, K.E. *Cornish Mining Heritage*. Adelaide: South Australian Government Department of Mines and Energy, 1985.

Lenton, D.A., and C.J. Frieman. *Australian Cornish Mining Heritage Site: Burra State Heritage Area, South Australia*. National Heritage Research Report. Canberra. The Australian National University School of Archaeology and Anthropology, 2014.

Lenton, D.A., and C.J. Frieman. *Australian Cornish Mining Heritage Site: Moonta and the Copper Triangle, South Australia*. National Heritage Research Report. Canberra: Australian National University School of Archaeology and Anthropology, 2014.

Lingenfelter, Richard E. *The Hardrock Miners: A History of the Mining Labor Movement of the American West 1863–1893*. Berkeley: University of California Press, 1974.

Migration Museum. *From Many Places: The History and Cultural Traditions of the South Australian People*. Adelaide: Wakefield Press, 1995.

National Trust SA. "Moonta Mines Museum." Accessed 30 May 2020. http://moontatourism.org.au/attractions/moonta-mines-museum.

National Trust SA. "School of Mines/Resource Centre." Accessed 30 May 2020. http://moontatourism.org.au/attractions/school-of-mines-resource-centre.

Payton, Philip. *The Cornish Overseas: A History of Cornwall's Great Emigration*. Exeter: University of Exeter Press, 2020.

Payton, Philip. "Bal-maidens and Cousin Jenny: The Paradox of Women in Australia's Mining Communities." In *Australia, Migration and Empire: Immigrants in a Globalised World*, edited by Philip Payton and Andrekos Varnava, 207–228. Basingstoke: Palgrave Macmillan, 2019.

Payton, Philip. *One and All: Labor and the Radical Tradition in South Australia*. Adelaide: Wakefield Press, 2016.

Payton, Philip. *Making Moonta: The Invention of Australia's Little Cornwall*. Exeter: University of Exeter Press, 2007.

Payton, Philip. "Cousin Jacks and Ancient Britons: Cornish Immigrants and Ethnic Identity." *Journal of Australian Studies* 68 (2001): 54–64.

People's Weekly.

Pryor, Oswald. *Cornish Pasty: A Selection of Cartoons*. Adelaide: Rigby, 1976.

Pryor, Oswald. *Australia's Little Cornwall*. Adelaide: Rigby, 1962.

South Australian Register.

Taska, Lucy. "Remembering and Incorporating Migrant Workers in Australian Industrial History." *Labor* 16, no. 1 (2019): 81–105.

TRC Tourism and Locales. *Moonta Mines Heritage Area Site Development Plan*. Jindabyne (NSW): TRC Tourism, 2018.

Wales On-line.

Yorke's Peninsula Advertiser.

5

'GO AND TAKE A LOOK AT MILLIE NOW'

Murder, tattooed remains and museum ethics in Quebec

Jamie Jelinski

Introduction

The remains of a woman named Mildred Brown, who died in 1929, are buried without a headstone near the easternmost point of the Island of Montreal in Hawthorn-Dale Cemetery. According to Brian Young, Hawthorn-Dale's 'mission was to provide an accessible, attractive site for modest burials' that the most destitute could afford.[1] The interment of Brown's remains in this cemetery and without a gravestone suggest that she did not have many assets and that her family, who paid for the burial, did not either. Brown's socio-economic status also impacted her body's posthumous treatment. When laid to rest, a small piece of her corpse was missing and now resides in a museum storage facility over two hundred kilometres away. Investigating the circumstances surrounding the removal and preservation of Brown's tattooed skin, I show that this object provides a counterpoint to the 'official' history of Quebec's medicolegal apparatus, which otherwise overlooks how one of the province's foremost physicians collected and displayed bodily pieces from the corpses of those victimised by crime.

Brown relocated to Montreal from Sydney on Nova Scotia's Cape Breton Island. It is unclear why she moved, but by the late 1920s the region's shipbuilding, coal and steel industries were declining and Cape Bretoners dispersed across Canada for employment.[2] Women's work outside the home was an established feature of Montreal life by the time she arrived.[3] Sydney and Montreal's respective economies likely played a role in Brown's move. Montreal was at the height of a pre-Depression economic boom and the city's factories, shops and garment industry employed working class women like her.[4] Simultaneously, Brown exemplifies how some women navigated and resisted gender and class barriers created by religious, medical and legal institutions, since her lifestyle – as an unmarried woman living and working far from her birthplace – was a noticeable deviation from the Catholic conservatism expected of women in Montreal.[5]

DOI: 10.4324/9781003029519-8

The events leading to Mildred Brown's death began early on 3 July 1929 at a residence that doubled as a speakeasy. The twenty-eight-year-old was drinking alcohol with two other women, a waitress named Doris Campbell Morrison, who went by Nancy, and Margaret Laird. Alongside them were two men, Thomas Stevens, a ship steward and Brown's boyfriend who she lived with in the Irish working-class Point Saint Charles neighbourhood, and a sailor named Emmanuel Borga. According to newspapers, Brown accused Morrison of trying to steal Stevens, creating tension between friends. After comings and goings and continued drinking, Morrison returned in the evening and confronted Brown. She picked up a wooden beam, struck Brown several times, and invited the others to, 'Go and take a look at Millie now'.[6] Brown was taken to hospital and died within hours. Police arrested Morrison, who the Coroner's Court found responsible for the death, thus sending her to trial for murder that September. Before trial, she pled guilty to the lesser charge of manslaughter. 'Millie was my best friend', she told Justice C. A. Wilson, 'but we were both drunk at the time and I did not know what I was doing'.[7] Wilson sentenced the twenty-two-year-old to five years in prison and in December she was transferred to Quebec City's Saint-Vincent-de-Paul Penitentiary to serve her sentence.[8] She faded into obscurity after her release but the implications of her actions still reverberate, raising issues about how museums collect and display body parts from crime victims from over a century ago to the present day.

A cause célèbre

Brown's deceased body was transported from hospital to the provincial medicolegal lab, which opened under the Directorship of physician Wilfrid Derome in 1914. Abrasions on her body told the story of a violent assault. Derome also discovered marks she had acquired voluntarily. Brown had tattoos, which many Western women – from sex workers to the bourgeoisie – began to wear by the turn of the twentieth century.[9] Tattoos, in other words, transcended class but records of these markings have skewed Western tattooing's history in that they typically come via people whose bodies were inspected by those in positions of power over them, namely lower and middle working-class male groupings such as criminals and sailors.[10] Much less is known about tattoos that belonged to normal working-class women like Mildred Brown because their bodies were not systematically examined in comparison. Brown's tattoos therefore straddle this schism: due to her death, we come to learn about one otherwise ordinary woman's tattoos and, more particularly, one doctor's interest in them.

Derome photographed Brown's body, believing that photographs had investigative value for identification.[11] He believed tattoos had a similar use. 'The value of tattoos as identifiers is highly important', he indicated prior to Brown's death.[12] But the doctor's attention to her tattoos was not for this purpose: Brown's identity was always known. Derome nevertheless removed at least one professionally rendered tattoo from her body, which depicted an American flag with her initials, 'M.B'.[13] There was already a model for such an act. An unidentified male cadaver found in Montreal's Saint

Lawrence River during 1920 bore several tattoos: a heart with a sword, an anchor, clasped hands over a heart and a rose.[14] Without leads regarding his identity, one newspaper reported that the tattoos were 'cut out by the doctor and placed to dry to enable the reading of the marks'.[15] This instance establishes that the removal of tattooed skin from deceased bodies in the city was done under the direction of a doctor, likely Derome, and underscores that such an undertaking was, apparently, to help identification. Subsequent actions, however, strongly hint that identification was not the reason the doctor collected Brown's skin.

Derome placed a photograph of Brown's corpse in a scrapbook he maintained, the *Album des causes célèbres*, wherein he juxtaposed images of victims of crime alongside coinciding newspaper reportage, obscuring boundaries between personal and professional interest. Documenting murder through photographs, media coverage and retained body parts was a practice the doctor engaged in well before Brown's death. Aside from Brown, other cases in the album that correspond to human remains Derome kept include that of Rita Dupuis, a victim of an unsolved murder in 1925; Charles Bernard, who was slain alongside his wife in 1925; Antonia Poitras, who was shot to death by her husband in 1926; eight-month-old Laurisse Roy and her four-year-old brother, Roger, who died from injuries inflicted by their father in 1929; and Thilnā Scobeil, who was killed by her husband in 1929.[16]

Legislation provides insight into the scope of authority given to those who investigated death in the province, which may have impacted the doctor's ability to save parts of deceased people's bodies. The *Coroner's Act* explicitly stated that 'for the purposes of an inquest the coroner shall take possession of the body and *everything* [emphasis added] that may be useful as evidence'.[17] Derome was not a coroner, but the Coroner's Court invested substantial power in him as the province's *foremost* expert in forensics – having testified on a near weekly basis – and this status ensured little oversight over his work. Brown's murder was one of seven in the city during 1929, but what made it so intriguing to the media and legal system was its commission by a woman.[18] Taking a piece of Brown's body may have been a way for Derome to extend his fascination with this *cause célèbre* and add to his growing assortment of human remains associated with crime, accentuating the sense of ownership the doctor felt over bodies at his lab and the power he held to do so.

Alongside Brown's skin, Derome amassed bones, internal organs, parts of men and women's reproductive systems, and foetuses at varying stages of development. They entered what he described as 'a museum where hundreds of articles, specimens of anatomy and instruments, all connected with crimes, are carefully set up and classified'.[19] Crime museums of this sort emerged across the world by the twentieth century. Police, criminologists and doctors established them for reasons that ranged from research to signifiers of professional accomplishment. Generally, institutional crime museums were not open to the public, shielding them from outside scrutiny of their holdings. The collections these museums developed reflect the access those who managed them had to certain objects and the authority they had to retain and display them. Police, for instance, kept evidence but did not typically have the ability to accumulate body parts in the same way that doctors like Derome did. The remains the physician collected came predominantly from that he had regular access to as a medicolegal physician: corpses of working-class crime victims like Mildred Brown.

There was a long precedent for collecting tattooed skin and displaying it in crime museums by the time Derome did so. Italian criminologist Cesare Lombroso founded a crime museum at the University of Turin in the late nineteenth century.[20] Lombroso collected remains of criminals to support his contention that criminality was a born trait and his assortment of tattooed skin was presumably to bolster his contention that tattoos were an atavistic manifestation of a biological criminality.[21] Lombroso's French contemporary Alexandre Lacassagne collected tattooed skin that he likewise displayed in a museum at his medicolegal laboratory in Lyon. Lacassagne differed from Lombroso in that he viewed tattoos as signifiers of a learned, socially acquired criminality.[22] Derome diverged from the two men in that he did not believe – so far as his available writing suggests – that tattoos denoted criminal tendencies and he did not publicly ascribe to them any inherent qualities regarding the personality of a wearer such as Mildred Brown. Consequently, Derome's pragmatic emphasis on tattoos as marks of identification supports my contention, reinforced by his cataloguing of Brown's death in a scrapbook, that he did not remove her tattoos for this purpose.

Helen MacDonald has shown that dissection became a cultural activity for many doctors and the circulation and display of body parts had a social component.[23] Not far from Derome's museum, the Maude Abbott Medical Museum at McGill University had pieces of tattooed skin in its collection that predated Brown's. Similar to the tattoos Derome collected, these came from people on the margins of society, so much so that their names were not even recorded in coinciding textual records – their body *parts* mattered more than their *whole* bodies as once living human beings. One specimen Abbott received from the Army Medical Museum in Washington, D.C. was referred to as 'tattooing of skin of negro'. Two obtained from New York's College of Physicians and Surgeons were catalogued simply as 'skin with tattooing'.[24] Unknown bodies, racialised bodies, criminal bodies and the bodies of poor, working-class people like Mildred Brown who died without financial means were the predominant sources of tattooed skin that these institutional museums collected and displayed. Outside museums, gathering and exhibiting human remains was normalised in Montreal's medical profession. A recurrent event at the Société Médicale de Montréal's meetings was the presentation of anatomical specimens. Physicians displayed these objects to their colleagues and gave a narrative of the patient's medical condition from who they came. In 1909, Derome showed his colleagues an ovarian cyst he removed from a woman.[25] Over successive years, his collecting continued. A label on another surviving object – a pregnant uterus encased in plastic – indicates that Derome obtained the specimen in 1911, during which time he worked at a local hospital. When his laboratory opened three years later, the institution and his position as its Director afforded him nearly carte blanche to continue collecting pieces from the bodies of people such as Mildred Brown to a greater degree while also providing space to display them.

The laboratory's museum may have had an educational impetus, but the peculiarities of the objects collected and the methods used to display them reveal that Derome and his successors considered aesthetic factors as well. Alike objects were grouped together and often affixed alongside one another on wooden supports, forming sculpture-like assemblages. Brown's skin was nailed to a piece of vinyl that was then fastened to a wooden display plaque. Brown, or at least part of her, literally became objectified. Alongside Brown's, additional pieces of tattooed skin were mounted to this object. Some of these tattoos closely match descriptions of those that belonged to the above-mentioned man whose skin was removed after he was found dead in the Saint Lawrence River. Wood discolouration on nearly the entire apparatus, except for a small rectangular section near the bottom, indicates the removal of a label previously fastened to the object. If Derome believed, at least in part, that the value of tattoos was for identification, perhaps it bore names of those the skin once belonged to, and, as I come to show, ascertaining their identities has been an endeavour that government and Museum employees want to prevent.

Objet d'emotion

Physician Rosario Fontaine assumed responsibility for the laboratory after Derome's death in 1931. Over successive decades, the Museum increasingly fell by the wayside. When plans were afloat for a new building in the 1940s, the Museum's contents were considered integral to the institution and needed appropriate storage.[26] During the early 1950s, Fontaine and his protégé, Jean-Marie Roussel, stressed that the laboratory needed better facilities for this 'invaluable' collection.[27] Notwithstanding their pleas, the collection fell into disrepair by the 1960s, with one observer referring to it as 'an obsolete, antique museum which no one has visited for a long time'.[28] The decreasing interest in the institution's museum hints at shifting norms regarding the collection and display of bodily remains and the importance – or lack thereof – that Derome's successors ascribed to them. By the 1960s, Brown's tattoos would have had little research use to doctors, but, over time and alongside dozens of other remains, they acquired historical importance as objects of institutional memory.

In 1969, Quebec's Ministère de la Sécurité publique opened a fifteen-floor complex for its departments. The Wilfrid Derome Building created space for and renewed interest in the museum collection. Acknowledging its historical, educational and research value, by the early 1970s plans were developed for a public institution named the Quebec Provincial Crime Museum. Around the same period, and perhaps to generate interest and secure finances and a location for the proposed museum, the Ministère admitted several journalists to the collection. One noted that proprietors 'recognize its value as part of the province's history' but were 'aware that some of the exhibits may lead to controversies and protests'.[29] By conceding that the collection raised ethical issues due to holdings of human remains, which needed acknowledgement if the collection was made publicly available, its caretakers faced an impasse. How could they – or would they – explain, for example, how five pieces of tattooed human skin ended up mounted to a wooden plaque? In the end, they did not have to. The Quebec Provincial Crime Museum never came to fruition and the collection remained with the Ministère de la Sécurité publique for the time being.

Finally recognising its importance to Quebec's history, during 1997 the Ministère transferred the entire collection, including the plaque with Brown's tattooed skin, to Quebec's provincially mandated public history museum, the Musée de la civilization in Quebec City, on a twenty-five-year loan. Human remains from murders Derome investigated appeared in exhibitions such as *Autopsie d'un meurte* (2005) and *Copyright humain* (2009). In early 2018, the Museum opened *Sortir de sa réserve: 400 objets d'émotion*, a permanent collection show with a breadth of objects spanning centuries and representing a cross-section of Quebec society. As a text panel stated, 'Objects tell us about the living environments, daily lives, work, knowledge and know-how, leisure activities, aspirations, accomplishments and mindsets of the people living in Quebec'. The exhibition included several remains Derome collected: the disinterred skull of Raoul Delorme, who was murdered in 1922 – his half-brother, a priest named Adélard Delorme, was tried for the crime but acquitted[30]; and pieces of sawed bone that belonged to Louis-Philippe Lafontaine, a teenager killed and dismembered in 1930.[31] The latter was displayed above the wooden plaque that includes Mildred Brown's tattooed skin, which was presented next to a single piece of unprofessionally tattooed skin encased in a plastic block. Despite the text indicating what objects in the show revealed about Quebec's citizens, more telling is how the Museum soon attempted to hide what the tattoos could divulge: namely, information about their wearers' identities – specifically Brown's – and their collection by one of the province's preeminent physicians.

After visiting the show in the spring of 2018, I contacted the institution about the tattoo objects and coinciding text panels, wanting to know more about their provenance and the sources from which the information in the text was gleaned. The response was obstructive. Emails obtained through Quebec's *Act respecting access to documents held by public bodies and the protection of personal information* reveal how, within days of my inquiry, the Museum removed both tattoo objects from exhibition to thwart attention adverse to the institution and the provincial medicolegal laboratory, which operates under the auspices of the Ministère de la Sécurité publique. The collection's loan agreement specifies that the laboratory retains ownership of the collection and therefore the ability to dictate how, when and why it is – or is not – displayed or accessed.[32] Yet, there is no indication that it ever intervened in the Museum's handling of the collection until this instance. Dany Brown, the Museum's Director of Collections, wrote to curator Valérie Laforge, 'It will be necessary to remove the works from *Sortir de sa réserve* that can reveal a person's identity (for example, Mrs. Brown's tattoo). We will need to validate how things stand in regard to pieces classified as "anatomical"'.[33] Days later, Laforge told the Museum's exhibition manager, 'I've been told that we should take out the tattoos from the section *Se perdre* for reasons linked to the possibility of identifying people. It's a question of ethics and legality.

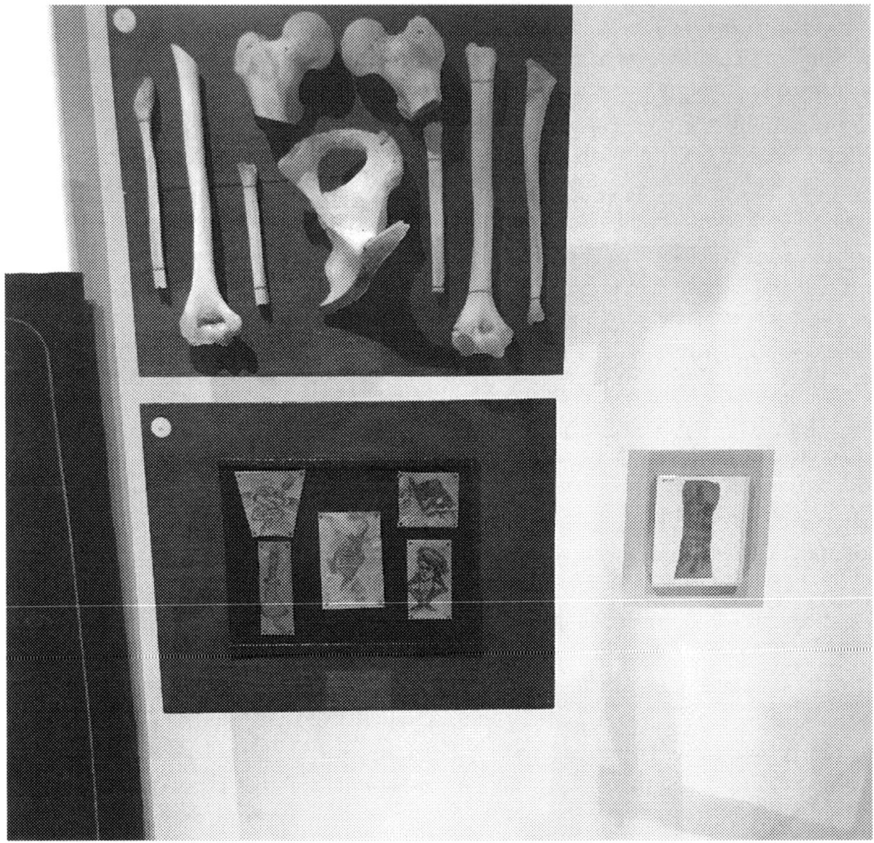

FIGURE 5.1 Installation view of *Sortir de sa réserve: 400 objets d'émotion* (2018). Photograph by Jamie Jelinski.

You must have already heard about this'.[34] Curator Sylvie Toupin confirmed to staff that the request to remove the items came from Yves Bob Dufour, Director of the laboratory. Outlining concerns raised by the coroner's office, who were also privy to these conversations, Toupin specified that the issue was that people the skin formerly belonged to could be identified because of the tattoos. She indicated that future access to objects from this collection should only be permitted for 'serious (and historical) studies' – implying that mine were neither – and that staff should 'be careful of voyeurism, and unhealthy curiosity',[35] descriptors that reveal how the Museum and government agencies comprehend such remains and perceive research that does not fit their institutional agendas. Curiously, although the institution removed the tattooed skin fragments from the exhibition, Raoul Delorme's skull and Louis-Philippe Lafontaine's bones remained, implying that *my* research on Brown's tattoos was understood to be contentious, rather than an institution-wide ethical stance on human remains more generally.

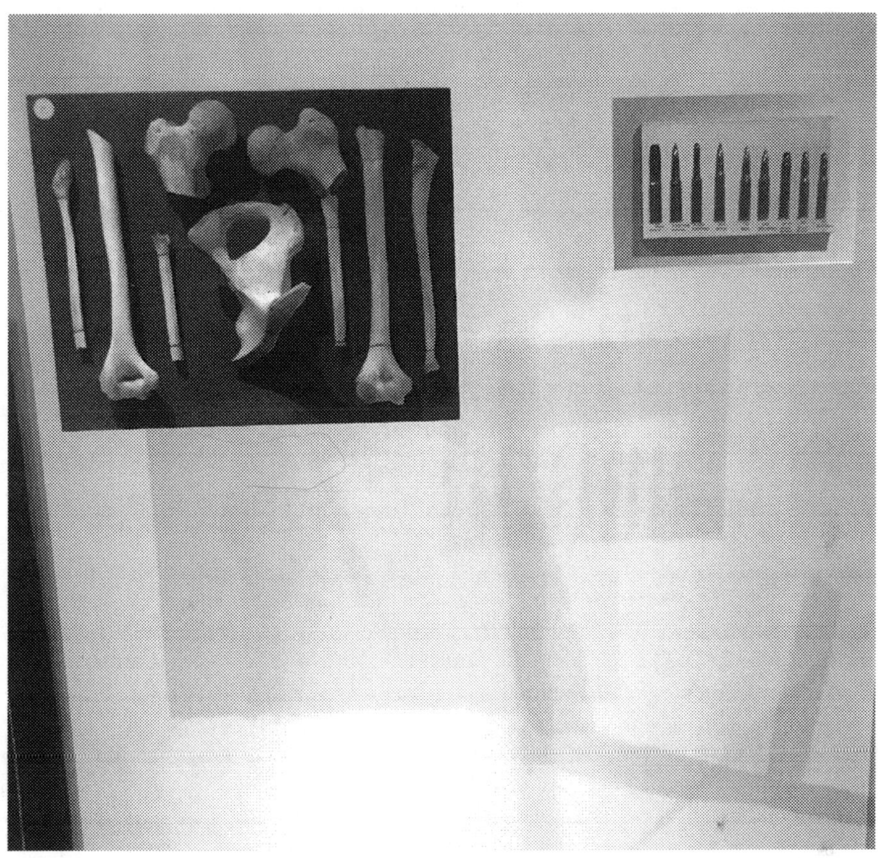

FIGURE 5.2 Installation view of *Sortir de sa réserve: 400 objets d'émotion* (2018) after removal of tattoo objects from exhibition. Photograph by Jamie Jelinski.

The removal of these objects from display echoes a similar pattern in New Zealand when, beginning in the 1980s and coinciding with Maori decolonisation efforts, many museums removed Maori remains from view to preempt protest.[36] The difference between these instances is telling: whereas New Zealand museums later conceded authority over remains to Maori communities and permitted research into their history,[37] the Musée de la civilization and government stakeholders have solidified their position and continue to restrict access to these objects and coinciding archival material. As his namesake building attests, the Ministère de la Sécurité publique has carefully cultivated Derome's legacy. Recent publications the Ministère and its laboratory have supported to valorise him as a trailblazer but fail to discuss the museum he created and or acknowledge how he retained remains from the bodies of people like Mildred Brown that he attended to.[38] Rina Knoeff and Robert Zwijnenberg argue that despite provocative histories, anatomical collections must be understood as fluid, 'their purpose, appearance and meaning continuously change according to the cultural and scientific ideas of their keepers'.[39] While I agree that the meaning of such collections should be in constant flux, I disagree that this process should be restricted to 'their keepers' because, as Brown's skin demonstrates, such keepers have ideological, institutionally driven motivations. The Wellcome Collection in London holds three hundred pieces of tattooed skin – many of unknown origin – and has taken a drastically different approach by supporting scholarship on the collection.[40] From this perspective, the Musée de la civilization believed that the tattooed skin fragments are displayable when nameless, yet unfit for viewing when the identity of those it belonged to, in this case Mildred Brown, and the questionable circumstances surrounding its acquisition become potentially knowable.

The Canadian Museums Association, an organisation the Musée de la civilisation is a member of, maintain *Ethics Guidelines* (1999) that provide direction for the treatment of 'culturally sensitive objects and human remains' by museums in the country. The recommendations suggest that museums consult 'appropriate cultural groups' before using such objects and that all presentations and research be 'accomplished in a manner acceptable to the originating community'.[41] These suggestions appear to guide how museums deal with human remains from Indigenous groups – many of which are held by museums across Canada – but provide no advice on how to approach human remains from other social or cultural contexts, such working-class crime victims like Mildred Brown. This framework, though, could easily be adapted for other instances, for example, by seeking out Brown's surviving relatives. Yet, the Musée de la civilisation's liaising with the Ministère de la Sécurité publique's divisions demonstrates that this government body is the only 'originating community' – a direct institutional lineage from Wilfrid Derome – the Museum feels accountable to when displaying remains he collected.

Conclusion

What does Mildred Brown's tattooed skin tell us now that it has been relegated to storage once more? The response that its display created may prove to be its most enduring legacy, counteracting the otherwise dubious circumstances of its removal. Viv Golding and Jen Walklate have suggested that museums need to think less negatively about conflict because 'transformation does not arise without some form of agitation and disruption: acknowledging the conflict zone might be a way to effect real and lasting change' by giving voice to those oppressed by these institutions and their partners.[42] Brown's tattooed remains cannot speak for themselves, nor is there any indication that surviving relatives of the hundreds of people whose body parts are held at the Museum are aware of this situation. However, human remains amassed from the deceased bodies of victims of crime, such as Brown's tattooed skin, expand and provide nuance to the institutionally told history of Derome, his laboratory and its museum. As *the* museum for Quebec history, the Musée de la civilisation has taken it upon itself – with help from the Ministère de la Sécurité publique – to portray the province's history, including Derome's part in it, favourably. When preserved tattooed skin is presented as part of medicolegal advancement, it contributes to this narrative. When such remains shed insight into the circumstances through which bodily pieces were systematically acquired and displayed in a purpose-built museum, this narrative shifts significantly and, as their efforts reveal, becomes one that government mandataries have worked to suppress. Mildred Brown may not have a headstone marking her final resting place in Hawthorne-Dale Cemetery, but her preserved tattooed skin has drawn posthumous attention to her in a way that no grave marker could and to a degree that members of the working class are rarely afforded in their afterlives.

Postscript

As this book was going to press, the author discovered that the Musée de la civilisation had quietly transferred Mildred Brown's tattooed skin, alongside all other human remains that Derome collected, back to the Ministère de la Sécurité publique in December 2020.

Notes

1 Young, *Respectable Burial*, 117.
2 MacEwan, *Miners and Steelworkers*; Palmer, *Working-Class Experience*, 218.
3 Bradbury, *Working Families*, 13–14.
4 Kealy, *Workers and Canadian History*, 337–38; Copp, *The Anatomy of Poverty*, 44.
5 Baillargeon, *A Brief History of Women in Quebec*, 103–28; Lévesque, *Making and Breaking the Rules*, 11–22.
6 "Woman Held for Murder of Friend," 3 and 12.
7 "Woman is Guilty of Manslaughter," 4.
8 "Woman Sentenced for Manslaughter," 4; Saint-Vincent-de-Paul Penitentiary inmate ledger.
9 DeMello, "The Carnivalesque Body"; Braunberger, "Revolting Bodies"; Osterud, *The Tattooed Lady*; O'Neill, *London*, 27–50; Gilbert, *Victorian Skin*, 318–49; Caplan, "'Educating the Eye'."
10 Kent, "Decorative Bodies"; Maxwell-Stewart and Bradley, "'Behold the Man"; Maxwell-Stewart and Bradley, "Convict Tattoos"; Breathnach and Farrell, "'Indelible Characters'"; Rogers, "'A Very Fair Statement of His Past Life'"; Burg, "Sailors and Tattoos in the Early American Steam Navy"; Burg, "Tattoo Designs and Locations in the Old U.S. Navy"; Dye, "The Tattoos of Early American Seafarers, 1796–1818"; Newman, "Reading the Bodies of Early American Seafarers"; Newman, "Wearing Their Hearts on Their Sleeves."
11 Derome, "Le lieu du crime," 278–81.
12 Derome, *Le Precis de Medecine Legale*, 251. Translated from French.
13 On the formal properties of preserved tattoos, see Angel, "Recovering the Nineteenth-Century European Tattoo."
14 Inconnu ("Windmill Point").
15 "Still Unidentified," 7.
16 *Album des causes célèbres.*
17 *An Act Respecting Coroners*, section 3479g.
18 *Rapport annuel du Service de la police 1929–30*, 22 and 29.
19 Derome, "The Laboratory of Legal Medicine and Technical Police of Montreal," 220.

20 Regener, "Criminological Museums and the Visualization of Evil"; Ystehede, "Contested Spaces"; Montaldo, "The Lombroso Museum from Its Origins to the Present Day."
21 Horn, *The Criminal Body*, 48–51.
22 Angel, "In the Skin," 136; Caplan, "'Speaking Scars'"; Angel, "The Tattoo Collectors"; Gilbert, *Victorian Skin*, 318–49.
23 MacDonald, *Human Remains*.
24 Abbott, *Curator's Report of Donations Received in the Museums of the Medical Faculty of McGill University*, 21 and 25; Accession Logbook, 43 and 139; Reception Book, 98.
25 "Presentation de Piece," 22.
26 "Plans for New Morgue Discussed; Would House Medico-Legal Work," 11.
27 Thomson, "Better Facilities Planned for Coroners, City Morgue," 12.
28 Guérin, "Le carnet," 17. Translated from French.
29 Dubois, "Crime Museum Not for the Squeamish," 37.
30 Monet, *The Cassock and the Crown*.
31 "Police Clear Up Brutal Murder," 3.
32 *Convention de prêt à usage*.
33 Dany Brown, email to Valérie Laforge, 24 May 2018. Translated from French.
34 Valérie Laforge, email to Anouk Gingras, 28 May 2018. Translated from French.
35 Sylvie Toupin, email to Valérie Laforge and Anouk Gingras, 31 May 2018. Translated from French.
36 Tapsell, "Taonga."
37 Tapsell, "Out of Sight, Out of Mind."
38 Côté, *Wilfrid Derome*; Cimon et al., "One Hundred Years of Forensic Sciences in Quebec."
39 Knoeff and Zwijnenberg, "Setting the Stage," 5.
40 Angel, "In the Skin."
41 Canadian Museums Association, *Ethics Guidelines*, 11.
42 Golding and Walklate, "Introduction," 11.

Bibliography

Abbott, Maude. *Curator's Report of Donations Received in the Museums of the Medical Faculty of McGill University*, 1910.

Accession Logbook. Maude Abbott Medical Museum.

Album des causes célèbres, 96–1183. Musée de la civilisation à Québec.

An Act Respecting Coroners. Quebec, 1922.

An Act Respecting the Study of Anatomy. Quebec, 1925.

Angel, Gemma. "Recovering the Nineteenth-Century European Tattoo: Collections, Contexts, and Techniques." In *Ancient Ink: The Archaeology of Tattooing*, edited by Lars Krutak and Aaron Deter-Wolf, 107–129. Seattle: University of Washington Press, 2017.

Angel, Gemma. "In the Skin: An Ethnographic-Historical Approach to a Museum Collection of Preserved Tattoos." PhD diss., University College London, 2013.

Angel, Gemma. "The Tattoo Collectors. Inscribing Criminality in Nineteenth Century France." *Bildwelten des Wissens* 9, no. 1 (2012): 29–38.

Baillargeon, Denise. *A Brief History of Women in Quebec*. Translated by W. Donald Wilson. Waterloo: Wilfrid Laurier University Press, 2014.

Bradbury, Bettina. *Working Families: Age, Gender, and Daily Survival in Industrializing Montreal*. Toronto: University of Toronto Press, 2007.

Braunberger, Christine. "Revolting Bodies: The Monster Beauty of Tattooed Women." *NWSA Journal* 12, no. 2 (2000): 1–23.

Breathnach, Ciara, and Elaine Farrell. "'Indelible Characters': Tattoos, Power and the Late Nineteenth-Century Irish Convict Body." *Cultural and Social History* 12, no. 1 (2015): 235–254.

Burg, B.R. "Tattoo Designs and Locations in the Old U.S. Navy." *Journal of American Culture* 18, no. 1 (1995): 69–75.

Burg, B.R. "Sailors and Tattoos in the Early American Steam Navy: Evidence from the Diary of Philip C. Van Buskirk, 1884–1889." *International Journal of Maritime History* 6 (1994): 161–174.

Caplan, Jane. "'Educating the Eye': The Tattooed Prostitute." In *Sexology in Culture: Labeling Bodies and Desires*, edited by Lucy Bland and Laura Doan, 100–115. Chicago: University of Chicago Press, 1998.

Caplan, Jane. "'Speaking Scars': The Tattoo in Popular Practice and Medico-Legal Debate in Nineteenth-Century Europe." *History Workshop Journal*44 (1997): 106–142.

Cimon, Denis et al. "One Hundred Years of Forensic Sciences in Quebec: The Evolution of Scientific Techniques Since 1914." *Canadian Society of Forensic Science Journal* 47, no. 3 (2014): 148–169.

Convention de prêt à usage. Ministère de la Sécurité publique and Musée de la civilisation, 1997.

Copp, Terry. *The Anatomy of Poverty: The Condition of the Working Class in Montreal, 1897–1929*. Toronto: McClelland and Stewart, 1974.

Côté, Jacques. *Wilfrid Derome: Expert en homicides*. Montreal: Boréal, 2003.

DeMello, Margo. "The Carnivalesque Body: Women and Tattoos." In *Pierced Hearts and True Love: A Century of Drawings for Tattoos*, edited by Don Ed Hardy and Margo DeMello, 37–52. New York and Honolulu: The Drawing Center and Hardy Marks Publications, 1995.

Derome, Wilfrid. "The Laboratory of Legal Medicine and Technical Police of Montreal." *American Journal of Police Science* 216 (1930): 216–223.

Derome, Wilfrid. "Le lieu du crime." *L'union médicale du Canada* 57, no. 1 (1928): 278–281.

Derome, Wilfrid. *Le Precis de Medecine Legale*. Montreal: La Compagnie d'Imprimerie des Marchands, 1920.

Dubois, Paul. "Crime Museum Not for the Squeamish." *Montreal Star*, 26 June 1971, 37.

Dye, Ira. "The Tattoos of Early American Seafarers, 1796–1818." *Proceedings of the American Philosophical Society* 133, no. 4 (1989): 520–554.

Garlandi, Alberto, and Silvano Montaldo. "The Lombroso Museum in Turin: A Reflection on the Exhibition and Scientific Study of Human Remains." In *Museums, Ethics and Cultural Heritage*, edited by Bernice L. Murphy, 322–331. London and New York: Routledge.

Gilbert, Pamela K. *Victorian Skin: Surface, Self, History*. Ithaca: Cornell University Press, 2019.

Golding, Viv, and Jen Walklate. "Introduction: Crossing the Frontier: Locating Museums and Communities in an Age of Migrations." In *Museums and Communities: Diversity, Dialogue and Collaboration in an Age of Migrations*, edited by Viv Golding and Jen Walklate, 1–18. Newcastle upon Tyne: Cambridge Scholars Publishing, 2019.

Guérin, Raymond. "Le Carnet." *La Presse*, 29 March 1963.

Horn, David G. *The Criminal Body: Lombroso and the Anatomy of Deviance*. New York: Routledge, 2003.

Inconnu ("Windmill Point"). 26 May 1920. TP12, S2, SS26, 1992-1907-005\29. Bibliothèque et Archives nationales du Québec.

Kealy, Gregory S. *Workers and Canadian History*. Montreal and Kingston: McGill-Queen's University Press, 1995.

Kent, David. "Decorative Bodies: The Significance of Convict's Tattoos." *Journal of Australian Studies* 21, no. 53 (1997): 78–88.

Knoeff, Rina, and Robert Zwijnenberg. "Setting the Stage." In *The Fate of Anatomical Collections*, edited by Rina Knoeff and Robert Zwijnenberg, 3–9. Farnham: Ashgate, 2015.

Lévesque, Andrée. *Making and Breaking the Rules: Women in Quebec, 1919–1939*. Toronto: University of Toronto Press, 2010.

MacDonald, Helen. *Human Remains: Dissection and its Histories*. New Haven: Yale University Press, 2005.

MacEwan, Paul. *Miners and Steelworkers: Labour in Cape Breton*. Toronto: A.M. Hakkert Ltd., 1976.

Maxwell-Stewart, Hamish, and James Bradley. "Convict Tattoos: Tales of Freedom and Coercion." In *Convict Love Tokens: The Leaden Hearts the Convicts Left Behind*, edited by Michele Field and Timothy Millett, 37–52. Kent Town: Wakefield Press, 1998.

Maxwell-Stewart, Hamish, and James Bradley. "'Behold the Man': Power, Observation and the Tattooed Convict." *Australian Studies* 12, no. 1 (1997): 71–97.

Monet, Jean. *The Cassock and the Crown: Canada's Most Controversial Murder Trial*. Montreal and Kingston: McGill-Queen's University Press, 1996.

Montaldo, Silvano. "The Lombroso Museum from its Origins to the Present Day." In *Cesare Lombroso Handbook*, edited by Paul Knepper and Per Jørgen Ystehede, 98–112. London: Routledge, 2013.

Newman, Simon. "Reading the Bodies of Early American Seafarers." *The William and Mary Quarterly* 55, no. 1 (1998): 59–82.

Newman, Simon. "Wearing Their Hearts on Their Sleeves." In *American Bodies: Cultural Histories of the Physique*, edited by Tim Armstrong, 18–31. New York: NYU Press, 1996.

O'Neill, Alistair. *London: After a Fashion*. London: Reaktion, 2007.

Osterud, Amelia Klem. *The Tattooed Lady: A History*. Golden: Fulcrum Publishing, 2009.

Palmer, Bryan D. *Working-Class Experience: Rethinking the History of Canadian Labour, 1800–1991*. Toronto: McClelland and Stewart, 1992.

"Plans for New Morgue Discussed; Would House Medico-Legal Work." *The Gazette*, 17 January 1945.

"Police Clear Up Brutal Murder." *Montreal Daily Star*, 26 May 1930.

"Presentation de Piece." *L'union médicale du Canada* 4, no. 2 (1909): 22.

Rapport annuel du Service de la police, 1929–30. Archives de Montréal.

Reception Book. MM-8371. National Museum of Health and Science.

Regener, Susanne. "Criminological Museums and the Visualization of Evil." *Crime, History, and Societies* 7, no. 1 (2003): 43–56.

Rogers, Helen. "'A Very Fair Statement of His Past Life': Transported Convicts, Former Lives and Previous Offences." *Open Library of Humanities* 1, no. 1 (2015). https://olh.openlibhums.org/articles/10.16995/olh.27.

Saint-Vincent-de-Paul penitentiary inmate ledger. RG73, 1996–97/878. Library and Archives Canada.

"Still Unidentified." *The Gazette*, 28 May 1920.

Tapsell, Paul. "Out of Sight, Out of Mind: Human Remains at the Auckland Museum." In *Looking Reality in the Eye: Museums and Social Responsibility*, edited by Robert R.Janes and Gerald T.Conaty, 153–173. Calgary: University of Calgary Press, 2005.

Tapsell, Paul. "Taonga: A Tribal Response to Museums." PhD diss., University of Oxford, 1998.

Thomson, Joe. "Better Facilities Planned for Coroners, City Morgue." *The Gazette*, 19 July 1952, 12.

"Woman Held for Murder of Friend." *Montreal Daily Star*, 5 July 1929.

"Woman is Guilty of Manslaughter." *The Gazette*, 27 September 1929.
"Woman Sentenced for Manslaughter." *The Gazette*, 29 October 1929.
Young, Brian. *Respectable Burial: Montreal's Mount Royal Cemetery*. Montreal and Kingston: McGill-Queen's University Press, 2003.
Ystehede, Per Jørgen. "Contested Spaces: On Crime Museums, Monuments, and Memorials." In *The Oxford Handbook of the History of Crime and Criminal Justice*, edited by Paul Kenepper and Anja Johansen, 338–352. Oxford: Oxford University Press, 2016.

6

MUSEUMS IN LATE POPULIST DEMOCRACIES

The photographic archive and the working class

Paolo Magagnoli

Held at the State Library of Queensland in 2019, *Home: A Suburban Obsession* and *Plantation Voices: Contemporary Conversations with Australian South Sea Islanders* shared a penchant for representing the lives of the ordinary man.[1] *Plantation Voices* told the story of the South Sea Islanders who were forcefully brought to Queensland in the mid-nineteenth century to work as indentured labour for cotton and sugar-cane plantations (Figure 6.1); *Home* offered an exhaustive record of Brisbane suburbs and vernacular architecture (Figure 6.2). Both exhibitions relied on the communicative and affective power of archival photographs: *Plantation Voices* drew on rarely seen nineteenth-century pictures of South Sea Islanders working in plantations; *Home* employed the collection of Frank Corley, the owner of a small business specialising in the photography of houses and operating between the 1950s and 1980s. While both exhibitions represented working-class or lower middle-class subjects, their curatorial logic privileged family, individuality and ethnicity over class as the categories through which to understand their historical subject matter.

The Museum's desire to reveal the life of the underdog is evidenced by the language used in the exhibitions' advertising materials. These stressed that the shows offered visitors the rare opportunity to access the history of the little 'h'. In *Home*, one curator declared, 'we hear stories of people who may not appear in big histories but are, nevertheless, the people who made Brisbane – people that we do not often hear the stories of'.[2] The examples could be multiplied many times, but this alone points to the democratic impulse at work in contemporary Australian museums and libraries. How was the *demos* represented in the exhibitions? In the imaginary of the people evoked by *Home* and *Plantation Voices*, class was simultaneously conjured and denied: class was evoked insofar as images of work and workers appeared throughout the shows; it was denied insofar as the Museum tended to rely on other categories for the representation of the people's identity. Family – rather than class – was at the centre of *Home* while ethnicity and nation

DOI: 10.4324/9781003029519-9

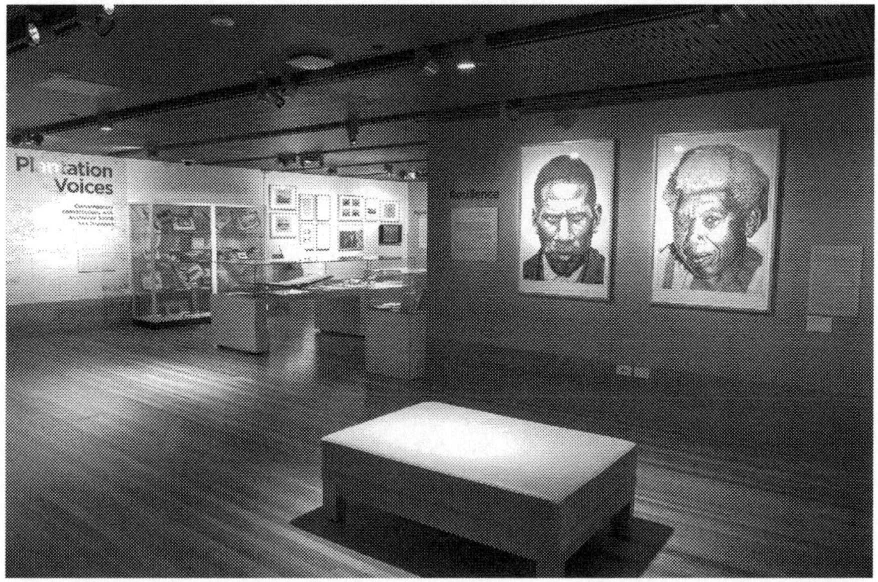

FIGURE 6.1 *Plantation Voices: Contemporary Conversations with Australian South Sea Islanders*, exhibition shot, 2019. Courtesy of State Library of Queensland.

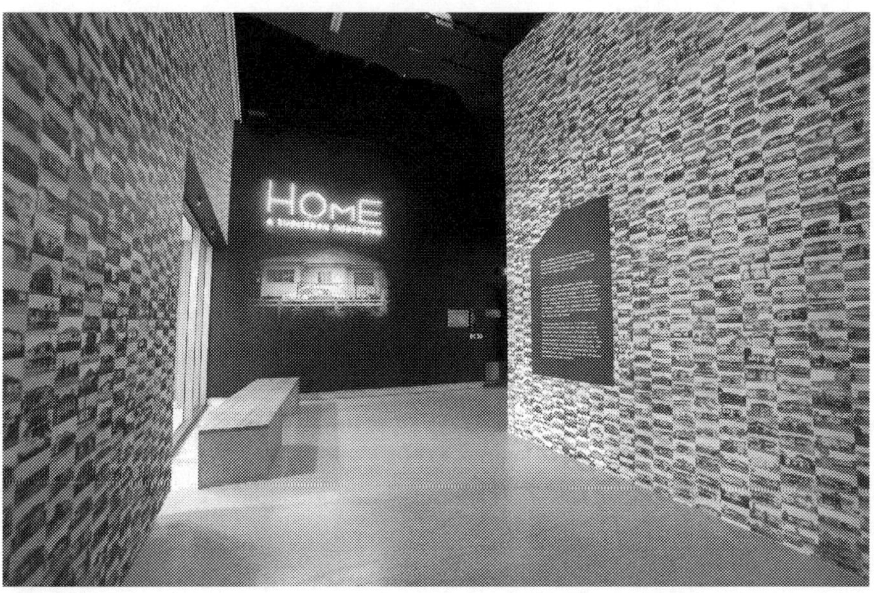

FIGURE 6.2 *Home: A Suburban Obsession*, exhibition shot, 2019. Courtesy of State Library of Queensland.

were at issue in *Plantation Voices*. Here, I use the term 'class' in the historical materialist sense: that is to say, as a construct that refers to one social group's relations to production and the ownership of capital. Within this notion, class is inseparable from questions about wages and work conditions. In both shows, however, these questions were marginally addressed. The Museum celebrated the underdog but downplayed class as the source of social and political identification. In the process, it lessened the perception of socio-economic inequalities and conflicts, relegating them firmly into the past.

Social identities such as class are as much about abstract concepts as about shared images and imaginaries. It is not unsurprising, therefore, that photography played a crucial role in the exhibitions' attempt to evoke the spirit of the people. The Museum relied extensively on vernacular photography. Like the subjects of the images, the authors of the photographic documentation deployed by the Museum were rather anonymous individuals: Frank Corley was virtually unknown until his death in the mid-1990s; similarly, many of the pictures of South Sea Islanders were taken by photographers whose names have been unidentified. The anonymity of the photographic materials accorded well with the democratic impulse at the heart of the exhibitions. Additionally, photographs were arranged into panels, magnified and enlarged to mural size, reproduced as artists' drawings and paintings. Assembled with nostalgic soundtracks, confessional interviews, family albums and recollections, photography emerged less as a Foucauldian tool of surveillance than as iconic images: archetypal crystallisations of collective memory that evoked emotional responses from viewers.

The State Library's use of images recalled the performative model of knowledge and democracy described by Dipesh Chakrabarty.[3] Built upon an emphasis on individual sensory experience rather than on the interpretative abstract categories of the social sciences, the performative model, for Chakrabarty, reflects the democratisation of the museum brought forward by the emergence of identity politics at the end of the twentieth century (a point to which I will return). *Home* and *Plantation Voices* epitomise the performative model of museum education theorised by Chakrabarty in that they attempted to give visibility to the experience of neglected and marginalised social groups. Yet, might the exhibitions' tendency to avoid questions around class weaken the democratic impulse at the heart of the performative approach to museum knowledge? Does the omission of class undermine the democratising effects of the model, reducing it to empty populism? My goal is not to dispute the noble intentions of the two exhibitions. Rather, I want to highlight the challenges that curatorial projects such as *Home* and *Plantation Voices* face in the current historical context, a context whereby the notion of class has virtually lost the political dimension that used to inform it.

Home: reviving the myth of Australia as a classless society

Home explored local suburban architecture through the photographic archive of Frank Corley. Operating between the late 1950s and the 1980s, Frank owned the

Pan American Home Photographic Company together with his wife and collaborator Eunice Reid. Throughout his career, the Corleys took about 300,000 photographs of houses in the Brisbane area and in east Queensland. Using a portable Leica 35mm camera, Frank drove the streets of the city taking quick snapshots of every house that could be seen from his Cadillac. Afterwards, a team of salesmen would have visited the house owners to sell the prints, developed by Eunice in the company darkroom van. Importantly, the photographs were not sold as stand-alone pictures but were inserted into personal greeting cards and calendars, often carrying various advertisements for local shops on the back. Frank's practice was by no means unique at the time: since at least 1958 commercial photographers had sold individual house photos inserted into calendars and some businesses also used home photographs as an advertising technique.[4] By inserting the photographs on personalised cards and calendars, Pan American was able to claim that its products were unique items, for which the company did not have to pay for an expensive hawking licence.

The survival of Corley's collection owes less to documentary purposes than economic reasons. To make profit, Pan American needed to produce photographs at high speed and quantity because not all of them could be sold. Additionally, Corley had to keep the unsold prints in the basement of his house to claim tax deductions.[5] Thus, the project's original intention was merely commercial, and not the preservation of the state's architectural heritage. After Frank and Eunice's retirement in the 1990s, sixty-thousand unsold prints from Pan American Home were donated to the State Library of Queensland. After years of painstaking restoration, the prints were digitised by the Museum librarians and shown for the first time in 2019 in the exhibition *Home*.

In the show, despite their commercial nature, Corley's photographs were presented as a testament to the spirit and beauty of popular architecture. Shot at middle distance, Corley's pictures have a resolute and 'honest' frontality and an obvious aspiration for clarity. They illustrate the typical features of Queenslander houses, with their simple materials such as corrugated tin roofs and attractive decorative elements such as lattice screenings. The simplicity of the architecture was mirrored by the snapshot quality of Corley's photography. The archive's content and form, then, made it an ideal symbol of 'popular culture' against 'elite taste', epitomised by big and modernist developments and luxury apartment units. In fact, despite its apparent objectivity and neutrality – Corley has been called 'the man who photographed every house in Australia' – Corley's archive never features modernist luxury architecture, despite the fact that this had emerged in the increasingly gentrified urban landscape of Brisbane from the early 1960s.[6]

The exhibition was organised by a diverse team of curators: Chenoa Pettrup and Adam Jefford from the State Library, Deborah van der Plaat, Nicole Sully and Andrew Wilson from the ATCH Research Centre and School of Architecture at the University of Queensland, and Denis Peel from the Annerley-Stephens History Group. Widely publicised through a gigantic banner placed on the Museum façade, the exhibition was the highlight of the Museum's programme. Shown over a period of seven months, *Home* was presented as more than a simple survey of local architecture: Corley's archive was introduced to the public as a monument to the life of the common man. Consider the statement made to the press by the Chief State Librarian in occasion of the exhibition opening: '*Home: A Suburban Obsession* is so much more than a story of bricks and mortar, it is about the everyday hopes and dreams of Queenslanders and how it [*sic*] has changed over the decades'.[7]

The curators deployed a variety of exhibition design strategies that aimed at fostering identification. Through labels and captions, the Museum downplayed the commercial nature of Corley's practice and, instead, deployed the images as a platform to probe 'the social and emotional foundations of our houses'. 'There's no place like home', the exhibition website declared, 'and there's no sense of nostalgia quite like the one we feel when we see a photograph of a home – our house, the house of someone close to us, the house where we spent our formative years'. Consequently, Corley's pictures were not displayed in their original commercial format – within calendars filled with advertisements or family cards – but, instead, were re-photographed, enlarged and arranged into large grids. In the darkened foyer of the gallery, spectators were literally surrounded by thousands of images of suburban homes that were plastered on the walls from floor to ceiling. 'I look at the style of the houses', one curator announced in the loud audio recording played in the hallway, 'I look at the simplicity of the house. I just feel so emotionally attached'. Through sound effects and the installation design, the Museum glorified Frank's photographs as expressions of popular culture.

The exhibition included a variety of interactive features, which echo Chakrabarty's performative model of museum education. At the entrance of the gallery, a computer platform – called the Corley Explorer – enabled the visitors to browse the digitised archive, identify their family house and add their personal story as well as other pictures. A virtual reality display guided visitors through a 3D animation that overlaid present photographs of Brisbane streets with views from the Corley collection. Through these devices, the show appeared as an open-ended, participatory project, which aimed to give voice to the general public. Shying away from the unsolicited nature of the photographs, *Home* was a feel-good show that played upon visitors' nostalgic memories of childhood.[8]

Home's nostalgia for 1960s Brisbane tended to gloss over class divisions. Rarely did the curators address the social status of the inhabitants of the suburban houses. Only one of the wall-texts hinted at class distinctions. As the label read, 'shifting social needs and trends have produced multiple styles and forms of the Queensland house and just as many incarnations of home, from sprawling share-houses to elegant family piles and austere workers' cottages'. Additionally, the display format contributed to the erasure of class distinctions. The pictures were arranged into big panels according to formal similarities and not according to the household's income. Class differences were thus reduced to stylistic differences. The uniform size of the prints – together with their repetitive frontality – further reinforced the impression of equality evoked by the panel display. The uniformity of Corley's images has led photography historian Doug Spowart to note that Frank's camera treated every house as the same, regardless of their appearance. The legacy of the

Pan American Home enterprise, Spowart has remarked, 'is an extensive collection of images that indiscriminately captures everyday Queensland homes – *from the architecturally beautiful to the ramshackle* (emphasis mine)'.[9] However, this claim is inaccurate. In fact, Corley's apparently exhaustive inventory of Brisbane houses does not show run-down properties, because the purpose of his project was merely commercial and not documentary: that is to say, its goal was neither the recording of the city architectural heritage nor the revelation of the social conditions of its slums to promote social reform.[10]

The homogeneity of Corley's archive could evoke, in a positive register, the democratic levelling of class differences; alternatively, the archive uniformity entailed a loss of meaning. Because of their repetitive quality, Corley's pictures did not really tell us much about the social and political changes of Australia after the War. Their superficial and stereotypical character recalls Pierre Bourdieu's analysis of family and amateur photography. In his 1965 book *Photography: A Middle Brow Art*, Bourdieu argued that family photography erases from images any specific historical trace. The logic of family photographs, Bourdieu wrote, 'tends to turn the photograph into an ideogram which eliminates from the environment all circumstantial and temporal aspects, such as people moving, in short everything that constitutes life'.[11] Bourdieu's analysis is valid for Corley's photography as well. Paradoxically, the most interesting pictures in *Home* are those rare ones that contain unforeseen accidents, such as the sudden appearance of the house owners, children playing in the backyard and so on. Although they were taken over three decades, Corley's images show a world immune to any change and conflict. If one looks at the past only through the lenses of Corley's photographic archive, Australia emerges as a rather static society without racial and class divisions.

A better glimpse into post-World War II history could have been provided by the stories of the three families interviewed by the curators. Cec Fox told the story of growing up in Mooroka; he recounted how, as he grew older, he had to duck his head to walk beneath the houses that stood six feet off the ground. Robyn Jenkinson narrated the lives of her ancestors, who had lived in Fairfield for 150 years; she also told how her daughter Sonia, during the construction of her new house, discovered the foundation of her great-great parents' first cottage. A sliver of the reality of working-class life was offered by the story of Walter Stubbings. A unionist and former communist activist – in the 1950s he travelled to Moscow with a delegation of other Australian radicals – Stubbings lived in one of the modest wood-and-fibre cottages built by the government in 1943. The section included photographs of Stubbings during his speeches at the Waterside Workers Federation in Brisbane. Another picture showed him attending a meeting of the Queensland Council for the Advancement of Aborigines and Torres Strait Islanders. Except for Stubbing's story, however, the interviews collected by the curators tended to focus on private events rather than on significant or controversial social issues.

Home constructed a nostalgic image of suburbia as a classless utopia. This image is hardly new: the discourse equating suburbia with Australian 'civilisation' can be traced as far back as the writings of Louis Esson and Vance Palmer of the 1910s and

1920s. As Tim Rowse remarked, while 'there is something undeniably authentic in any observation of Australia as suburbia' insofar as the country is perhaps one of the most suburban nations in the world, 'relying on "suburbia" as a summary image and as an explanation of Australia has entailed the unquestionable acceptance of an ideology of society' for which there are no class differences and antagonisms and for which the good life is reduced 'in terms of what goes on inside the spirit or at least within one's suburban plot'.[12] It is this very idealised image of suburban society that *Home* attempted to evoke. While this utopia betrays some positive democratic aspirations, it also seems to gloss over the existence of class inequalities and social injustice.

Plantation Voices: psychologising recognition, racialising class

Plantation Voices provided a poignant account of the labour trade of South Sea Islanders and their deprivation of civil rights following the infamous White Australia policy.[13] In the period between 1863 and 1904, an estimated 62,500 South Sea Islanders – originally from more than 80 Pacific Islands, including Vanuatu and the Solomon Islands – were brought to Australia to work on sugar-cane and cotton farms in Queensland and Northern New South Wales.[14] Some of them were forcibly removed from their land through kidnapping and trickery (a practice called 'blackbirding'). Once in Australia, they were paid almost nothing compared to white workers. In the later decades of the century, the indentured labour system became increasingly regulated by the government. However, under the new legislations, Islanders were still paid a meagre wage and hired under three-year contracts. According to government records, almost 15,000 Islander labourers died in Queensland between 1868 and 1906 due to the poor conditions in which they had to live and to frequent diseases. This is by far the highest death rate for any group of immigrants in Australia. *Plantation Voices* acknowledged the immense suffering of South Sea Islanders and, while not using the word slavery too openly, the exhibition represented a strong antidote against prevailing historical amnesia and recent revisionist histories that have granted a high degree of agency and resistance to South Islander labourers.[15]

The history of South Sea calls attention to the historical overlap between categories such as race, nation and class.[16] For a long time, Islanders were the subject of a double exclusion: because of their black skin, they were an unrecognised working-class group, contributing significantly to the state economy, but nevertheless treated as alien to the nation; at the same time, because of their ethnicity, Islanders were also excluded from representation in the labour and trade movement. The discourse about improved labour conditions and the protection of South Sea Islanders' human rights intersected with a nationalism based on the desire to create a racially homogenous Australia. During the last decades of the nineteenth century, the increasingly powerful Australian workers movement pressed the government to reduce recruitment of South Sea Islanders in the sugar industry. Fears of racial miscegenation combined with fears of competition from Islanders: by the early

1900s, some Islanders had become more apt at negotiating higher wages and were viewed as a threat by white workers. The labour movement condemned plantation owners for being interested in maximising profit through the use of Islanders' cheap labour to the detriment of both the white worker and the white nation. Pressures from trade unions to limit black labour led to the Commonwealth's 1904 decision to begin the deportation of most South Sea Islanders to their native lands. Only about 2,000 Islanders managed to stay in Australia while the rest – some of whom had lived in the country for decades – were forcefully repatriated. Those who succeeded to stay in Australia were not any luckier than those who were forced to leave: for six decades, legislation prohibited their employment in the sugar industry that they had built through their hard labour; it restricted them from voting at both the state and federal level, cultivating and leasing property, accessing social benefits, gaining legal employment, and receiving financial assistance from banks. Starting in the 1970s, after decades of active lobbying and protest, a range of fundamental social, economic and legal rights began to be gradually recognised to South Sea Islanders. The 1990s was a seminal decade in the history of this community: in 1994, the Commonwealth officially recognised Australian South Sea Islanders as a distinct ethnic group with its own history and culture, acknowledged the injustices, disadvantage and prejudice experienced by Islanders because of the indentured labour system and the White Australia policy.

Curated by Imelda Miller, *Plantation Voices* attempted to show the violence of colonialism through a dizzying array of written and visual records from the Queensland State Archive. The exhibition included maps with handwritten numbers indicating where and how many South Sea Islanders were taken on board, a list of Islanders 'recruited' on these voyages, registers of the arrival of vessels bringing Pacific Islanders to various ports, plantation accounting reports listing the wages of indentured labourers, and the names of employers and estates. The exhibition also relied on photographic records. These were mostly group portraits of Islanders made by civil servants and plantation owners during ceremonial activities and visits from government officials. Like *Home, Plantation Voices* devoted scant attention to the context in which the photographs were produced, the institutions for which they were originally made, and the potential blind spots in the photographic archive. In fact, despite their apparent immediacy and straightforward quality, the photographs do not reveal the implicit, silent and institutionalised violence of the labour trade. Made by white people and government agencies for a wide range of public relations purposes, the photographs do not show the 'inadequate diet, appalling sanitation, swampy and unhealthy living quarters, and negligent treatment of the sick and dying', that were, according to historian Banivanua-Mar, 'the legal and regulated standards that contributed greatly to Islanders' bloated mortality'.[17]

Yet, photographic portraiture played a central role in the exhibition narrative. Portraits appeared throughout the exhibition and one representing a group of Islander labourers on a sugar-cane field was even magnified to mural size. The plethora of photographic portraits epitomised the humanist impulse at the heart of *Plantation Voices*. The exhibition aimed to restore dignity and individuality to the anonymous and powerless faces of Islanders appearing in these anonymous group portraits. 'For too long their ancestors' faces', read one of the wall-texts at the entrance, 'have been hidden, disregarded, and dishonoured in historical photographs and documentation'. The kind of humanistic approach to the photographic archive adopted by *Plantation Voices* was also articulated by the curator, Imelda Miller, in her introductory statement ('I am curious about the people in the photos, the names in books, names on papers and I wondered if they thought I would sit here 150 years on and look at their faces and think about their story').[18]

Yet, one could argue that, because of the original function of the photographic documents, it was hard to find instances of resistance in the pictures magnified to mural size by the curators. Some of the images depict de-individualised workers and they show disciplined subjects arranged into orderly lines. The pictures seem to suggest the inexhaustibility of labour and thus advertise the plantation and its well-organised productivity. Thus, the display of those documentary photographs may reiterate the economic objectification that motivated their creation in the first place. Hence, the exhibition curators attempted to 're-animate' and 're-frame' the documents by relying on contemporary artists' interventions in the archive (a point to which I will return).

Having as its primary audience the contemporary community of Australian South Sea Islanders, *Plantation Voices*' humanist impulse was consistent with the language of recognition that has informed much political discourse on this diverse ethnic group. Held in occasion of the twenty-fifth anniversary of the official recognition of South Sea Islanders by the Commonwealth Government, the show's implicit argument was that the acknowledgement cultural identity and memory is fundamental to social justice. Therefore, portraits of Islanders wearing dapper Sunday dresses and military uniforms – a testament to Islanders' contribution to seminal nation-building events such as World War II – hold a powerful symbolic meaning in the show. The exhibition's two conclusive sections focused on the last 50 years of the history of the community and celebrated the Islanders' path towards redemption. The sections were titled 'Reclamation' and 'Resilience' and praised the first generations of migrants for their resistance in the face of adversity: 'With courage and tenacity, strength and determination', one caption read, 'Australian South Sea Islanders fought for the empowerment and recognition and for acknowledgement of their experiences and stories to be woven into the broader Australian history'.

Nevertheless, *Plantation Voices*' emphasis on cultural and historical recognition, although acknowledging the community role in nation building, overlooked the persistent economic disadvantages that South Sea Islanders still face today – disadvantages that could have been addressed if the exhibition's conceptual framework had included the notion of class. To put it differently, the view of recognition brought forward by *Plantation Voices* was marred by a too restrictive, 'culturalist' notion of recognition. This is also the notion that successive Australian governments have tended to embrace. Like in other settler nations such as Canada or the United States, in Australia 'the state role in defining recognition regimes has tended to "culturalize" communities' interest in self-determination in ways that preserve and advance a particular model of political economy, namely a capitalist one whose surplus depends heavily on resource extraction'.[19] Likewise, *Plantation Voices* followed the dominant discourse about Australian South Sea Islanders' equity and access, a discourse which considers the cultural recognition of distinctive ethnic identities as the main form of social justice while downplaying the importance of redistributive claims. As Emelda Davis has recently remarked in 2017, despite official recognition and two decades of state initiatives and inquiries aimed at improving Islanders' social conditions, the community's grievances and demands have not been fully addressed by the Queensland and Commonwealth governments:

> The government realises the likelihood of class action being taken over its disgraceful behaviour in the nineteenth century, when the state seized the wages of the 15,000 dead ASSI to pay for the administration of the Sugar Slave trade and ultimately the forced deportations in the 1900s. In today's money the Queensland and Australian governments have misappropriated tens of millions of dollars, in the same way as Aboriginal wages were misappropriated.[20]

Additionally, the exhibition's insistence on reading the history of South Sea Islanders according to terms such as trauma, resilience, strength and empathy tended to 'psychologise' recognition, that is, to reduce it to mere individual 'psychological' damage.[21] This lens further displaced class as a crucial dimension of the politics of recognition.

In its account of the history of South Sea Islanders, *Plantation Voices* gave priority to the psychological individual experience of the victims over a reflection on the systemic overlaps between colonialism and capitalism. The story of Australian South Sea Islanders demonstrates the dependency of capitalism on cheap labour. It also reveals the influence of racist ideologies on the origins of the Australian working-class movement. As Stefanie Affelds has pointed out, the deportation and repression of Islanders could not have been possible without the activity of an emerging labour and trade union movement. This deployed a variety of methods – including cultural propaganda through a plethora of publications and printed media – to persuade the government that Islanders represented a threat to white Australia. Paradoxically, 'it was only by asserting their whiteness that the European cane cutters eventually succeeded in their fight for improving working conditions'.[22]

Through its use of photographs and other documentation, *Plantation Voices* acknowledged the infamous White Australia Policy; and yet, it seemed also to forget the numerous instances in which solidarities between the white and non-white working class were forged. From the 1940s to the 1970s, several left-wing leaning unions as well as political movements opposed the White Australia policy.[23] Walter Stubbings was just one of the many white workers and activists who fought for the recognition and rights of Aboriginal Australians: indeed, many unions and the Australian Communist Party in the 1960s and 1970s campaigned in their favour and advocated for equal rights between workers, regardless of their ethnic background. These solidarities continue today but, unfortunately, the relations between South Sea Islanders and the contemporary white working class were not dealt with by the exhibition, whose focus remained on the politics of difference and recognition – and this constituted yet another symptom of the invisibility of the white working class from museum discourse.

The museum in late neoliberal democracies

Class was the elephant in the room in *Plantation Voices* and *Home*. The former exhibition lingered on the diasporic history of South Sea Islanders and emphasised psychological damage over material loss; the latter celebrated the ordinary man through Frank Corley's extensive photographic archive of suburban homes and rehashed the long-standing myth of a classless Australia. In their own ways, both exhibitions tended to eschew questions around class differences, work and the redistribution of wealth.

The erasure of class might have owed to the type of visual documentation deployed by the curators. In fact, Corley's photographic archive as well the South Sea Islanders' portraits were not originally produced with the intention to memorialise working-class life and values. Corley's photographs were meant to be used as symbols of family identities. Likewise, the pictures of Islanders were meant to be, for the most part, bureaucratic records. In other words, the kind of images chosen by the Museum might have been ill-suited to the task of representing the working class. As Allan Sekula remarked, the photographic archive possesses strong affinities with the ideological mindset of the capitalist, the scientist and the bureaucrat.[24]

Regardless of the implicit ideologies inscribed in the photographs, the Museum attempted to 'reframe' and subvert the power of the photographic archives. Consider for instance the numerous artistic projects commissioned by the State Library and displayed in both exhibitions. The projects remediated some of the photographs in the archive and thus reclaimed archive as a repository of counter-memory. *Home* included a gigantic charcoal rendition of a Queenslander house based on one of Corley's photographs and made by contemporary artist Ian Strange. Monumental in size, Strange's tryptic *Sixteen* (2019) formed the centrepiece of the exhibition. The beautifully executed black-and-white drawing showed the house under the moonlight and turned the ordinary house into a melancholic and almost magic apparition. Commenting on the piece, Strange emphasised the universal sentimental value of the picture. As he remarked, 'I think everyone has this sort of imagined nostalgic sense of home in them, which is a connection to place or childhood'.[25] Also relying on the power of art to undo the clinical and objectifying gaze of documentary photographs was *Plantation Voices*. The exhibition showcased artistic projects made by contemporary artists whose ancestors were South Sea Islander plantation workers. In *Stop and Stare* (2018), artist Dylan Mooney blew up mugshots of various anonymous South Sea Islanders and turned them into large-size drawings. Through this intervention, the artist softened the cold forensic gaze of the photograph. A similar approach characterised Jasmine-Togo Brisby's series *The past is ahead, don't look back* (2019). Deploying the collodion wet plate process, commonly used in the mid-nineteenth century at the time of South Sea Islanders' coerced migration to Australia, Brisby inserted pictures of herself in old photographs of indentured labours.

All these projects shared the desire to bring viewers into intimate contact with the past. By relying on the artists' haunting images, the Museum aimed to overcome the cold abstraction and neutrality of the archive. In so doing, the Museum seemed to follow the performative model of democracy and museum education discussed by Chakrabarty almost 20 years ago. Chakrabarty theorises two opposed models of museum knowledge, the 'pedagogic' and the 'performative model', which correspond to different stages in the development of liberal democracies. The pedagogic model places emphasis on the brain over the senses, abstraction over embodied knowledge; the 'performative model', on the contrary, draws from the domain of the sensual and embodied experience, and privileges personal memory over the objectivity of numbers, dates, statistics and tables. While the former model dominated the nineteenth and early twentieth-century museum, the latter corresponds to the emergence of the civil rights movement and identity politics in the 1960s and 1970s and it is currently the prevailing model. The performative model is, according to Chakrabarty, a reaction to the discourse of the conventional social and historical sciences, viewed as elitist, authoritative and, ultimately, complicit with power. In conclusion, the performative model gives expression to late democracies' de-colonising impulse.

Class, however, does not fare well in the performative model of democracy. The pedagogic approach of the old 'conservative' museum is based upon the belief that it is 'only through analytical reasoning that one reach[es] the deeper, general and invisible "truths" about society, whatever they are – *class*, economic forces, natural laws (emphasis mine)'.[26] For Chakrabarty, the discourse of the social sciences is fundamentally compromised. 'It is precisely against such politics of knowledge that the cry goes up from time to time from the ranks of the historically oppressed, "to hell with your archives, we have the experience!"'[27] Chakrabarty welcomed the performative turn as a sign of the democratic opening of once-elitist institutions; by embracing sensory knowledge and a focus on individual testimonies and personal memory, Chakrabarty concluded, museums have become a beacon of true democracy: 'Museums, more than archives and history departments, have travelled the distance needed to keep up with the changes that mark late democracies'.[28]

Chakrabarty's essay was written in a time of hope for the emerging politics of reconciliation between Aboriginal and non-indigenous Australians. After 20 years and a series of dramatic events – such as two major global financial crises, the exponential growth of income inequalities, the rise of right-wing populism and, last but not least, the dismantling of the humanities in the neoliberal university – Chakrabarty's theory might have lost traction. Is the performative model of democracy still the symptom of multiculturalism or has it become a way by which the museum panders to the taste of the audience? More crucially, does the performative model of knowledge accord too well with a mainstream media discourse that denies the existence of class for fear that acknowledging social inequalities might lead to anomie?[29] In light of these questions, *Home* and *Plantation Voices* demand critical attention. As I hope this chapter has made clear, a close examination of the exhibitions demonstrates that we need a more nuanced approach to museum education – one that would consider the risks of curatorial strategies that shun the complex theoretical language of the social sciences and an historical materialist approach to class.

A vague populism seemed to inform *Home* and *Plantation*. In their attempt to give visibility to the experience of humble workers, the exhibitions carried the genuine desire to democratise the Museum. This desire is not to be dismissed: populist discourses – Ernesto Laclau has suggested – are not necessarily symptomatic of a reactionary and conservative ideology. There can be a progressive left-wing populism that, in fact, aspires to radical social change. Laclau goes as far as claiming that a certain element of populism is essential to the existence of democracy as such, as long as democracy always implies the discursive construction of a people or a *demos*. 'No political movement', Laclau has remarked, 'will be entirely exempt from populism because none will fail to interpellate to some extent the people against an enemy, through the construction of a social frontier'.[30]

However, the Museum's populist-democratic impulse was hard to pin down. While the pictures' captions celebrated the personal strength, character and resilience of working-class people, rarely did they name the cause for their discontent. Equally, the implicit demands made by the exhibitions were unclear because the Museum suggested that social conflicts and divisions had already been resolved. *Home* projected the dream of a classless society; it alluded to the possible end of this dream as the show's final photographic panel – showing contemporary photographs of Brisbane suburbs – alluded to the recent gentrification of the city; and yet, the show failed to explore this phenomenon, opting for a nostalgic escape into the past. Likewise, *Plantation Voices* projected racial conflict firmly onto the past, suggesting that material recognition was a *fait accompli*.

Perhaps the most disquieting feature of the State Library's exhibitions was not just their veiled populism but the reduction of happiness to family values and private property. Specifically, *Home*'s monument to Australian suburbia possessed some affinities with the neoliberal claim for extension of the personal private sphere over the public sphere. As Wendy Brown has remarked, neoliberalism subordinates democracy to personal freedom and views the idea of the social and the state as inimical to it: 'the existence of society and the idea of the social is precisely what neoliberalism set out to destroy conceptually, normatively, and practically'.[31] For their reluctance to talk about class and the tendency to psychologise reconciliation issues, *Home* and *Plantation Voices* might be read as symptoms of the broader retreat from the social that have characterised the dominant world view in the last 40 years.

Notes

1 *Home* was held at the State Library of Queensland, Brisbane, from 17 December 2018 to 14 July 2019; also organized by the State Library of Queensland, *Plantation Voices* ran from 16 February to 8 September 2019.

2 Curator statement drawn from the audio recording played in the foyer of the exhibition *Home*.
3 Chakrabarty, "Museums in Late Democracies."
4 Peel, "The Frank Corley House Project."
5 Spowart, "Backstory on the Frank and Eunice Corley House Photograph Collection."
6 Spowart, "The Man Who Photographed Every House in Australia: Back Story on the Frank & Eunice Corley House Photograph Collection."
7 McDonald as quoted in Chirgwin, "Snapshot of Our History."
8 See Lush, "State Library of Queensland: Home, A Suburban Obsession."
9 Spowart as cited in Brown, "Never-before-seen Photos Bring 1960s Queensland Back to Life."
10 Peel, "The Frank Corley House Project," 19.
11 Bourdieu, *Photography. A Middle Brow Art*, 37.
12 Rowse, "Heaven and a Hills Hoist: Australian Critics on Suburbia," 4.
13 The literature on the history of South Sea Islanders is by now vast and it will be impossible to mention all of it in an endnote. See Moore (1985), Mercer (1995), Saunders (1984) and Banivanua-Mar (2007) for some examples of the most significant work in this area.
14 Data sourced from Flanagan, Wilkie and Iuliano, "Australian South Sea Islanders: A Century of Race Discrimination under Australian Law (2003)."
15 On the risks of historical revisionism in relation to South Sea Islanders history see Banivanua-Mar, *Violence and Colonial Dialogue*, 12.
16 On the intersectional quality of race, nation and class, see Balibar and Wallerstein, *Race, Nation, Class.*
17 Banivanua-Mar, *Violence and Colonial Dialogue*, 13.
18 Curator statement accessible at: www.slq.qld.gov.au/discover/exhibitions/plantation-voices-contemporary-conversations-australian-south-sea-islanders
19 Williams, "On the Use and Abuse of Recognition in Politics," 5.
20 Davis, "Australia's Hidden History of Slavery: The Government Divides to Conquer."
21 For the problems with recognition discourses that pay excessive attention to the 'psychological' and 'existential' needs of indigenous minorities, see Webber, "The Generosity of Toleration," 273.
22 Affeldt, "Making Black White," 93.
23 Dixon, "Immigration and the 'White Australia Policy'."
24 Sekula, Allan, "Photography between Labor and Capital", 197.
25 Strange as cited in Storie, "The Art of the Build: Ian Strange Interrogates Our Ideas of Home."
26 Chakrabarty, "Museums in Late Democracies," 8.
27 Chakrabarty, "Museums in Late Democracies," 9.
28 Chakrabarty, "Museums in Late Democracies," 11.
29 On the avoidance of class in Australian media discourse, see Winton, "The C Word."
30 Laclau, "Populism: What's in a Name?," 110.
31 Brown, *In the Ruins of Neoliberalism*, 28.

Bibliography

Affeldt, Stefanie. "Making Black White: Sugar Consumption and Racial Unity in Australia." *Zeitschrift für Australienstudien/Australian Studies Journal* 31 (2017): 87–100.

Balibar, Etienne, and Immanuel Wallerstein. *Race, Nation, Class. Ambiguous Identities.* London: Verso, 1991.

Banivanua-Mar, Tracey. *Violence and Colonial Dialogue. The Australian-Pacific Indentured Labor Trade.* Honolulu: University of Hawaii Press, 2007.

Brown, Alison. "Never-before-seen Photos Bring 1960s Queensland Back to Life." *Brisbane Times*, 27 November 2018.

Brown, Wendy. *In the Ruins of Neoliberalism: The Rise of Antidemocratic Politics in the West.* New York: Columbia University Press, 2019.

Bourdieu, Pierre. *Photography: A Middle Brow Art.* Cambridge: Polity Press; Stanford: Stanford University Press, 1989.

Chakrabarty, Dipesh. "Museums in Late Democracies." *Humanities Research* 9, no. 1 (2012): 5–12.

Chirgwin, Sophie. "Snapshot of Our History." *The Courier Mail*, 7 December 2018.

Davis, Emelda (Waskam). "Australia's Hidden History of Slavery: The Government Divides to Conquer." *The Conversation*, 31 October 2017. Accessed 29 June 2021. https://theconversation.com/australias-hidden-history-of-slavery-the-government-divides-to-conquer-86140.

Dixon, Richard. *Immigration and the 'White Australia Policy'.* Sydney: Current Book Distributors, 1945. www.marxists.org/history/australia/comintern/sections/australia/1945/white-australia.htm.

Flanagan, Tracey, Meredith Wilkie, and Susanna Iuliano. "Australian South Sea Islanders: A Century of Race Discrimination under Australian Law (2003)." Accessed 29 June 2021. https://humanrights.gov.au/our-work/race-discrimination/publications/australian-south-sea-islanders-century-race.

Laclau, Ernesto. *On Populist Reason.* London: Verso, 2007.

Laclau, Ernesto. "What's in a Name?" In *The Populism Reader*, edited by Cristina Ricupero, Lars Bang Larsen, and Nicolaus Schafhausen, 101–112. Berlin: Lukas and Sternberg Press, 2005.

Lush, Rebecca. "State Library of Queensland: Home, A Suburban Obsession." *Curate Your Own Adventure: Reviewing Museums and Heritage Places*, 8 December 2018. Accessed 29 June 2021. https://curateyourownadventure.com/2018/12/08/state-library-of-queensland-home-a-suburban-obsession/.

Mercer, Patricia. *White Australia Defied: Pacific Island Settlements in North Queensland.* Townsville, Queensland: James Cook University Press, 1995.

Mooney, Dylan. "Stop and Stare." *State Library of Queensland Blog*, 9 March 2020. Accessed 29 June 2021. www.slq.qld.gov.au/blog/stop-and-stare.

Moore, Clive. *Kanaka: A History of Melanesian Mackay.* Port Moresby, Papua New Guinea: University of Papua New Guinea Press, 1985.

Peel, Denis. *The Frank Corley House Project.* Annerley, Qld: Annerley-Stephens History Group Inc., 2015.

Rowse, Tim. "Heaven and a Hills Hoist: Australian Critics on Suburbia." *Meanjin* 37, no. 1 (April 1978): 3–13.

Saunders, Kay, ed. *Indentured Labour in the British Empire, 1834–1920.* London: Croom Helm, 1984.

Sekula, Allan. "Photography between Labor and Capital." In *Mining Photography and Other Pictures: A Selection from the Negative Archive of Shedden Studios, Glace Bay, Cape Breton: 1948–1968*, edited by Benjamin H. D.Buchloh and Robert Wilkie, 193–286. Halifax: Press of Nova Scotia College of Art and Design, 1983.

Spowart, Doug. "The Man Who Photographed Every House in Australia: Back Story on the Frank & Eunice Corley House Photograph Collection." *Wotwedid*, 19 December 2018. Accessed 29 June 2021. https://wotwedid.com/2018/12/19/the-man-who-photographed-every-house-in-australia/.

Storie, Edwina. "The Art of the Build: Ian Strange Interrogates our Ideas of Home." *ABC*, 17 February 2017. Accessed 29 June 2021. www.abc.net.au/news/2017-02-17/the-art-of-the-build-ian-strange-interrogates-our-ideas-of-home/8281682.

Webber, Jeremy. "The Generosity of Toleration." In *Recognition versus Self-Determination: Dilemmas of Emancipatory Politics*, edited by Avigail Eisenberg, JeremyWebber, Glen

Coulthard, and Andrée Boisselle, 269–292. Vancouver and Toronto: University of British Columbia Press, 2014.

Williams, Melissa. "On the Use and Abuse of Recognition in Politics." In *Recognition versus Self-Determination: Dilemmas of Emancipatory Politics*, edited by Avigail Eisenberg, Jeremy Webber, Glen Coulthard, and Andrée Boisselle, 3–18. Vancouver and Toronto: University of British Columbia Press, 2014.

Winton, Tim. "The C Word: Some Thoughts about Class in Australia." *The Monthly* (December 2013–January 2014): 24–31.

7

WOMEN'S WORK IN COASTAL GALICIA

Shining a light on the unseen at the Marea Museum

José Manuel Vázquez Lijó

Throughout the history of Spain and Europe, the region of Galicia has maintained an important role for its fishing traditions. This explains the high concentration of ethnographic museums in this territory dedicated to a diverse and rich maritime heritage. However, only in a very few instances is the work of people engaged in the fishing industry captured in these collections, which in the case of women's labour translates to a complete absence from a sector that fundamentally relied upon the work of women for its development and sustainability. The cheap and readily available work of women has been key for the growth of the salting and conservation industries, while the selling of fish and shellfish, net making and the manufacture of waterproof clothing were predominantly entrepreneurial activities of women. At the Marea Museum in Porto do Son, a small town in the south-west of Galicia, we have researched and attempted to identify some of these shortcomings, paying particular attention to the latter two above-mentioned occupations thanks also to the involvement of the local community wishing to rediscover and preserve their histories. This work speaks to a wider imperative for social history museums. It is not enough to simply re-present working-class history that is already understood and recognised. A rigorous approach to museums and the working class requires investigation and inclusion of working-class identities and narratives that have been overlooked.

When speaking of non-agricultural labour in Galicia, its presence in historiography is limited due to the overall socio-economic influence of traditional agriculture and long period of industrialisation.[1] The lack of available historical studies is particularly limited in reference to the work of women in the region, the analysis of which is hampered by the 'invisibility' of documented evidence. Such 'invisibility' is a consequence of the secular and absolute subordination of women under the guardianship of men and of prevailing social norms (particularly with regard to their domestic duties) that overshadowed their work, along with many other facets of their lives. In

DOI: 10.4324/9781003029519-10

terms of the role of women in the Galician maritime industry of modern times, the scarcity of research is connected to the limited amount of attention devoted to this subject in the museums, with the notable exception of Luisa Muñoz Abeledo's analysis of work management in the fish processing industries of salting and canning,[2] among a few others.[3] This recently received recognition through a travelling exhibition that showed the wide range of women's trades in coastal areas and the result of a project in the Campus do Mar at the University of Vigo.[4] Although no artefacts were exhibited, it displayed a series of photographic images with brief explanatory texts accessed via QR codes, all sourced from the Massó Museum collection and the private albums of the Italian Attilio Gaggero – a photography aficionado and fish salting and canning entrepreneur. The photographs can now be seen together with a selection of items from the Museum of Pontevedra in the highly regarded exhibition 'Arredor do Mar', organised in 2002 by the Museo do Mar de Galicia (Vigo).[5] The images in the Museum's photographic library prior to 1920 are especially valuable, as are those of the Pacheco Archive,[6] as the very limited amount of photography in Galicia at that time was produced in the provincial capitals and ports of industrial or commercial significance such as El Ferrol, Vigo and Vilagarcía de Arousa. The data recorded in trade directories confirms that only 15 Galician municipalities (eight of them coastal) with under 10,000 inhabitants had opened one or more photographic studios between 1910–1919.[7] This did not include Porto do Son, which adds more value to archives of Ramón Caamaño, whose work is a point of reference for the Marea Museum's research and dedication towards the subject.[8] The Museum is also in the process of reproducing digital files of family albums for reference on the progressive changes in the landscape around the fishing villages, traditional crafts and trades, and pastimes and social events such as processions and races, among others.[9]

The municipally owned Marea Museum opened its doors in 2012 following construction and equipment co-financed by the EU's European Maritime and Fisheries Fund. A relatively small building spanning 330 square metres, the Museum is home to a collection of more than 200 items of fishing equipment, mainly donated by residents of Porto do Son. The exhibit is complemented by ample audio-visual material, some of which depicts the work experiences of the men and women of the maritime trades. Although rather inconsequential, the work of the women also features in a rare film shot in Porto do Son in 1962 and shown at the Marea Museum.[10] Unfortunately, examples of women's work in Galicia documented on film were few and far between until the latter half of the twentieth century. For this reason, the documentary short film *Talleres Alonarti. La Artística Sociedad Ltda* deserves special credit. Filmed in 1928 by José Gil in Vigo, it was recovered and restored by the CGAI – Centro Galego de Artes da Imaxe (the Galician Centre of the Imaging Arts) – in 2001, and documents the activities of a company dedicated to the manufacturing and pressing of tin for the canning industry, with a workforce comprised entirely of women.[11]

Footage of the documentary shot in Porto do Son 60 years ago includes scenes of work in a canning factory mostly conducted by women. As with fish salting, the canning industry is characterised by the overwhelming predominance of women in the workplace (comprising over 80% of seasonal employees), as Muñoz Abeledo's research has shown. The temporary employment of these workers is evidenced in each record of employment registration and completion at the Antonio Pérez Lafuente S.A. canning company, established in Porto do Son in the 1950s. This documentation has recently been transferred to the Marea Museum, to be reformatted digitally and exhibited as an audio-visual representation of the largest women's workforce of the second half of the twentieth century.

The predominance of women among cannery workers can be attributed to their willingness to work for low pay – key to Galicia's competitiveness in this sector – and by the small fraction of women in the unions, which grew substantially until the governance of the Popular Front.[12] In reference to this, two recently donated union cards can be seen in the permanent exhibition at the Marea Museum (Figure 7.1). The cards originally belonged to two sisters, Josefa and María Piñeiro Millán, representatives of the Union of Miscellaneous Trades – the socialists' trade union which forms part of the UGT (General Union of Workers). These small-size prints (approximately 10×6cm) remained hidden for more than 80 years in a metal box under the wooden floor of the sisters' family home, until their discovery in 2017 during renovation work on the property acquired by this author's sister-in-law and donated to the Marea Museum. The concealing of these documents was almost

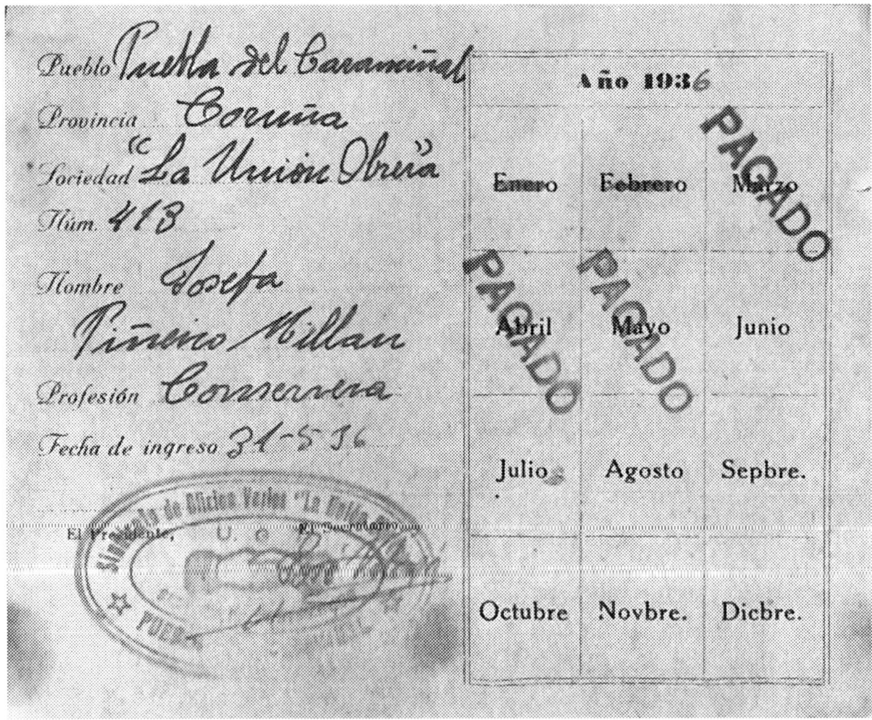
Pueblo Puebla del Caramiñal
Provincia Coruña
Sociedad «La Unión Obrera»
Núm. 418
Nombre Josefa Piñeiro Millan
Profesión Conservera
Fecha de ingreso 21-5-36
El Presidente,

Año 1936

Enero	Febrero	Marzo PAGADO
Abril PAGADO	Mayo PAGADO	Junio
Julio	Agosto	Sepbre.
Octubre	Novbre.	Dicbre.

FIGURE 7.1 Union card of a woman canner, 1936.

certainly motivated by the looming threat of suffering some form of punishment at the hands of the Francoists. The cards show that the sisters, then unmarried young women, joined the union at the beginning of 1936 and had paid their monthly dues just as General Franco was to lead his historic 'Alzamiento', or 'Uprising'. His coup d'état eradicated the democratic achievements of the Second Republic, condemning Spaniards to a 'longa noite de pedra' (the long stone night) – in the words of the revered Galician poet Censo Emilio Ferreiro – and served as a metaphor for a dictatorship that suppressed the fundamental rights of the country's citizenship for the next 40 years. The Millán sisters' cards remained hidden at the time of the constitutional regime of 1978, probably forgotten, and did not come to light until the aforementioned renovation work in 2017 when Josefa and María were subsequently identified as affiliates (nº 173 and 413 respectively) of the Postmark Section of La *Unión Obrera* (The Worker's Union). There are not many cards available of that nature within that particular numeric sequence, owing to the loss of many trade union files, or because they have simply been forgotten or misplaced by family members. Therefore, we are dealing with rare documents as an interesting source of historical information, particularly when taking into account the low number of women union members at that time. In 1932, the UGT brought together 231 workers' associations consisting of 41,948 members, just 4% of all union members at the UGT.[13]

Part of the exhibition at the Marea Museum is dedicated to shellfish-gathering, an ever-present element of Galician culinary culture since records began, as evidenced by the remains of molluscs in the *'concheiros'* – shell heaps where the shells were stored after eating – found at the many Castro archaeological sites[14] across the region. With the exception of the pickled oyster (a popular delicacy among the religious communities of the Modern Age), seafood in this region was rarely distributed and sold outside the local area until more recently. Until then, women were legally prohibited from sailing, fishing or shellfish-gathering from boats – or even on foot from the shore – due to the Maritime Registration Act established in the 1750s which granted maritime trading exclusivity to any man registered on the official lists of the Secretariat of the Navy.[15]

Galician women have a long history of exploiting the natural resources of the coasts, although documentary evidence of this has been very scarce and has only recently come to light, as defined by the various types of instruments covered by the term 'Rastro', as seen in the well-known *Diccionario de los artes de la pesca nacional* – Dictionary of the National Fishing Arts, published in the late eighteenth century, which states that knives, hooks and sickles were used to dig into the sand and remove stones, and that young men and elderly women used to make a living by the sea scouring the beaches with basket in hand, extracting clams and other bivalve shellfish from the sand.[16] However, the women shell-fishers were not necessarily of advancing years, and may have had other skills to speak of. Traditionally, the most commonly used tool for fishing bivalves in intertidal zones was the 'sacho', a type of small hoe. A 'sacho' with a short wooden handle, tarnished by the passage of time and continued use, can be seen in the permanent exhibition at the Marea Museum. As with most of the pieces in the collection, it was donated by a family of fishermen and probably took shape on the anvil of a blacksmith due to the fact that, until a few decades ago, it was not regularly manufactured as an industrial tool as it could easily be acquired in the abundant number of market fairs held all over Galicia, as with the tools of tillage. The sight of people crowded into the sandy areas of the beaches uncovered by the lowering tide handling these and other tools is one of the most enduring images of working life on the beaches of Galicia. This buzz of the shell-fishers digging out tonnes of the then little sought-after cockle (a 'gift from God' which helped the poor stave off hunger) from the coastal area of Cambados, Pontevedra (in the south-west of the region) was the subject of one of the poems of 'A gaita galega'[17] – *The Galician Bagpipes* (1853) – entitled 'Os birbirichos e os birbiricheiros' by Xoán Manuel Pintos Villar, an outstanding precursor to the *Rexurdimento*.[18]

According to Pintos Villar, among the crowds of people who came in from the areas surrounding the rich natural habitat that provided them with food, the majority were women congregating in great numbers and swirling around each other. Their husbands and young children were employed in other maritime trades, mostly fishing – a reliable economic resource on the coasts of Galicia. Fishing generated more income than just from the gathering of clams and cockles, although shellfish were not in particularly high demand by the canneries until the twentieth century, lacking a certain culinary profile and national exposure that would later be achieved with the introduction of the railways. In 1884, the photographer Francisco Zagala immortalised in pictures the arrival of the first steam locomotive to Pontevedra on a newly built iron track and, in the years to follow, a small group of barefooted women on the beach during breaks from work, with seafood tucked into their skirt pouches and resting on the handles of their hoes.[19]

Later, during the 1920s, the American Ruth Matilda Anderson also directed her attention towards Galician women's exploitation of the natural resources of the coast, not only of the shellfish, but also of the seaweed, traditionally used as a fertiliser. These unkempt, barefooted women are anonymous figures in an extraordinary photographic album of great referential value for historical, anthropological and ethnographic studies. The latter was of particular interest to Anderson, a young scholar of the Hispanic Society of America who sailed across the clipped coastline on passenger boats, and drove for many miles across the bumpy roads of Galicia – a land that was gradually approaching modernisation.[20]

Prior to the 1970s, the availability of imagery related to seafood fishing is minimal due to the limited commercial appeal of the topic, the small number of amateur photographers dedicated to the subject, the loss of many archives of film, and the lack of awareness regarding the work of others. One of the better-preserved collections, although only partially catalogued, was provided by the photographic expertise of Xosé Piñeiro Priegue, *Pepe Esteiran* (1930–2002). A small section of his archived work revealed part of a series of images centred around the cockle-gathering campaign in the bay of Noia (in the north-west) in 1975, with particular focus on the women as a collective. The use of such snapshots as a museographic resource is yet to be implemented.[21]

Women's pluriactivity in coastal communities during the Modern Age was investigated by the sadly deceased Serrana Rial García, with the help of documentation from the registry of the Marquis of the Ensenada in the mid-eighteenth century,[22] and filed as a list of trades by the administration department of the Treasury. Members of each family can now be identified in each port, including the women with roles in the processing and trading sections of the fishing companies, such as the picklers and resellers. The resellers in particular are high in number but low in profile.[23] Notably, they encompassed only a fraction of the women employed in such roles, and very little detail has been uncovered regarding their work in salting. In the case of the resellers, confirmation of undeclared earnings can be obtained from the records of the amounts of fish sold daily in the dock of Porto do Son from six boats owned by a company whose brief existence in the summer of 1789 served as an alternative to the suppliers of imported cod.

By 1752, Porto do Son had registered the tenth highest number of maritime tradesmen in the towns of Galicia. 183 of those were registered on the lists of the Secretariat of the Navy, a significant figure for a community of only 318 households. Aside from those in rural areas, the vast majority of families in Porto do Son made a living – or were simply able to survive – exclusively from fishing. However, the Ensenada Land Registry does not contain specific records of any reseller of fish or shellfish, although they do have records of the contributions of women in the local retail sector and particularly fresh produce during the 1780s. In June 1789, 31 of the 48 purchasers of spider crabs consisted of women, four of whom acquired 30 per cent of the supply from the handful of boats on the port. Extracts of these accounts from a recent monograph on the marine collective of Porto do Son between the sixteenth and nineteenth centuries[24] are part of the latest temporary exhibition at the Marea Museum[25] and have provided much scope for analysis.

The rather more unsung work of the netmakers in said documentation is particularly significant. They were provided with netting by members of the family who would then assist with the binding and repairing of the mesh without any financial gain. On the municipal records of the inhabitants, the occupation of most of these women is labelled generically as 'housewife' or *'sus labores'* – their work. During the sixteenth and seventeenth centuries, the local unions decreed that the day of the Sabbath would be set aside for the essential drying, maintenance and repair of the equipment in the main ports of Galicia, where surrounding the fish with large gillnets (cercos) was commonplace and usually took place in the territories known as 'campos de redes' (the net fields), co-owned by the members of the union collective.[26] This technique was never traditionally used in Porto do Son as the fishing was managed by small companies that exploited the resources of the sea with their trawlers and nets,[27] as with the *'Tendedeiro'* – fences built for curing eel and octopus and for the drying of ropes and nets; a method still employed to this day. Nets were also woven in evening gatherings, combining work with chat and song and dance, and subsequently frowned upon by the custodians of moral Catholic values. For the most part, the fishing tackle was made and repaired in wide open spaces, while the netmakers worked on the Tendedeiro, by the dock, and on the village streets. A photograph of five of the netmakers plying their trade was taken in 1959, donated to the Marea Museum by the then 20-year-old *Solita* (Avelina Avilés Fajardo), who can be seen in said photograph as the only one not in mourning dress. Solita has also donated a collection of needles and wooden mesh moulds – a typical yet rare sample of the tools of their trade (Figure 7.2). These pieces form part of the permanent exhibition at the Museum, along with of two short video interviews with *Solita* and her apprentice, *Ginocha* (Regina Mariño Fernández)[28] – recordings of a trade that is now practised with tools made of plastic in interior working environments by the dozen or so women of the Virxe do Carmo of Porto do Son Association, one of the few associations of this kind that exist in Galicia.

In addition to this, much material can be found deep within the Marea Museum gathered from the wealth of information and research regarding trades associated fundamentally with Galician women but also driven by the needs of the fishermen, particularly in terms of what they wore. Towards the end of the nineteenth century, waterproof clothing came into production in the town of Porto do Son, A Coruña and became a growth industry.[29] Made of linen – the go-to material of the Galician textile industry – and popular in rural households, it enjoyed a period of great success during the second half of the eighteenth century, eventually to be eclipsed by the mass production of cotton towards the end of the Napoleonic Wars.[30] In the small textile workshops that made Porto do Son famous, Galician women in their tens of thousands had spun the linen and then weaved it manually, which later evolved into the machine-made fabric produced in factories in

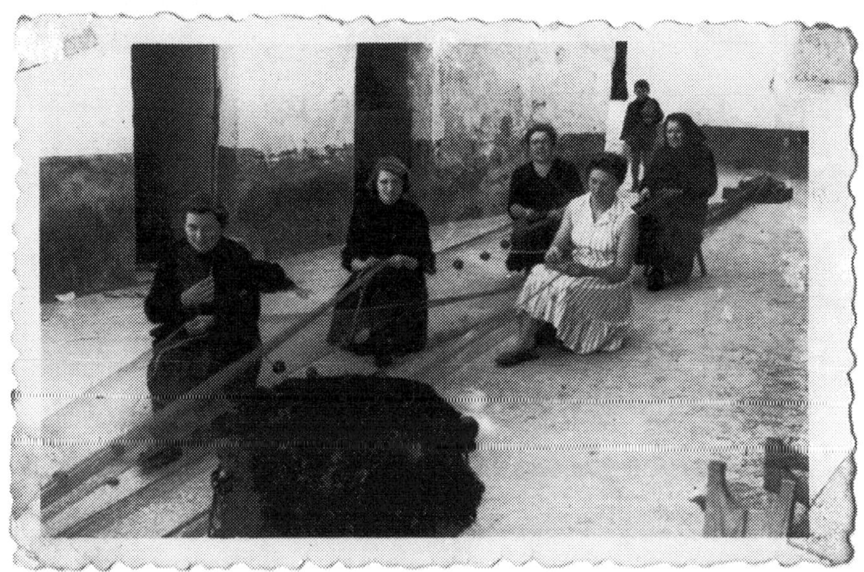

FIGURE 7.2 Netmakers on one of the streets of Porto de Son, 1955.

Barcelona and Xuvia near El Ferrol. The likelihood is that the vast majority of the machines they used were the American-made Singer, a brand popularised in Galicia in the 1870s and promoter of sewing courses across the region ever since. Today, these small mechanical artefacts are kept as decorative memorabilia in many homes, some weathered by time and some reconditioned by their owners.[31]

Starting a business such as this was simple: only a small amount of capital was needed for payroll, acquiring the fabric and the necessary materials for waterproofing, as well as the installation of a couple of well-ventilated sewing rooms where the fabric could be oiled and left to dry. It is thought that the first waterproof clothing business of this kind was established by Ana María Castro García (1857–1923) – wife of a modest shipowner and with a long line of fishermen in her family, her entrepreneurial spirit provided the fishing industry with protective garments that improved their working conditions in the open air. The visionary Ana Maria appears in an old portrait inherited by one of her granddaughters; her achievements remain undervalued as a result of tax infringements – part and parcel of all fields of industry and commerce in those days – or inaccurate documentation by the public administration when women were registering such activities on behalf of their husbands, as was the case with many other women who held the reins of these businesses (Pepa la Gallega, Josefa da Pancha, Regina Mariño, to name a few).

One of the highest production outputs of the first half of the nineteenth century can be attributed to the workshop established by Joaquina García García (1879–1939) – more commonly known as 'A Gaxola' – which not only supplied fishermen and seamen with protective clothing, but also the tin and tungsten miners of San Fins de Lousame. Unfortunately, there are hardly any documented images of the work in the workshops of Porto do Son as the first photographic studio did not appear until the 1950s, with the brief exception of one local studio that opened during the period of the Second Republic. By then, the waterproof products of Porto do Son had extended to further production in important national ports such as Marín, Vigo, A Coruña, Gijón, Pasajes, Las Palmas and Cádiz, but were soon to be replaced by the arrival of plastic raincoats.

During his stay in Porto do Son in November 1933, photographer Ramón Caamaño had the good fortune of meeting and befriending the family of 'A Gaxola' and gifted them with two snapshots of the interior of their workshop. It was one of the countless businesses where he directed his camera, making a living by taking and selling photographic portraits upon request, as was the case with everyone in his profession. Some of the clothing that appears in his photographs are part of the Marea Museum collection, including 'suestas', the typical sombrero-style hats that complemented the jacket and trousers worn by the increasing number of people working on small coastal fishing boats. One of these canvas hats was donated by Joaquina García´s great-granddaughter and another was custom made from textile patterns and preserved by one of the daughters of the founders of a waterproof clothing workshop established in 1954 in Pasajes in the Basque Country, an important fishing port and home to a large colony of Galicians. In the name of fairness and righteousness, the business was named in the female gender: *La Sonesa*.[32]

Skilled labour in these workshops was almost non-existent as the seamstresses were the same people who had previously washed the canvas to remove the coating and waterproofed the clothing with flaxseed oil. This is confirmed by testimonies of family members and employees who were interviewed and can now be found in the audio archives of the Marea Museum along with visual material that includes a number of commercial letterheads and advertisements, pieces of correspondence, notes and bookkeeping related to these clothing workshops. With the help of biographical accounts and the breadth of roles that they took on, it has finally been possible to identify the women who led this unique manufacturing industry and to understand changes in pricing, their target markets and product distribution methods.[33]

In short, the exhibition at the Marea Museum highlights the importance of the role of women in the economic history of coastal Galicia, but there is still much work to be done in terms of documentation, research and disclosure regarding these 'invisible' workers.

Notes

1 For an overview of workers' rights in connection with this subject see Villares, *O mundo*, 14–21.
2 Muñoz Abeledo, *Género*; Muñoz Abeledo, "Actividad."
3 Highlighting the Massó Museum's exhibition of materials from the canning industry (Museo Masso, "Conquista do Mar e Explotación dos Seus Recursos").
4 Sustentabilidade de Feminino, "As achegas das mulleres á sustentabilidade do mar."
5 Museo do Mar de Galicia, "Arredor do Mar."
6 For a selection of his extensive body of work, see López Mondéjar, *Pacheco*.
7 Data obtained from Pazos Labrador and Santos Solla, *Poboación*; Rodríguez Molina and Sanchís Alonso, *Directorio*, 731–80.
8 Soutelo Vázquez and Vázquez Lijó, *O Son*.
9 Marea, Museo da Memoria Marineira de Porto do Son, "Fotografia Historica."
10 www.youtube.com/watch?v=2VC-6_TTZoM&t=12s
11 https://vimeo.com/266444274.
12 Pereira, *Loita*, 160–61, 193–94, 201, 40–42.
13 Núñez Pérez, *Trabajadoras*.
14 González Gómez de Agüero and Bejega García, "Pesca."
15 Vázquez Lijó, "La matrícula," 305–7.
16 Sáñez Reguart, *Diccionario*, Vol. 5, 157.
17 "Os fillos dos pobres brincan/ De alegría e de contento/ E sahen en coiro a fóra, cando ven os pais de lexos/Que traen os birbirbirichiños/ Das areas do Castrelo" (The children of the poor jump/ for joy and contentment/ and go out, when they see the parents from afar/ That they bring the little cockles/ From the land of Castelo). Cockles were consumed raw or simply cooked, without any dressing (in contrast to the meals of the more affluent, which were full of aromatic spices). For a digital copy go to http://biblioteca.galiciana.gal/es/consulta/registro.do?id=8425.
18 The resurgence of Galician language and literature in the nineteenth century.
19 This image is from the large photographic library of the Pontevedra Museum and one of the first to document this activity in Galicia. It can be seen in Cabrera López, *Mujer*, 230.
20 Anderson, *Unha mirada*, 233, 305.
21 In 2013–2014, a selection of Pepe Esteiran's work was part of the photographic exhibition "Un estudo chamado Galiza," "Esteirán," Xosé Piñeiro Priegue e José Vázquez Arias "Rizo," Un estudo chamado Galiza: a modernidade a través das imaxes.

22 Rial García, *Las mujeres*, 123–29, 230–32.
23 Rey Castelao and Rial García, *Historia de las mujeres*, 128–32.
24 Vázquez Lijó, *Donos de seu.*
25 Marea, Museo da Memoria Marineira de Porto do Son, "Exposición temporal: Donos de seu. A xente de mar de Porto do Son (1580–1830)."
26 Canoura Quintana, *A pesca*, 59–62.
27 Examples of dragnets used to catch fish along the sea bottom are "volantas" and "raeiras," while driftnets used to catch sardines are "xeitos." For references to work differences within the fishing companies of Porto do Son, see Vázquez Lijó, *Donos de seu*, 67–88.
28 Marea, Museo da Memoria Marineira de Porto do Son, "Historias de redeiras. Porto do Son."
29 Soutelo Vázquez and Vázquez Lijó, *O Son*, 390–409.
30 Carmona Badía, *El atraso industrial.*
31 Several Singer machines are kept as part of the collection of the Marea Museum, but they are not exhibited due to lack of space and because the general theme of the collection is centred around the maritime workers and their trades.
32 A portrait of a fisherman wearing this equipment can be seen as part of the Mariñeiros series by well-known photographer José Suárez. https://josesuarezfernandez.files.wordpress.com/2013/05/maric3b1eiros-31.jpg
33 Soutelo Vázquez and Vázquez Lijó, *O Son*, 390–409.

Bibliography

Anderson, Ruth Matilda. *Unha mirada de antano: fotografías de Ruth Matilda Anderson en Galicia.* A Coruña: Fundación Caixa Galicia; New York: The Hispanic Society of America, 2010.

Cabrera López, Luis Alberto. *Mujer, trabajo y sociedad (1839–1983).* Madrid: Fundación F. Largo Caballero, 2005.

Canoura Quintana, Andrés. *A pesca na Galicia do século* XVII. Santiago de Compostela: Xunta de Galicia, 2008.

Carmona Badía, Xoán. *El atraso industrial de Galicia: Auge y liquidación de las manufacturas textiles.* Madrid: Editorial Ariel, 1990.

Concello de Vigo. "Arquivo fotográfico Pacheco." Accessed 17 December 2020. https://hoxe.vigo.org/movemonos/m_pacheco.php?lang=gal#/.

Díaz de Rábago, Joaquín. *La industria de la pesca en Galicia: Estudio sociológico.* Santiago de Compostela: Sociedad Económica de Amigos del País, 1885.

"Esteirán," Xosé PiñeiroPriegue, and José Vázquez Arias, "Rizo." "Un estudo chamado Galiza: a modernidade a través das imaxes." Outone Fotografee. Accessed 18 December 2020. www.outonofotografico.com/2013/web/galicia-entra-na-modernidade-2/.

González Gómez de Agüero, Eduardo and Víctor Bejega García. "Pesca y marisqueo en la Ría de Arousa (Galicia) durante la cultura castreña." In *Actas de las II Jornadas de Jóvenes en Investigación Arqueológica.* Madrid: OrJIA, Tomo I (2009): 295–302.

López Mondéjar, Publio, ed. *Pacheco: A memoria dun tempo e dun país.* Vigo: Concello de Vigo; Barcelona: Lunwerg, 2002.

Marea, Museo da Memoria Marineira de Porto do Son. "Exposición temporal: Donos de seu. A xente de mar de Porto do Son (1580–1830)." Accessed 18 December 2020. http://mareamuseo.com/es/exposicion-temporal-donos-de-seu-a-xente-de-mar-de-porto-do-son-1580-1830/.

Marea, Museo da Memoria Marineira de Porto do Son. "Fotografia Historica." Accessed 17 December 2020. http://mareamuseo.com/gl/fotografia-historica-galego/.

Marea, Museo da Memoria Marineira de Porto do Son. "Historias de redeiras. Porto do Son." 28 August 2020. YouTube, Accessed 18 December 2020. www.youtube.com/watch?v=DcJodUG2QIY.

Mariño del Río, Manuel. *A industria derivada da pesca no Concello de Porto do Son*. Noia: Toxosoutos, 1996.

Muñoz Abeledo, Luisa. *Género, trabajo y niveles de vida en la industria conservera de Galicia, 1870–1970*. Barcelona: Icaria, 2010.

Muñoz Abeledo, Luisa. "La actividad femenina en industrias pesqueras de España y Portugal (1870–1930)." *Historia Contemporánea* 44 (2012): 49–71. Accessed 20 November 2020. https://ojs.ehu.eus/index.php/HC/article/view/6602/6040.

Museo do Mar de Galicia. "Arredor do Mar." Accessed 17 December 2020. http://museodomar.xunta.gal/es/explora/993/arredor-do-mar.

Museo Massó. "Conquista do Mar e Explotación dos Seus Recursos." Accessed 17 December 2020. https://museomasso.blogspot.com/p/expo-permanente.html.

Nuñez Pérez, Mª Gloria. *Trabajadoras en la Segunda República. Un estudio sobre la actividad económica extra-doméstica (1931–1936)*. Madrid: Ministerio de Trabajo y Seguridad Social, 1989.

Pazos Labrador, Alberto X., and Xosé M. Santos Solla. *Poboación e territorio: As parroquias galegas nos últimos cen anos*. A Coruña: Difux, 1995.

Pereira, Dionisio. *Loita de clases e represión franquita no mar (1864–1939)*. Vigo: Edicións Xerais de Galicia, 2010.

Rey Castelao, Ofelia, and Serrana Rial García. *Historia de las mujeres en Galicia: Siglos XVI al XIX*. Vigo: Nigratrea, 2009.

Rial García, Serrana. *Las mujeres de las comunidades marítimas de Galicia durante la época moderna: Una biografía colectiva*. Alcalá de Henares: Ayuntamiento de Alcalá de Henares, 2005.

Rodríguez Molina, Mª. José, and José Ramón Sanchís Alonso. *Directorio de fotógrafos de España (1851–1936)*. Valencia: Archivo General y Fotográfico de la Diputación de Valencia, 2013.

Sáñez Reguart, Antonio. *Diccionario histórico de los artes de la pesca nacional*. Tomo V, Madrid: Imprenta de la Viuda de Ibarra, 1795.

Soutelo Vázquez, Raúl, and José Manuel Vázquez Lijó. *O Son que coñeceu Ramón Caamaño. Xentes e espazos dentro e fóra do marco fotográfico*. A Coruña: Deputación Provincial, 2018.

Suárez, José. "Mariñeiros.ca 1936." Accessed 18 December 2020. https://josesuarezfernandez.wordpress.com/series/marineiros/#jp-carousel-1719.

Sustentabilidade de Feminino. "*As achegas das mulleres á sustentabilidade do mar*." Accessed 17 December 2020. https://marenfeminino.campusdomar.gal/un-breve-percorrido-pola-exposicion/.

Vázquez Lijó, José Manuel. *Donos de seu. Loitas, arelas e froitos da xente de mar de Porto do Son (1580–1830)*. Vigo: Edicións Xerais de Galicia, 2019.

Vázquez Lijó, José Manuel. "La matrícula de mar y sus repercusiones en la Galicia del siglo XVIII." *Obradoiro de Historia Moderna* 15 (2005): 289–322. https://dialnet.unirioja.es/servlet/articulo?codigo=2161154.

Villares, Ramón, ed. *O mundo do traballo en Galicia*. Santiago de Compostela: FEUGA, 2007.

PART III

Know your place: Site-specific narratives

Questions pertaining to heritage not only concern which sites are conserved but who is entrusted with these decisions and how the preservation and interpretation are realised. Those heritage policies and practices that are confined to the aesthetics of architectural discourse may disavow the experiences – both past and present – of those who inhabit certain sites. When heritage work is informed by historical narratives, the implications are: Whose stories? Who gets to decide? What is the process for making these decisions? Are there any community consultations? Which groups are invited to the decision-making table and who are overlooked or deliberately excluded?

Imperatives such as 'Don't get too big for your boots' and 'Don't rise above your station' are familiar to the working classes. Such demands are often, and ironically, ordered by their class peers. The working and poverty classes have been scrutinised for generations, so much so that such regulation has been internalised. The title of Part III aims to apply, as an illuminating metaphor, a phrase that may be used to dictate expectations of class behaviour to the restraints, definitions and interpretations of heritage sites that were/are inhabited by the working classes.

The authors of the chapters in Part III examine the implications for the working class of the development of historically significant sites. One chapter exemplifies that the consequences are severe for those of low income who are forced to relocate. In other case studies, it is community groups and labour activists that campaign for the conservation of sites of importance for the working class. But once preserved, what is the site's purpose? The other three chapters in this section analyse the house of a famous labour politician, convict barracks and a factory that have all been repurposed as museums. Contributors to this section relate the consequences of interpretations of heritage sites that compartmentalise the associated narratives either to the past and/or to simplistically constructed boundaries of identity. Part III

DOI: 10.4324/9781003029519-11

emphasises that the 'knowing of place' in heritage work requires an understanding that the working classes are not confined to the past. This is not a mere ideological preference. This linking, on heritage sites, of the working class to the present, is central to a meaningful and relevant social justice.

8

ERASURE OF WORKING-CLASS HERITAGE IN CONSERVATION PLANS

Absent presence in the Walled City of Lahore

Rabia Nadir

'The planned city sweeps the poor away...'[1]

The Walled City of Lahore (WCL) is the nearly 2000-year-old historic core of Lahore,[2] the capital of the Pakistani province of Punjab. Spatially it lies on the periphery of the sprawling footprint of the modern metropolis but remains a hub of urban activity and looms large in the cultural imaginary. Half a dozen regional wholesale markets, dozens of specialised bazaars, small manufacture, and over 150,000 persons are packed within an enclosure of 2.5 square kilometres. A wide road swollen with traffic and bristling with commercial activity defines the WCL now without the walls that marked its identity. The clearly bounded space of the WCL preserves an organic layout of ancient streets, a rich sprinkling of historical buildings and iconic monuments including mosques, palaces and temples dating from the sixteenth to the early twentieth centuries. Socially, it is home to a dense population of working classes.[3]

The socio-spatial genealogy of the WCL coils with the evolution of the dual city of colonial modernity.[4] Colonial urbanism initiated a process of elites migrating to the new suburbs and the aggregation of working classes in the WCL and physical neglect of the built fabric. The cataclysmic exodus of the non-Muslim population in 1947 was a watershed moment. It changed the socio-spatial ecology. There was massive destruction of buildings and influx of poorer residents. The city lost its elite classes but small manufacturing businesses and markets grew and became concentrated as greater urbanisation spurred the growth of Lahore city.[5] Many products for daily use, work implements, building components, toys, clothing and shoes produced through small-scale, mainly artisanal means, were manufactured in and around the WCL. The WCL became the destination of choice for urban artisans displaced from India. It was, and continues to be, both home and workplace for local artisans and petty commodity producers who live in historical neighbourhoods often characterised by trade identities

DOI: 10.4324/9781003029519-12

such as *Mohallah Patrangaan* (neighbourhood of silk dyers), *Sirki Bandaan* (reed screen makers) and *Thatti Malahaan* (abode of boatsmen).

Formal urban planning in Pakistan has been subordinate to trends in Europe and North America.[6] The history of the urban development initiative in the WCL follow significant shifts in urban planning discourse. Following the modernist spatial planning paradigm, the dense historical areas damaged by arson in the 1947 riots were cleared inside the Shah Alami gate and supplanted by a contemporary shopping arcade and apartments along a motorised boulevard in the early 1950s. In addition, two wholesale cloth markets were also constructed inside the Delhi gate in anticipation of the growth of an indigenous textile industry.

Since the 1970s, conservation of historical built fabric has been undertaken *de rigueur* in urban plans for cities.[7] In 1978, the World Bank funded the 'Lahore Urban Development and Traffic Study' (LUDTS). The 'Walled City Upgrading Study' (WCUS) was part of this larger project in recognition of the concentration of low-income residents and high-value historical built fabric. In 1988, a conservation plan for the WCL based on the recommendations of the earlier study was finalised and implemented. The outcomes of the project comprised an extensive documentation and mapping of the WCL, and upgrade of the infrastructure of water supply and sanitation infrastructure. The ambition of creating a social balance by stemming the flight of the middle classes and restricting unregulated commercial and manufacturing activity, however, remained unrealised.[8]

Since the 1980s, liberalisation and deregulation of the economy accelerated the spread of wholesale markets and growth of shoe manufacture.[9] This has meant a radical change in the diversity and scale of economic activity. This increased attention to non-residential purposes has created swathes of neighbourhoods with tall, multi-storeyed commercial buildings interspersed with vacant lots which serve as temporary parking for the thousands of motorcycles used by commuting workers and buyers and sellers in the markets. However, still countless micro-enterprises producing vermicelli, sweetmeats, drinks, medicine, oil presses, earthen stoves, jewellery, clothing, furniture, luggage, musical instruments, printing, packing, finishing and waste recycling continue to survive. The WCL, the former centre of imperial and cultural capital of north India with its associated remnants and traces of grand architecture as well as the memories of artistic and literary culture, is also part of the life of new and old working-class residents.

Along with this 'informal'[10] development, a formal project for the development of the WCL entitled 'Sustainable Development of Walled City Project' was launched in 2006 with the support of a loan from the World Bank. The aims of the project were to 'preserve, restore, protect and develop' the WCL with the aim of attracting tourism and creating economic opportunities for the poor residents. Heritage tourism of the WCL was proposed as a double blessing: paying for conservation and generating income for residents. Based on the Strategic Plan developed through a Public Private Partnership with Agha Khan Cultural Services Pakistan (AKCSP), a new authority was created through an Act of provincial legislature to control and plan development inside the WCL, which was designated a Special Historic Area.[11]

Class as an economic category and 'heritage' of a place is central to the planning discourse in both the 1978 and current plans for the WCL. The planners highlight the issue of divergent needs and relationship of classes to the 'heritage' conservation plans for the WCL. For the planners, the primary heritage of the WCL is the historical built fabric and the poor lack the capacity to maintain it. Rather, their lifestyle aspirations, work requirements and sheer numbers are seen as a threat to fragile old buildings.

This chapter is based on an extended ethnography of those who live and work in the WCL. It presents an empirical account of the life of the local populous, highlighting the living conditions, nature of work, use of WCL space and relationship to state and planning authorities. It concludes by arguing that the WCL residents, petty commodity producers, owners of micro-businesses, skilled artisans, wage workers and lowly service sector employees, express nostalgia for a culture rooted in space and modes of production associated with the WCL. The expressed objectives of the planners involved seizing space from those who inhabit it and erasing the conditions for a *recognised* presence of the working class.

The WCL: a 'field' of tales untold

I offer two vignettes of my encounters in an extended ethnography of the WCL to introduce a class presence I found 'at home' in the WCL. I was in the WCL with some friends, chatting casually with some men sitting amidst a pile of cardboard shoe boxes on the extended platform of a tiny shop in Sootar Mandi. Somehow, the conversation became dominated by a slightly plump young man and very soon we found ourselves in his house, unable to resist his insistent hospitality.

> These are tough times, the new pre-cut, fold and staple variety of boxes has robbed us of work. They want to make people deskilled! I have poor health. I am a heart patient and not even 40 years of age. My three young boys are not going to school. They are between nine to 12 years of age. The younger two are apprentices in Suha bazaar (Gold Market), the eldest lives with his maternal grandparents in Mozang (an old neighbourhood outside the WCL) and works as a shop assistant.[12]

Butt lives in the Sootar Mandi neighbourhood inside the Lohari gate. He has a small business making shoe boxes on order from the many shoe factories in the city. Work has dwindled and remuneration has also declined. His home is a one room with a mini kitchenette, the ground floor of a two-storey house, a joint property of less than 200 square feet. His estranged father lives alone on the first floor. The place is damp and dark due to electrical load shedding. It is furnished with a double bed, fraying upholstered sofas and a few racks, one of which has a small television set. The air is filled with a faint smell of urine and everything is a shade of grey from age and use but organised with meticulous care. The wedding portraits and family snapshots displayed on the racks seem to belong to another time. Butt is characteristically generous and hospitable and offers tea to our party of five. As we left we caught his wife quietly adding water to the left-over milk in the kitchen. His wife undertook home-based work such as making *samoosas* (a local snack), stringing beads for jewellery or piecework for shoe factories, but lately she too has had difficulty in finding work.[13] She was keen to know if we could find work for her and she shared her dreams of educating her sons.

Along the narrow street entering Mori Gate WCL, a row of men sit making shellac cakes by melting pellets of resin over open earthen stoves. One of them has a more ample workspace, a shallow portico outside a small one-room shrine[14] (see Figure 8.1). A conversation with him is invariably joined by his string of regular visitors, and even newcomers who come to share a puff at the *hookah* (water pipe

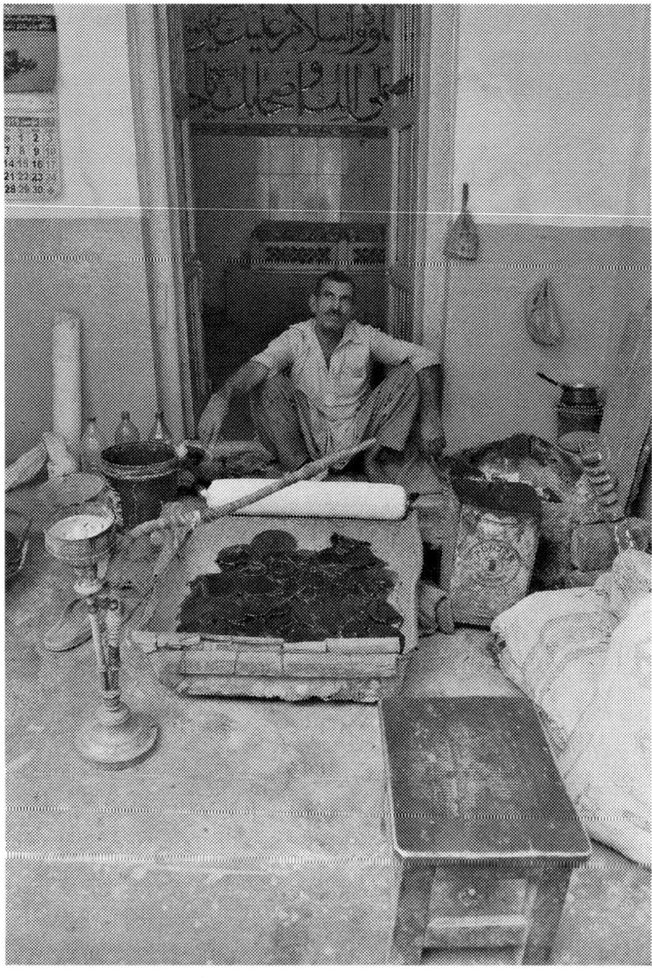

FIGURE 8.1 Shellac maker, Mori Gate, Lahore, 2019. Photograph: author.

for smoking tobacco) that he keeps by his side. Here, I was introduced to Mairaj, as one of the old residents of the area.

> They called me 'Hero'. I had two passions: dressing well and eating well. I don't mean fancy clothes but wearing things with style and cooking the simplest meal with skill. I was a kite maker till they banned the *basant* [a local spring festival celebrated with kite flying, which was banned in 2005[15]]. My skill is still in demand but I cannot do anything illegal. Everyone knows me and they would pick me up in the first raid on illegal kite manufacture. No one ever inquired how we fared after the ban. We were all too poor to start a new business. My sons work, one works in a mobile phone shop, the other has no permanent job. He lives separately in a portion upstairs in this same *mandir* (Hindu temple). You are impressed with my Urdu accent, but I am plain illiterate. In my youth I liked to spend time with learned people and poets. I used to go to Ustad Daman's *baithak* (a famous Punjabi poet's circle). A friend of mine was a candy floss hawker, his poetry became a hit film song and an actress married him. I also practise *hikmat* (traditional medicine) but not for money, I just like to help people.[16]

Mairaj lives in a Hindu temple inside the Mori Gate neighbourhood of the WCL. The dilapidated temple is the property of the Evacuee Property Trust Board (EPTB) and has been occupied since 1947 by partition migrants who sought shelter here. These illiterate rural migrants from the Amritsar district, including Mairaj's father, never managed to claim any property in their new homeland and continued to live in the abandoned Hindu temple. Mairaj's father worked as a vegetable hawker. At a young age, Mairaj was apprenticed to become an expert kite maker. He is illiterate but claims to have always sought the company of literary figures in the city. He had a passion for cinema and dreamt of becoming an actor, in addition to being an amateur herbal medicine man for the neighbourhood. A raconteur par excellence, he enjoyed telling tales to a captive listener. His sons know nothing of the Radio Pakistan literary gatherings or the well-known Punjabi poet whom their father talks about.

Mairaj's grandfather had found shelter in an abandoned Hindu temple inside the Mori Gate, just like many other migrant families who continue to occupy the large number of non-Muslim religious buildings left by the rich Hindu and Sikh community of the WCL. Even those who leave continue to keep a foothold in the space and sublet it to others. Over time, extended clans have added structures, continuously subdividing the spaces, paying little or no rent to the state department responsible for the sites' administration. The state, until now, had hardly any interest in the properties, except for individual officials who keep a messy and fluid paper trail as the local politics and rampant practices of rent-seeking allow. The sorry state of the buildings and communities within keep the rich away, and powerful commercial interests may strive to occupy the space but this is an exception. Complex negotiation and sheer number of occupants has assured minimal changes to the area (Figure 8.2).

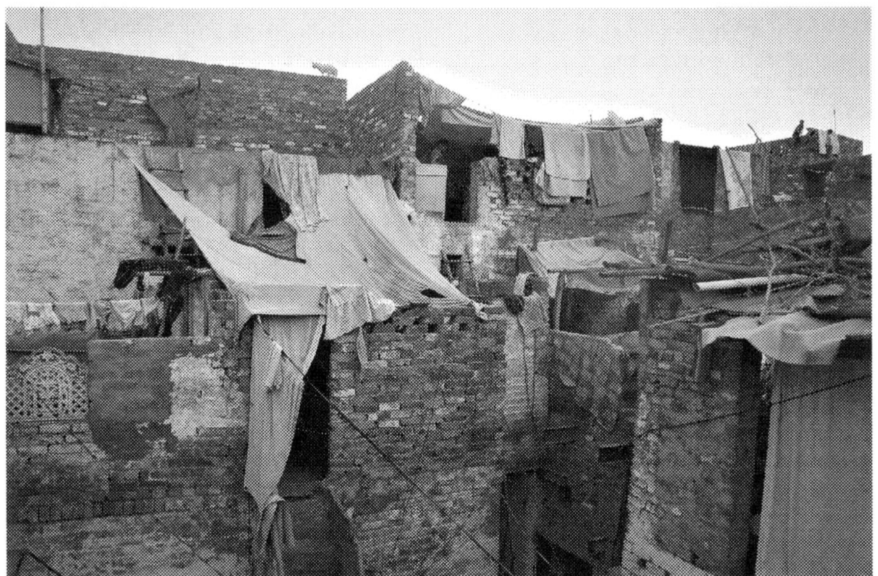

FIGURE 8.2 Mandir in Moti Bazaar, Lahore, 2019. Photograph: author.

WCL built space is not a uniform urban fabric: land use, the scale and quality of building and infrastructure differ both inside and across neighbourhoods. Shoes and allied manufacture of boxes, materials, printing, sale and transport can adjust to the small spaces in the old houses in the WCL. Families such as Butt from Sootar Mandi depend on work from the shoe market and can conduct their businesses in the small premises and open spaces of the WCL. Most, including Butt, are keen to rent their decaying homes for a higher rent to a shoe-making workshop or as a dormitory for migrant workers and move to better accommodation in nearby areas outside the WCL but they cannot exercise this option if their young children and wives also need to work. Life inside the WCL means that they do not have to supervise their children's travel for school, play and even shopping for minor needs.

Work is changing inside the WCL. Traditional craftsmen and micro-producers of small metal, wood and food items no longer introduce their children to the family business. These businesses include the manufacture and repair of musical instruments, knives, metal engraving, embroidery, toys and herbal medicines, for example. The predicament of local craft workers is the result of low returns from their work and a disappearing market. Traditional shoe makers, who have no clientele for the expensive handmade shoes, now make shoes from parts in a shoe assembly kit, all imported in bulk from China. Schooling the children is everyone's aspiration, including the traditional craftsmen. However, poverty pushes many children, like the young sons of the Butt family, to become helpers, apprentices in new repair businesses, servicing and sorting, or in shops in the bazaar. The new workshops service modern technologies such as motorcycles, mobile phone repair, energy saver bulbs, UPS (uninterrupted power supply) units and batteries. The work and living conditions of most of the residents living in the WCL are not very different from those of Butt and Mairaj. Even the handful of upper middle or minority middle-class residents share walls with tiny dilapidated homes and businesses. They see you noticing the utter squalor of their surroundings – dilapidated buildings and garbage-strewn streets. But they dwell at length on the advantages of living in the WCL; an oft-heard refrain is, 'this place is kind to the poor'. They mention the advantages for the poor: the easy access to cheap goods, pedestrian streets, access to health facilities and schools, security and, above all, community. They describe the WCL environment as a place of *bhai chara* (brotherliness) and *lihaaz* (respect). This brotherliness translates into sharing minor items of use, food and, most importantly, support in time of need. Respect and recognition are often conflated and attributed to the endless encounters in the dense living spaces which force life to spill onto the neighbourhood street.

The small shops in the markets sell many unpackaged items and quantity is tailored to the pocket of each buyer. The pace of the WCL and its culture allows purveyors of the cheapest and, until recently, more traditional goods, unavailable in other city neigbourhoods. Ghazi, the *miswaak* (strip of bark or twig used to brush teeth) seller, stands at the entrance of the Delhi gate WCL, with his bundle of thin strips of bark slung over his shoulder. Every 10 or 15 minutes, on average, someone stops and buys a piece of bark that he cuts and simply hands to the customer. This traditional item of teeth hygiene sells at less than ten cents a piece. At the end of the day, it earns him the equivalent of a day's wage (in 2019) of approximately five dollars. Even plastic toothbrushes and toothpaste are unaffordable for the majority of the poor in Pakistan and are especially difficult to use in the shared or bathroom-less accommodation where most migrant workers and residents live.

The economic activity of the WCL is a prime generator of employment in Lahore city. An owner of a small workshop making school bags put it that 'the walled city carries the whole Lahore on its head'. The WCL's economy is mostly small-scale micro-enterprises and is often referred to as 'informal'. However, it varies in scale and seamlessly extends from the 'informal' to more 'formal' businesses. Some of the richest individuals in the city run businesses in the tiny shops of the Azam Cloth market developed by the state for local traders. The rich traders pay taxes and run legally registered entities, but many of their operations and transactions may be undocumented and take place in traditional networks based on bonds of trust.

The WCL bazaar and streets with multiple chances of face-to-face encounters make up a place of shared cultural activities involving diverse classes. Many of these activities centre around religious activities, forms of traditional charity and local fairs mostly associated with specific communities. The presence of many mosques, *imambargahs* (Shia Muslim congregation hall used for preaching but not prayer) and shrines weigh against spatial class segregation found in the modern spaces outside the WCL. These activities have and are changing in scale and class composition as part of wider changes in society. However, they have for a long time been dominated by the lower classes, especially since the hegemonic onslaught of colonialism.

Master planning a new WCL

In 2017, 'Walled City of Lahore: Master Conservation and Redevelopment Plan' (MCRP) was prepared by the WCLA and their partners Agha Khan Trust for Culture (AKTC) as mandated by law.[17] While the WCLA and its consultants could not share the plan, as it had not been 'legally' passed by the appropriate body,[18] it has been described as an effort to cherish and preserve the distinct identity and character of the WCL. The primary emphasis is on the visual presentation of the place as a valuable asset with a distinct historical architecture. The aim of planning interventions is to minimise external pressures which endanger the selected historical built fabric in order to preserve and enhance its presentation as a historical townscape. Its value as a townscape is seen to derive from its well-preserved pre-modern morphology.[19]

The plan spells out the need for revalourisation of historical precincts and monuments in the WCL, which would be realised through the creation of suitable conditions for tourism as an economic activity. Development of tourism is deemed a 'smokeless industry' and panacea for the economic uplift of the local population. It envisages a bigger role for WCLA, integrating it into the development plans of the larger city. It recommends phasing out the dense economic activity that surrounds the WCL as it is an impediment to physical access and mars the visual presentation of the WCL. The state had, back in 2006, much before the development of the plans by the planning partners, announced an economic development project to facilitate tourism and upgrade of the population by encouraging the well-heeled to move to the WCL for its architectural and cultural value.[20]

The actual interventions to date only cover a small area of the WCL, categorised as high-value heritage. Most work under this part of the greater plan is referred to as the *Shahi Guzargah* (Royal Trail), a heritage path stretching from the Delhi gate to the Lahore fort. Significant historical monuments such as the Delhi gate reconstructed during colonial rule, Mughal period *Shahi Hammam* (Royal Bath) and Masjid Wazir Khan and its courtyard are part of the royal trail. Conservation work started in the neighbourhoods of Gali Surjan Singh and Mohammedi Mohallah and involved installation of new underground services for water, sanitation and electricity, paving as well as restoration, preservation and remodelling of street facades. The work in these two neighbourhoods served as demonstration projects to motivate locals to conserve their historical homes and acted as lessons in good conservation practice. Work on the main bazaar, monuments and 57 adjacent streets started in 2012 after the completion of the neighbourhood project. By 2019, extensive conservation and spatial restructuring of the ensemble of iconic historical monuments, Lahore fort, Badshai mosque and adjoining Greater Iqbal Park had been accomplished.

The Shahi Guzargah project removed almost 130 shops which had been deemed 'encroachments'. These tiny shops had been built attached to the walls of two Mughal monuments, the *Shahi Hammam* (Royal Bath) and the Wazir Khan mosque, as well as in the courtyard in front of the mosque on 'public' land, that is, the street and open square were inhabited by the shopkeepers. The shopkeepers vacated reluctantly, agreeing after long negotiations to cash compensation, dispensed according to the resettlement guidelines of the World Bank.[21] Dozens of vendors who occupied the entrance gateway structure or used the open space of the mosque courtyard could not qualify for compensation; they resisted but finally gave in to persistent pressure and simply moved – most have not come back. Over time, some have managed to create space for themselves along the wall of a shrine in front of the Wazir Khan mosque; this 'encroachment' has been officially accommodated.[22] There are plans for renovating the shrine with a less garish, appropriate finish and they may have to move again.

The shopkeepers consider the 'compensation' unjust and describe themselves as weak in the face of state power. A widely prevalent refrain questioned the very notion of calculating the monetary value of businesses. They described business as a process of cultivating relationships and clientele over a long period of time, which cannot be measured. The shopkeepers described small businesses as a heritage of the WCL and the built space as devoid of value without the life it supports.

Those evicted have dispersed and moved to other locations. Some have no business anymore. Others have had to start a new business. A shopkeeper of the royal trail praised the female in charge of facilitating negotiations with the community for her sympathetic role and respectful conduct. He felt, however, with the expansion of the role of WCLA that the same officials have now become inaccessible and considered their previously friendly manner only a tactic to garner support for the project and not a commitment to alleviating their problems.

There has been a visible increase in the traffic of visitors to the WCL since the completion of the first package planned for the Delhi gate area. International tourism, the planned revenue generator, has never arrived given Pakistan's negative image, post 9/11, as a dangerous country plagued by terrorism and religious extremism. The tourists are mostly the local middle and upper classes, and even their visits are limited to the four months of good weather in winter and on Sundays when the throngs of lower-class shoppers and porters from wholesale markets are absent. The royal bathhouse is the prize of the conservation initiative and has received international acclaim for the quality of conservation effort. However, few WCL residents ever visit it. The less than 50 cents entrance fee is steep for large families, but they are proudly dismissive when queried if they have visited it. They declare: 'We have seen it for years. I used to fly kites on the roof, my uncle got married there. It is for tourists like you. Do you know its history?'

Production, class and heritage

'Heritage' as a social construct is ontologically and epistemologically tied to place. It is the heritage of a social formation in time and space. The socio-material realities of those who live and work in the WCL is pivotal to the question of WCL heritage. Their relationship with the bazaars full of cheap wares, dingy, noxious workshops of shoe manufacture, and magnificent frescoes inside the Wazir Khan mosque of the grand Mughal period cannot be separated from their concrete existence.

The expressed goals of the conservation plans for the WCL are the creation of a 'heritage zone' for tourist consumers of heritage sites. Juxtaposing the nostalgic voice of the residents and the unfolding plan and its immediate and long-term impact on the locals reveals a productive disjuncture. I interpret it as a split created by the contradictory interests of classes. In the graded spectrum of class under a regime of globalised capitalist production, the petit bourgeoisie shop keepers of Delhi gate WCL easily huddle within the broad spectrum of exploited lower classes.

A tight embrace of the neoliberal economic model at the start of the new millennium brought 'the new urban age' and idea of cities as 'engines of growth' to urban development plans in Pakistan.[23] Developments in larger Lahore present a poster image of neoliberal urbanisation. Wide boulevards, flyovers, underpasses, metro lines, gated housing and shopping malls promote a culture of rising consumerism.[24] Development such as the Delhi gate's royal trail has made the WCL a 'heritage' and authentic 'local Lahori' experience and a mine for the growing market of global entertainment, hospitality and fashion.

The authorised heritage discourse (AHD) approach informs these plans for conservation with a focus on the materiality and universality of the value and meaning of heritage. The AHD fits well with the 'urban entrepreneurialism' of post-Fordist urban economics where city space is the site of capitalistic growth. State-led conservation plans for the WCL have been criticised as being paradigmatic of this approach.[25] The state has facilitated and accelerated processes of 'flattening' and 'clearing' locales including historical landscapes to be a part of a planetary economy of tourism and entertainment which relies on a 'glocalisation' of urban space.[26] The plan pits the interests of the poor residents who stand to lose the right to prime urban land, independent livelihoods and historical sociocultural capital to rich consumers of heritage and the owners of businesses linked to local and global tourism.

The shopkeepers removed from the sides of the grand Mughal buildings were reluctant to move and finally moved under duress. They complained about loss of business, and the state's failure to relocate them to a comparable location. They speak of loss of liveliness, of the hectic traffic of buyers and generational accumulation of a social capital that allowed small businesses to flourish. Location, numbers, class and memory are wrapped in the many narratives of the locals. They seldom cohere into a sustained critique of the new development but there is suspicion and despondency.

Class is at the heart of the heritage plans and helps lay bare the dynamics of capitalist social relations. The development plans for the WCL created an all-encompassing and multi-dimensional mechanism for changing the WCL. It is a reconstruction of WCL space that is emphatically positioned against the interest of the resident poor who will be forced to move in the new walled city. Their lifestyle and needs are not sustainable in the new heritage 'value' of the WCL. The craftsmen and petty producers are being reduced to a dependent niche sector to be led by a glorious, professionalised class of designers, planners and entrepreneurs. The 'scalar' aspect is significant as the profits will accrue to larger global players, as many critical heritage scholars have observed. These global entities are airlines, hospitality business chains, entertainment and fashion media, for example.

A 'heritage' of local knowledge, deep linkages to a vast hinterland of small towns and villages, solidarities born of co-dependence of small businesses and local production is sedimented in the WCL. The liberalisation of the economy was already undermining local production and wider social change was no less impactful. However, the vision of the WCL Masterplan emphatically reorients the WCL away from its historical development as a hub of local production and lower-class culture towards a global socio-spatial order of the heritage tourism market. The plan is designed to end half a century of occupation of the socio-spatial capital of the WCL by the lower classes in favour of a new well-heeled class with global cultural capital. An alternate reading of heritage needs to bring production and its relations into the discussion to assert the presence of those who are exploited in the processes of material (spatial) accumulation. The presence of past production, space and memories is a living heritage of the WCL which will disappear in the planned enclosure of material heritage as a spectacle for tourist consumption.

Notes

1 Watson, "Planned City," 151.
2 Rehman, *Historical Towns*, 169.
3 Umney, *Class Matters: Inequality and Exploitation in 21st Century Britain*, 1.
4 See Beverley, "Colonial Urbanism," 495, for a discussion of colonial urbanism through a review of recent historiography of South Asian cities.
5 See Chattha, "Economic Change"; Qadeer, *Lahore*; Weiss, "Industrialization in Pakistan" for discussion on pre- and post-partition manufacturing work in the inner city of Lahore. Chattha discusses how artisans who migrated after partitions and came to settle in the Walled City where they had prior contacts. Also, it was the hub of artisanal work and its markets.
6 Qadeer, "Urban Policies Post 1947," 454, points to the increasing role of international agencies in guiding the urban policy and proliferation of international prescription. Even the local architects and planners are guided by either their training in institutions in Britain and North America or the local institutions had weak local moorings and followed a course of studies developed in Britain and North America. There was widespread looting and arson of non-Muslim areas of the WCL during partition in 1947. The rehabilitation and rebuilding plans totally disregarded the traditional urban morphology and inserted a modernist commercial street planned for access of motorized transport.
7 In the 1970s, World Bank funded conservation of the historical built fabric was in urban plans for cities in many countries with the view of making heritage tourism a part of the urban economies. Scholars place this trend in urban planning and development within the longer history of the development of capitalism. See Harvey, "Transformation in Urban Governance in Late Capitalism," 9.
8 Lahore Development Authority, *Walled City of Lahore*, 1; Hankey "Conservation of Walled City Lahore," 73.
9 Scott, "The Changing Geography of Low-tech, Labor-intensive Industry," explains how shoe manufacture lends itself to growth in inner-city dense urban enclaves and is located

in many decaying inner-city areas, especially with growth of an assembly kit of parts model with cheap components from China. In a contrast, it is interesting to note that the socio-economic profile given by the AKCSP imputes the 'skilled' nature of shoe manufacture for high incidence of child labour in the WCL rather than the poverty of the locals.

10 Roy, "Urban Informality," 149. Roy makes a strong case against the false binary of formal and informal in urban spatialities are developing through a complex mix of processes where legality and illegality are on a continuum.

11 Khan, "The Master Conservation and Redevelopment Plan for the Walled City of Lahore," 153.

12 Butt of Sootar Mandi, interview with author, 28 March 2012. Butt is a common surname in the WCL. Full name not given to ensure privacy.

13 Weiss, *Walls within Walls* records the extensive presence of home-based work by women in the WCL. It too was disappearing by 2012 when we visited the family of B.

14 While typically shrines exist outside the settlement, in the WCL, its long history and shifting edges have brought many shrines into the main settlement. However, that is not the only reason; many locally revered figures have been buried in spaces within the neighbourhoods and this practice continues to this day. These are often spaces they occupied in their life and served as a gathering area for their followers, even apprentices.

15 Salahuddin, "Ban or Bane."

16 Mairaj of Mori Gate, interviewed by author, 23 November 2012 and 17 August 2020. Real name changed to ensure privacy.

17 Walled City of Lahore Authority (WCLA) website, "Walled City of Lahore Act 2012," WCLA Act 2012 Chapter IV states 'The Authority shall, in consultation with the Heritage Conservation Board, in such form and in such manner as may be prescribed, prepare a master conservation and re-development plan for purposes of the Act and the Authority shall implement and execute the same, after the approval of the Government'.

18 Interviews with chief conservation architect and planner WCLA and AKTC senior architect by author conducted 21 February 2020 and 3 March 2020, respectively. The plan could not be shared as it was not a legal document yet and hence not available to the public. However, a publication titled 'Lahore: A framework for Conservation', which was launched at the high-visibility Lahore Literary Festival quotes extensively from the plan and the lead architect/planner of the masterplan has contributed to the publication.

19 Khan, "The Architectural Heritage of Lahore," 71. Khan, the lead architect of the Masterplan for conservation developed by AKTC, considers the Mughal period (sixteenth to late eighteenth century) and Mughal-derived historical buildings as the 'backbone' of the architecture and urbanism of the WCL. This guides the hierarchy of spatial planning with respect to townscape zoning for conservation. Contemporary buildings and spaces are relegated to a supportive role for enhancing and supporting the historical pre-modern cultural landscape (Khan, 'The "Master Conservation and Redevelopment Plan for Walled City Lahore," 156.)

20 "Sustainable Development of Walled City Lahore Project (SDWCLP)," Unpaginated. In this report, the main objective of the project is described as a plan to unleash the economic potential of the Walled City of Lahore through leveraging cultural heritage and sustainable tourism.

21 World Bank, "Resettlement Action Report," 61. The majority of those affected had demanded compensation in kind rather than cash for vacating the premises.

22 The author was not able to gain any conclusive information about the status of the few stalls that have appeared along the wall of a shrine in front of Masjid Wazir Khan. In an informal chat, the shopkeepers claimed that they were given these by the Walled City Lahore Authority but were reluctant to give further details.

23 Hassan, "World Class City Concept"; Haque, "Cities as Engines of Growth."

24 Jan, "Lahore Elite"; Mallick, "Urban Space and Middle Class."

25 Smith, *Uses of Heritage*, 6; Su, "Urban Entrepreneurialism and Commodification of Heritage," 4; Sohail, "Conservation-led Marginalisation in WCL," 15. Authorised Heritage Discourse (AHD) is described by Smith as a dominant Western discourse that is characterized by an emphasis on 'things' rather than intangible cultural practices and social processes as heritage. It is an assemblage of practices that select, validate and regulate a hegemonic discourse which helps sustain the status quo based on liberal capitalist relations. The importance given to material heritage helps to silence debates on class power and its histories and fits with neo-liberal urban entrepreneurialism discourse which uses commodification of heritage as a capitalist growth strategy. See Sohail for more discussion on the WCL in this context.

26 Swengedouw, "Neither Global nor Local: 'Glocalization'," 137.

Bibliography

AKCSP. *Lahore Walled City Project. Quality of Life. Baseline Socio-Economic Household Survey Report*. Lahore: Walled City Authority Library, nd.

AKCSP. *The Lahore Walled City: A Preliminary Strategic Framework*. Report submitted to Punjab Government Sustainable Development of Walled City Project Unit, February 2008.

Alavi, Hamza. *Class and State in Pakistan: The Roots of Dictatorship* (H. Gardezi and J. Rashid, eds.). London: Zed Press, 1983.

Ali, Reza H. "Urban Conservation in Pakistan: A Case Study of the Walled City of Lahore." In *Architectural and Urban Conservation in the Islamic World*, edited by Abu H. Imamuddin and Karen R. Longeteig, 74–88. Geneva: The Aga Khan Trust for Culture, 1990. Accessed 6 October 2020. https://archnet.org/publications/3811www.archnet.org/library/documents.

Beverley, Eric Lewis. "Colonial Urbanism and South Asian Cities." *Social History* 36, no. 4 (2011): 482–497.

Chattha, Ilyas. "Economic Change and Community Relations in Lahore before Partition." *Journal of Punjab Studies* 19, no. 2 (2012): 193–214.

Hankey, Donald. *Case Study: Lahore, Pakistan – Conservation of the Walled City*. No. 19253. Washington, USA: The World Bank, 1999.

Haque, Nadeem Ul. "PIDE Policy Viewpoint No. 2. January 2007: Renew Cities to be the Engine of Growth." *The Pakistan Development Review* 45, no. 3 (2006): 505–509.

Harriss-White, Barbara. "Awkward Classes and India's Development." *Review of Political Economy* 30, no. 3 (2018): 355–376.

Hassan, Arif. "The World Class City Concept and its Repercussions on Urban Planning for Cities in the Asia Pacific Region." Conference paper presented at IAPS-CSDE Network Symposia on Culture, Space and Revitalization, Istanbul, Turkey, October 2009. Accessed 23 November 2020. http://punjablaws.gov.pk/laws/2500.html.

Jan, Ammar Ali. "Lahore's Elite Logic." *Tanqeed* (2013). Accessed 6 October 2020. www.tanqeed.org/2013/08/lahores-elite-logic/.

Khan, Masood. "The 'Master Conservation and Redevelopment Plan for the Walled City of Lahore'." In *Lahore: A Framework for Urban Conservation*, edited by Philip Jodidio, 153–176. Munich: Prestel, 2019.

Lahore Development Authority (LDA). *Walled City of Lahore: A Socioeconomic Study*. Lahore: Metropolitan Planning Wing, Lahore Development Authority, 1979.

Mallick, Ayyaz. "Urban Space and (the Limits of) Middle Class Hegemony in Pakistan." *Urban Geography* 39, no. 7 (2018): 1113–1120.

Qadeer, Mohammad A. "An Assessment of Pakistan's Urban Policies, 1947–1997." *The Pakistan Development Review* 35, no. 4 (1996): 443–465.

Qadeer, Mohammad A. *Urban Development in the Third World: Internal Dynamics of Lahore, Pakistan*. Westport: Praeger Publishers, 1983.

Rahman, Taimur. *The Class Structure of Pakistan*. Karachi: Oxford University Press, 2012.

Rehman, Abdul. *Historic Towns of Punjab: Ancient and Medieval Period*. Lahore: Ferozsons, 1997.

Roy, Ananya. "Urban Informality: Towards an Epistemology of Planning." *Journal of the American Planning Association* 71, no. 2 (2005): 147–158.

Salahuddin, Saadia "Ban or Bane." *The News on Sunday*. Accessed 6 October 2020. https://jang.com.pk/thenews/sep2012-weekly/nos-09-09-2012/she.htm#1.

Scott, Allen J. "The Changing Global Geography of Low-technology, Labor-intensive Industry: Clothing, Footwear, and Furniture." *World Development* 34, no. 9 (2006): 1517–1536.

Smith, Laurajane. *Uses of Heritage*. London and New York: Routledge, 2006.

Sohail, Jannat. *Conservation-Led Marginalization: Making Heritage in the Walled City of Lahore*. Unpublished thesis, 2020.

Su, Xiaobo. "Urban Entrepreneurialism and the Commodification of Heritage in China." *Urban Studies* 52, no. 15 (2015): 2874–2889.

Sustainable Development of Walled City of Lahore Project. *Resettlement Action Plan (RAP) – (Draft Report)*. World Bank. Accessed 12 September 2020. http://documents1.worldbank.org/curated/en/527671468077335181/text/RP11380SAR1RAP1BOX358344B0component.txt.

Sustainable Development of Walled City of Lahore Project. *Exploring the Economic Potential of Walled City Lahore*. Unpublished Seminar Report. Planning and Development Department, Government of Punjab, 2007.

Swyngedouw, E. "Neither Global Nor Local: 'Glocalization' and the Politics of Scale." In *Spaces of Globalization: Reasserting the Power of the Local*, edited by Kevin Cox. New York: Guilford, 1997, 137–166.

Umney, Charles. *Class Matters: Inequality and Exploitation in 21st Century Britain*. London: Pluto Press, 2018.

Walled of City Lahore Authority. *The Walled City of Lahore Authority Act 2012*. Accessed 23 November 2020. http://walledcitylahore.gop.pk/wcla-act-2012/.

Watson, Vanessa. "'The Planned City Sweeps the Poor Away…': Urban Planning and 21st Century Urbanisation." *Progress in Planning* 72, no. 3 (2009): 151–193.

Weiss, Anita M. *Walls within Walls: Life Histories of Working Women in the Old City of Lahore*. Oxford: Oxford University Press, 2002.

Weiss, Anita M. *The Emergence of an Industrial Bourgeoisie in Punjab, Pakistan: Case Studies of three Industries*. PhD diss., University of California, 1983.

9

EUGENE V. DEBS' MUSEUM AND THE PRESERVATION OF RADICAL WORKING-CLASS POLITICAL MEMORY

Wesley R. Bishop

Introduction

In 1968, on the corner of the campus of Indiana State University, there sat a small home. Previously a member of Terre Haute's older downtown suburb, time and the University's expansion had witnessed the neighbourhood go from row upon row of upper-class homes, to areas annexed for the college's use. The home in question, located at 451 North 8th Street, was one of few remaining survivors of the old neighbourhood. It was also in the path of the University's dreams for development. In its place the University planned a new parking lot to service the state-of-the-art Statesmen Towers. When completed, these twin towers were to be affordable residences for students, a sign of the college's progress, and potential landmarks as the fifteen-story buildings would rise above the small town.

Just a few years earlier, the University would have had little problem removing the obstructing home. In 1936 the original owner, Kate (Metzel) Debs, had died. A faculty member of the college then bought the house, and lived in it for a number of years before selling it to a fraternity in 1948. Once in the possession of Tau Sigma Alpha, the home accrued the damage one would expect a college fraternity to inflict until, in 1961, it was sold again to a developer who renovated the home into a series of small apartments. If left to its own decline, the home would have likely continued its deterioration until the University rendezvoused with the structure, via wrecking ball, in the last years of the 1960.[1]

Fortunately, this did not happen. In 1962, a group of dedicated academics, labour activists and community members came together and purchased the home for the grand total of 9,500 USD. Why did this happen? Why would such a normally disparate group come together to buy a home? The answer was simple. For nearly 50 years, from its construction in the late nineteenth century to the 1930s, the home belonged to the family of Eugene Victor Debs. A five-time candidate for

DOI: 10.4324/9781003029519-13

the Presidency of the United States, a widely known labour leader and a world-renowned orator, Debs was one of the most famous socialist politicians ever produced by the United States.

This chapter examines the history, politics and issues surrounding one of the rare American museums dedicated to socialism, the working class and industrial workers' movement. Its survival, it will be shown, is a testament to the longevity of the labour movement, and the story of this Foundation and Museum presents an example of what is possible when academics, labour leaders and concerned community members come together to protect pieces of working-class history. Likewise, the life and career of Debs offers insight into how public historians can work with working-class history to examine issues of past figures, movements and who they have included and excluded. Figures like Eugene V. Debs, then, provide a personality to encapsulate broader social movements – such as labour, peace and social justice – and as a result a narrative to engage the broader public. As it will be shown, this use of a personality is not without limitations. Yet the Debs Foundation through the late twentieth century kept this history and public engagement alive, and in the early twenty-first century as Occupy Wall Street and the campaigns of Bernie Sanders rekindled interest in Debs, poised itself as a model for activist-oriented public history.

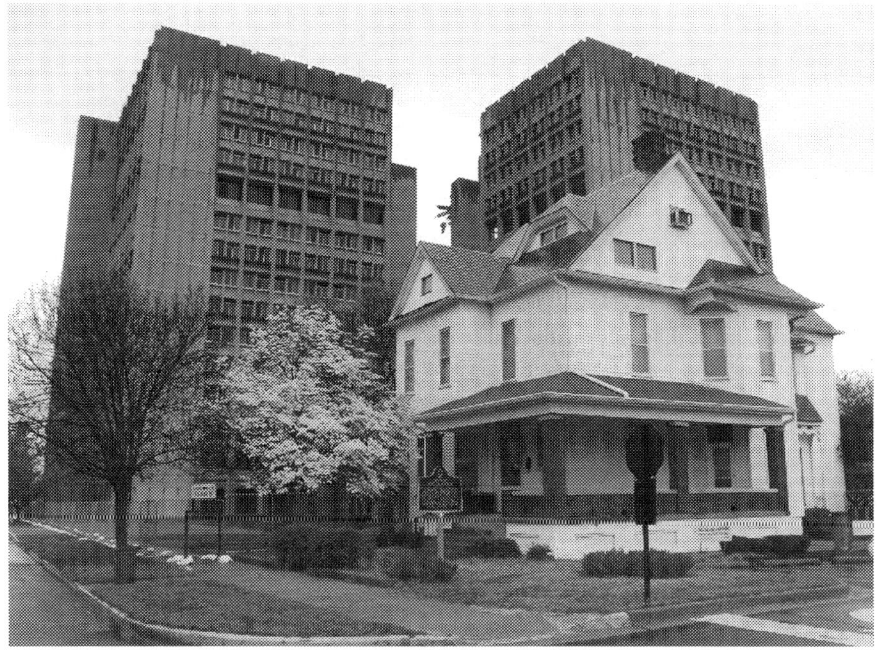

FIGURE 9.1 The Debs' home and Foundation in 2015 as Indiana State University began demolishing the Statesmen Towers. Photograph: author.

From trade unionism to industrial workers

Born in Terre Haute in 1855 to French immigrant parents, Eugene V. Debs had attended school until the age of 14 before dropping out and joining the Brotherhood of Locomotive Fireman. A young man with political ambitions, he rose in the ranks of his union, served two terms as city clerk and then one term as a Democratic representative in the Indiana General Assembly. Yet, after his term ended in 1889, he turned away from electoral politics and rededicated his work to labour organising. He did, however, marry during his time in the Assembly and in 1890 finished construction of his home. Large and elegant for its times, the home reflected the status of a rising political star. His new wife, Kate Metzel, was of upper-middle-class stock, and to anyone viewing Debs' rise in politics it would have been difficult to predict that just a few years later Debs would be one of the most famous, or infamous depending who was asked, radical political figures in US politics.

In fact, the size and placement of the home would become a political and historical controversy as Debs' career took off in the labour, populist and then socialist movements. Specifically, during his campaigns for president as well as his various challenges to the federal government, critics would sometimes charge Debs with hypocrisy for being for the working people while living in such a luxurious and affluent home. Of particular criticism was the various fireplaces and cobalt blue porcelain tiles.[2] The Foundation, and Debs himself, did not take too seriously these charges since having nice things, living in comfort and appreciating beauty are not incompatible with socialism, and in fact are the goals of the socialist movement. Yet, later critics would continue to search for blame for the house's appearance and their view of who Debs was as a political figure.

Not surprisingly, later critics would blame not Debs but instead scapegoat his wife, Kate. Born to the Metzel family, Kate was not of the same immigrant or working-class status as Eugene. Some later biographers and writers would depict Kate's marriage to Eugene as one of opportunity, where an upper-middle-class woman hoped to be the spouse of a new political star. In 1947, the novelist Irving Stone told the story of Eugene and Kate Debs, and used the trope of a troubled home, bitter woman and frustrated man to tell their story. Stone's portrayal depicted Eugene as having a horrible home life and having married the wrong woman. Kate was depicted as a bourgeois upper-class woman who hated socialism and hated her husband's political ideals. Likewise, Gene's dedication to Kate was also questionable since it implied an error in judgement, insofar as it pointed to a betrayal of his revolutionary ideas and an attempt to achieve social mobility through marriage. Entitled *Adversary in the House*, Stone used the Debs' home as the central point in the drama and as the story develops the reader is supposed to have an increasing anger towards Kate for not understanding the bigger social issues of Gene's political career.

> "But, Kate,'" Gene wails in one scene. "'I just want to earn enough for a comfortable living. Kate will have none of it".

"Money is the most important thing in the world, Eugene, because it controls everything in life."

"That's crass materialism."

"You can't throw me off the track by calling names... He was crushed. Kate sensed her triumph. She said more placatingly, "Eugene, it isn't as though I nag you to make more money. Now do I?"

"No, Kate."

"If I had been another kind of woman, it would have been easy to spend your salary on frivolities. But when I saved five dollars or twenty dollars, I knew just what it would buy: a beautiful lamp at the foot of the winding staircase..."[3]

Of course, the major issue with this depiction is that its validity is highly debatable. As one reviewer put it at the time of the novel's release:

> In a novel the writer is free to use devices that make for a convincing story, and the result is often more believable than the mere truth... It is possible that in this book Irving Stone made too much up. At least some authorities may disagree with his central thesis that Mrs. Eugene Debs was the adversary in her husband's house... Irving Stone has not enshrined Debs in this book. Rather, he has tried to explain him, and on the purely human side he has cast Mrs. Debs in the role of villainess.[4]

Despite this admission to fiction, and the fact that Irving Stone would be forced to write a letter explaining the fictitious elements to Eugene and Kate's niece Marguerite, the theme has to a certain extent taken hold.[5] Nick Salvatore in his work *Citizen and Socialist* argued a similar interpretation that Stone had, and the home has been periodically questioned for its use as a good representation of a working-class museum. It has not been until recently with the work of Michelle Morahn that this interpretation has been seriously challenged.[6] As such, the home sits as a good example of the continuing question over how best to represent working-class history, and how much the site adds to the story of the industrial workers' movement.

Yet despite this, examining Debs' actions after the completion of the home shows a serious commitment to the radical workers' movement. In 1893, Debs organised one of the first US industrial unions in the form of the American Railway Union (ARU), and made quick work of empowering previously ignored unskilled labourers. The ARU just two years later backed striking car construction workers of the Pullman Company. The Cleveland Administration, hostile to the workers, used federal troops and legal manoeuvrings to crush the strike. On 20 June 1894, citing a court injunction, the Administration claimed the strike disrupted the flow of mail and therefore posed a national security risk. The injunction also targeted anyone verbally supporting or inciting the strike. Dozens were either killed or injured in the resulting battles. Debs, for his leadership and outspoken support, was arrested, tried and sentenced to prison. It would not be the last time his democratic rights landed him in trouble with the law. He famously claimed that the time in prison resulted in his decision to connect labour issues with a quest for socialism. Once out of prison he became a key political figure in the American political arena moving from labour, to the Populist movement of the 1890s, to eventually the American socialist movement. As a figure in the Socialist Party, Debs was one of the key national figures in promoting socialism in an American context. In 1905, in Chicago, he was one of the founding members of the Industrial Workers of the World (IWW), and argued for an international, industrial and Marxist approach to working-class politics.

In 1918, with the eve of US involvement in World War I approaching, Debs gave a speech in Canton, Ohio where he spoke out against US entry into the war. Arrested, and tried for treason, Debs offered a passionate plea for social justice in his legal defence. Despite his appeal, the court sentenced Debs to ten years in prison. Warren G. Harding in 1921 commuted Debs' sentence and then Debs died just five years later, having never fully recovered his health. He is now buried in Terre Haute, not far from the home where he rarely lived during his life.

Debs in history

As evident, the legacy of Debs offers several questions to the historian presenting work on working-class history. As a figure of the radical Left, his politics and the punishment meted out by the state conforms to the similar experiences of Emma Goldman, Martin Luther King Jr., and John Brown. Like many of these figures, Debs' dedication to social justice was not something easily reducible to a single praxis. Debs argued socialism, labour and democratic practice should always be dedicated to the liberation of the total human. Yet, even a short biography reveals Debs was not often successful in his efforts for direct political and economic reform. Also, it is clear from Debs' arguments against white supremacists and his disagreements with figures like the suffragist Susan B. Anthony that Debs' approach to economic and social justice could be viewed as a type of class reductionism.[7] As such, what should we emphasise in a popular imagining? In essence, where does one place Debs in history?

Such questions faced the purchasers of the Debs' house. As it is stated above, the original members of the Foundation represented a mixture of academics, union leaders and community members. The answer was to first preserve the home, while eventually using the space as a new museum. The second task was to see Debs' legacy as not one simply of labour unions, although that was vital, but to communicate to the public that the history of economic and social justice could not be separated. The American labour movement, specifically the unionism Debs and many other Americans came to practice in the early twentieth century, took issues of social and cultural concerns seriously. Therefore, the causes of wages, work conditions and ownership of means of production had to be seen as tied to the issues of anti-racism, civil rights and peace and justice. Yet, before any of this could actually be achieved, the home which was to be the base of operations for the Foundation needed to be preserved.

With the financial support of local chapters of the American Federation of Labor and Congress of Industrial Organization (AFL-CIO) and the United Auto Workers (UAW), much of the damage caused by old age and the home's fraternity years was quickly fixed. As Bob Constantine, a member of the Foundation and historian, remembered years later, 'By 1967, the "remarkable progress" [of the Foundation]... included the near completion of the physical restoration of the Debs home...and the beginnings of the Foundation's work in the fields of education and research'.[8]

Although the Foundation eventually contributed thousands of dollars in maintenance and upkeep, which included a new roof and siding in 1989, the house was preserved enough by 1966 that it was made a National Landmark by the National Parks system. This protected the property from dangers such as seizure through eminent domain. Two years later, the demarcation proved to be a powerful designation, as the University developed the property around the home. Finding that the house was not able to be torn down, University officials offered to move the home to a location further away so as to make room for the development. The Foundation refused. As a result, the home still sits at its 1890 location where Debs had it completed. The house secure, the Foundation focused on how best to represent the legacy of Debs.

Aside from maintaining the home as a museum, the Foundation also contributed to the advancement of Debs in public memory through education. This included working with Indiana State University Library to establish and maintain the Debs collection, the largest deposit of Debs' papers. It also included awarding an annual Debs Award given every year to a figure 'whose work has been in the spirit of Debs and who has contributed to the advancement of the causes of industrial unionism, social justice, or world peace'.[9] Required to give a keynote address, the Foundation has archived these recipient speeches, creating a rich resource for any scholar interested in seeing how major figures of the Left view Debs' place in history.

Awarded at the annual banquet, this event ties Debs' legacy to current issues in social justice, labour and global politics. Beginning in 1962 and continuing to the modern day,[10] the Foundation has honoured such figures as A. Philip Randolph, Walter Reuther, Coretta Scott King, Kurt Vonnegut, Howard Zinn and Danny Glover. Aside from these well-known figures in US politics, art and academics, the Foundation has also honoured many less publicly known labour leaders and organisations such as Clayola Brown, Sara Horowitz, Brave New Films, and Jobs With Justice.

In 1967, A. Philip Randolph demonstrated this ability to create connections between Debs and the present by saying:

> This is hallowed ground... where Debs spent his life. He was one of the prophets of the world. Sometimes referred to as the lion-hearted agitator. Debs was a crusader of the poor, the oppressed, and the downtrodden workers. With a passionate dedication to peace, racial justice, and profound [socialism]... He was conscious that votes alone would not work...

Organization of people, Randolph summarised, was required for success. He then tied Debs' work in the labour movement to the then ongoing work in the civil rights movement, arguing that Debs' views were still pertinent to modern struggles.[11]

James Hightower argued Debs' relevancy in his 1995 acceptance speech. Using Debs' legacy as a way to understand global capitalism, Hightower spoke on corporations' use of outsourcing, demonstrating how capital and government work hand-in-hand to maintain a system of exploitation. Tying this back to Debs' work with Pullman, and his critique of the First World War, Hightower argued such historical understanding was necessary if people were to combat larger societal oppression.[12]

In 1998, when Howard Zinn was honoured with the award, he reflected on the legacy of Debs, both in American history and his personal life, by saying,

> Eugene Debs was the first socialist I ever heard of. See, when I went to work in the ship yard I was already a radical. And I, and a few other workers… would get together once a week and we would read. And we would read Marx… and we read Upton Sinclair and Jack London and it was very exciting. Then I came across Debs because he was not only a thinker and writer, but a man of enormous action.[13]

Taken together, the actions of the Foundation from the 1960s onwards present multiple ways to learn and engage with the history of Eugene Debs and American labour. Both as a museum, and an annual banquet honouring his legacy, the Foundation has simultaneously found a way to continue the memory of Debs while tying him into a continuing narrative of the American Left's development.

However, the Foundation's dedication to promoting Debs' life and legacy has not always been an easy task. As an essay decrying the state of America argued in the *Indiana Tribune-Star* in the year 2000:

> Eugene Victor Debs, Terre Haute's contribution to America's last populist gasp… Debs' words are already antiquated and it's hard to believe he will remain of much interest in a century where the accumulation of stuff [is] the scorecard for success… Who is our Eugene V. Debs today…?[14]

Debs, in this understanding, is only a populist reformer with Midwestern sensibilities. Society dupes Americans through their love of material things, the argument goes. Any kind of radical critique has exited politics, which has been captured by corporate interests. This poses problems for organisations such as the Debs Foundation. By collapsing Debs into a simple expression of American Midwestern belief, he becomes a socialist in name only.[15] The consequences of this belief are seen in the 2014 movie *The Drunk*. A low-budget film, the movie follows the life of the fictitious grandson of Eugene Debs. Arrested for drunk driving, Joe Debs (played by William Tanoos) eventually runs for governor of the state of Indiana against a corrupt prosecuting attorney (played by Tom Sizemore). The film, despite being based on a historical inaccuracy, is interesting nonetheless for its imagining of Debs, labour and radicalism in American history. Opening with a scene of the outgoing governor (played by Jesse Ventura), the governor argues the problem with modern politics is hyper partisanship. To solve the problems of the United States, the nation's politics needs to abandon partisanship and focus on the betterment of the American 'people'. Joe Debs echoes this sentiment throughout the film. For example, as Tanoos is preparing a campaign speech he writes, 'I do think we should all pull ourselves up by our bootstraps. But you know what? I think it's important we make sure everyone has boots'.[16] In this view, Debs and America's radical Left are fundamentally indistinguishable from populism or general reform.

In his own time, commentators also argued that Debs' largest contribution to politics was the adoption of his ideas by mainstream figures like Roosevelt, Wilson, the Progressives and Democrats. A cartoon from the period argues this by showing Debs, dully swimming in a small pond, gazing in amazement as he is told by William Jennings Bryant that Roosevelt has stolen his clothes, therefore leaving him naked and unable to leave. The clothes in the cartoon represent the political positions of socialism, the stealing an adoption of the ideas by others, and the nudity an inability to attract voters to his message.[17]

This imagining of Debs as a failed radical is also reflected in much historiography. Breaking the field into two main categories, one can see Debs emerge as either a utopian socialist, or the democratic citizen challenging the power of the state. As Ronald Lee and James R. Andrews have argued:

> We find Eugene Debs as an American democrat, running five times for President, speaking of revolution but abhorring violence, and spending his life organizing unions for the protection of the working people... Debs is the story of a man, confident in The People's sense of right, leading the country from the world of Rockefeller to the world of Reuther.[18]

The late historian of political economy, Martin Sklar, offered a theoretical interpretation of Debs as a utopian, arguing that the act of dissent in American history can be of a 'utopian' or 'realistic' nature. Breaking figures on the Left into three major categories of Right/Left, socialist/capitalist and utopian/realist, Sklar argued someone like Debs could be seen as a left-wing, pro socialist, utopian. 'The utopian mind', Sklar wrote, 'being ahistorical in its conception of the "good" or "true"... is static, essentialist, and closed'.[19]

Others, like Ray Ginger and Nick Salvatore, provide another interpretation of Debs by seeing him as an extension of American democratic thought, a reformer, who believed in the basic principles of American democracy. Whereas Ginger's work is mostly laudatory, Salvatore offers a critical view of the five-time candidate for president. Salvatore concludes that Debs is very much a product of American thought and culture. Debs' understanding of class struggle as pertinent to American democracy makes Debs as much a son of American democracy as it does Marxist socialism. This leads Salvatore to argue that throughout much of their careers

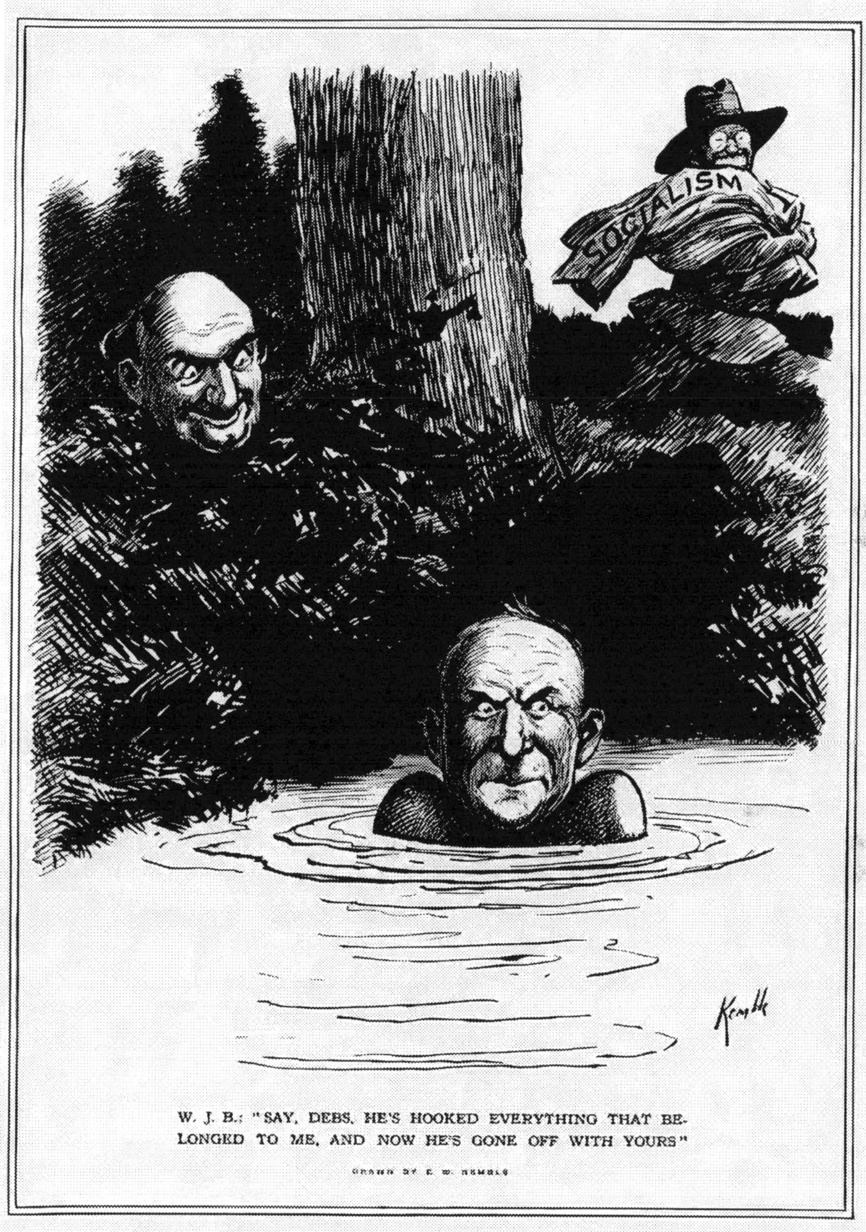

FIGURE 9.2 'W. J. B.: "Say, Debs…"'. This cartoon demonstrates the shift towards progressive politics in the United States, as well as the adoption of socialist policies to the determent of the Socialist Party's electoral efforts. *Harper's Weekly*, 21 September 1912. Cartoonist: Edward Windsor Kemble.

Samuel Gompers, the pure and simple trade unionist of the AFL, and not Debs the socialist candidate, was the more Marxist of the two. This raises an interesting discussion over how historians classify Marxist and radical. Although it is true that Gompers did acknowledge class divisions, while Debs typically couched his rhetoric in American ideals, Debs repeatedly made the case that capitalism, as a system of social relations between capital and labour, provided a fundamental relationship of exploitation. From this understanding Debs argued against such institutions and practices as imperialism, prisons and wage labour. Debs encouraged engagement with the state because of his belief in the transitive possibility democracy provided a general populace.

This faith in democratic reform via civic engagement is often what landed him in trouble through his use of the general strike and his criticism of US foreign policy. By viewing Debs in this manner, one begins to see that instead of separating Debs' views on American democracy and his views on socialism, they should be read together. When this happens a fuller vision of Debs emerges that combats the common declension narrative of the American Left and shows that not only are radicals like Debs capable of being fostered in American culture, but that they can access the larger cultural attitudes of the country to make their arguments. This has led some historians to express concern that Debs has been co-opted by more conservative forces. As Mark Lause has written, 'the transformation of Debs into a kind of pet rock for thoroughly domesticated labour organizations comes as no surprise'.[20] Lause views Debs as a transnational figure in a radical development in the Western world during the late nineteenth and early twentieth century. Therefore, attempts to explain him purely through an American lens of democracy are misplaced.

This fear over co-optation of various figures on the Left is understandable. A misrepresentation of radical thinkers, activists and leaders often leads to a series of heroic biopics that support the very systems of oppression the historic figure fought to end. Thus, white liberals depict Martin Luther King Jr. in twenty-first-century American media as a kind of apolitical hero spouting only feel-good inspirational quotes, a character for a meme to be shared during an uprising, while his ideas on labour and militarism are ignored.[21] The whitewashing can reach such a totality that figures like Helen Keller cease to be political actors at all. Instead, Keller is a socially disconnected autobiography. Keller's popular imagining becomes one of personal suffering, hardship and ultimate triumph. Yet this narrative utterly ignores Keller's contribution to social justice, the founding of the ACLU and radical politics.

Public history has a part to play in either furthering this simplification of political figures and movements or correcting it. As historian Megan Kate Nelson argues, we can either consume our history, or confront it. In this way, a dichotomy is established with consumption being the passive acceptance of a narrative or confrontation: a headlong engagement that requires the present to grapple with the past. Likewise, the questions of ethical memory in public history sites is one that has repeatedly come up in twenty-first-century societies. From memorials of slavers to Confederate generals, the toppling of statues demonstrates that some in the public, far from being apathetic about history and its representations, care deeply. Can the possible co-optation of say, Martin Luther King Jr. in a D.C. memorial, or Harriet Tubman on the 20 dollar US bill, or any various uses of Debs by modern political leaders, lead to a distraction from their history? Can it lead to a perversion where the systems these figures fought, and in many cases gave up life and freedom for, end up helping support those systems?

Public sites for labour history are uniquely charged in this regard. Even as a quick perusal of the most obvious public history labour sites demonstrates, sites of labour history are very much sites of partisan public memory. Much of this can be attributed to the nature of the broader labour movement itself. As a social movement that continues to seek political and economic change, sites of labour history are not simply memorials. They are places where memory is invoked with the potential of compelling the participant to engage with the unending continuation of social justice. Therefore, from the danger of co-optation is also opportunity. When figures are memorialised they gain a moral stature that allows them to be used as figures of authority. This in turn permits members on the Left to push radical ideas. This will, of course, mean that certain ideas are stressed over others but it also means the normalisation of previously fringe concepts. Figures like Debs, then, as a persona of public memory, provide a key site in our historic landscape for working-class people to fight inequality.

Conclusion

In 2013, Indiana State University announced the Statesmen Towers would be demolished. Although in the 1960s the University billed the towers as state of the art, times had not kept up with the architectural integrity. Rumours spread that the Foundation was unsafe for human occupation, a charge University officials denied. Instead the issue was given that the continued development of the college required a new place for University students. The University made plans to demolish the two buildings, gaining concern from the Foundation. Although the University offered to construct a 'barrier and netting or cover to protect the entire Museum site from flying debris',[22] several Foundation members opposed the idea, citing the risk the demolition posed to the historic site. In 2014, the University temporarily halted plans to demolish the towers, opting to explore the possible refurbishing of the buildings for continued use. Yet in April 2015 the University went ahead with demolition. At 11:00 AM a 7,000 pound wrecking ball slammed into the towers' east building sending debris crashing down. Initially sceptical of the demolition, the Foundation was at least placated that the University were not imploding the buildings.[23]

Indiana State University made quick work of the buildings, and after just a few months, the site of the towers was reduced to nothing more than an open, green lot. Currently the University does not have public plans for what to do with the land, but given its location it will most likely not remain empty for long. The Foundation has considered placing an extension of the Museum into the lot, perhaps a statue or some other monument. Yet, concerns exist in the Foundation of building a statue that centres Debs as a man, a lone individual, instead of a member of a larger ongoing social movement. Therefore, it has been suggested to create a memorial that is more inclusive, democratic and demonstrates that the history being preserved on the campus is not one of conquest, of white-washed figures, or of military triumph. Given the politics of public space, it is difficult to predict what will join the Museum as its new neighbour. Hopefully it will be something that centres the experiences of working-class people, justice and ultimately the longevity of labour.

The construction, and then demolition, of the towers provides an excellent illustration of capital's unstable growth, compared to the stability of arguments from labour. Replaced within only a few decades, compared to the centenarian Debs' house, one continues through community engagement to stand strong, while the other was abandoned in a mission of growth for growth's sake. It is an irony that Debs himself, and working-class public historians, can well appreciate.

Notes

1 Debs Foundation Newsletter, "The Debs Home:100 Years of History," 3.
2 Debs' Foundation, "First Floor of the Debs Home."
3 Stone, *Adversary in the House*, 143.
4 Weigel, "Novelist Employs Eugene Debs as Central Character of Book."
5 As Stone recounts in the letter, 'I don't think I ever told you what made me so ill for many months during the writing of the book. I shall do so now: it was the monumental difficulty of bringing forth a lucid and completely sympathetic novel, which would be read by a wide public which would not read a biography or a history about Eugene V. Debs, labor unions and socialism. It is no good having our book read only by those who already love and approve the work of Debs; it is necessary to reach millions of Americans with the book, Americans who are either prejudiced against the name and work of Debs, or who have never heard of him' (Irving Stone to Marguerite Debs Cooper, 14 July 1947).
6 Morahn, "Kate Debs: The Other Radical?" 296–310.
7 Although Debs was an ardent supporter of women's suffrage, and by the time he was a major socialist figure he was openly critical of white supremacists, including racist socialists who did not want to integrate the movement or unions, Debs often couched support for women and people of color in economic terms. Often Debs' depictions of sexism and racism would be reduced to the issues of capitalist class exploitation, and in his disagreement with Susan B. Anthony he would argue socialism had to come first before women's equality could be achieved. For more see: Debs, "The Negro in the Class Struggle," 5 and Debs Foundation, "Debs and Women's Rights."
8 Debs Foundation Newsletter, "Twenty Five Years Ago the Debs Foundation: 1967," 3.
9 Debs Foundation, "Eugene V. Debs Foundation."
10 With the exception of the year 1971.
11 Randolph, Debs Award Speech, 1967.
12 Hightower, Debs Award Speech, 1995.
13 Zinn, Debs Award Speech, 1998.
14 Debs Foundation Newsletter, "Where is the Eugene Debs of the 21st Century?," 3.
15 Debs Foundation Newsletter, "Where is the Eugene Debs of the 21st Century?," 3
16 *The Drunk*, 2014.
17 Kemble, "W.J.B.: 'Say, Debs...'"
18 Andrews and Lee, "A Story of Rhetorical-Ideological Transformation," 29.
19 Sklar, "Thoughts on Capitalism and Socialism," 363.
20 Lause, "New Introduction," 10.

21 Martin Luther King Jr'.s thoughts on various topics shifted during his life. Yet, as can be seen by his later works, such as his 1967 book *Where Do We Go From Here: Chaos or Community?* King was, by the end of his life, a committed activist and theologian to the ideas of democratic socialism, labor unionism, and anti-imperialism. Furthermore, he was increasingly critical of white liberals and saw the plight of African American people as part of a larger issue of economic oppression and US military aggression.

22 Loughlin, "Days are Numbered."

23 Loughlin, "Debs Home to be Safe During Towers' Demolition, All Parties Say."

Bibliography

Secondary sources

Andrews, James R., and Ronald Lee. "A Story of Rhetorical-Ideological Transformation: Eugene V. Debs as Liberal Hero." *Quarterly Journal of Speech* 77, no. 1 (1991): 20–37.

Ginger, Ray. *The Bending Cross: A Biography of Eugene Victor Debs*. Chicago: Haymarket Books, 2007.

King, Martin Luther. *Where Do We Go from Here: Chaos or Community?*Boston: Beacon Press, 1967.

Lause, Mark. "New Introduction." In *Eugene V. Debs Reader: Socialism and Class Struggle*, edited by William A.Pelz. Chicago: Merlin Press, 2014.

Morahn, Michelle Killion. "Kate Debs: The Other Radical?" *Indiana Magazine of History* 114:4 (December 2018): 296–310.

Nelson, Megan Kate. *Ruin Nation: Destruction and the American Civil War*. Athens, Georgia: University of Georgia Press, 2012.

Salvatore, Nick. *Eugene V. Debs: Citizen and Socialist*. Chicago: University of Illinois Press, 2007.

Sklar, Marin. "Thoughts on Capitalism and Socialism: Utopian and Realistic." *Journal of the Gilded Age and Progressive Era* 2, no. 4 (2003): 361–376.

Primary sources

Chicago Herald, 2 July 1894.

Debs, Eugene V. "The Negro in the Class Struggle." *International Socialist Review* 4, no. 5 (November 1903): 260.

Hightower, James. "Debs Award Speech." Annual Debs Award. Terre Haute, Indiana, 1995.

Kemble, Edward W."W.J.B.: 'Say, Debs…'" Illustration. *Harper's Weekly*, 21 September 1912. Accessed 30 November 2020. https://elections.harpweek.com/1912/cartoons-1912-list.asp?Year=1912.

Loughlin, Sue. "Debs Home to be Safe During Towers' Demolition, All Parties Say." *Terre Haute Tribune Star* (Terre Haute, Indiana), 29 January 2015. Accessed 27 April 2015. www.tribstar.com/news/local_news/debs-home-to-be-safe-during-towers-demolition-all-parties/article_9a6aff07-b593-5dcb-8884-7db70e540f56.html.

Loughlin, Sue. "Days are Numbered: ISU Asking for Towers Demolition Money." *Terre Haute Tribune Star* (Terre Haute, Indiana), 15 February 2013. Accessed 1 March 2015. www.tribstar.com/news/local_news/days-are-numbered-isu-asking-for-towers-demolition-money/article_0e6efd6e-f666-51a4-8aea-0380006d93aa.html?mode=jqm.

Perry, Henry Chapin. "Socialist Wrecked by His Wife." *Hartford Courant* (Hartford, Connecticut), 12 October 1947.

Randolph, A. Philip. "Debs Award Speech." Annual Debs Award. Terre Haute, Indiana, 1967.

Stone, Irving. *Adversary in the House*. New York: Doubleday & Co., 1947.

Stone, Irving to Marguerite Debs Cooper, 14 July 1947. Special Collections Department, Indiana State University Library, Terre Haute, Indiana.

The Debs Foundation. "Debs and Women's Rights—A Lifetime Commitment." Accessed 14 July 2020. https://debsfoundation.org/index.php/landing/debs-biography/womens-rights/.

The Debs Foundation. *Eugene V. Debs Foundation*. Accessed 12 March 2015. http://debs foundation.org/foundation.html.

The Debs Foundation. "First Floor of the Debs Home." Accessed 13 July 2020. https://debsfoundation.org/index.php/landing/visit-the-museum/virtual-tour/first-floor-of-the-debs-home/.

"The Debs Home: 100 Years of History." *Debs Foundation Newsletter* (Fall 1989). Debs' Foundation Archive. Terre Haute, Indiana.

"Twenty Five Years Ago the Debs Foundation: 1967." *Debs Foundation Newsletter* (Fall 1992). Debs' Foundation Archive. Terre Haute, Indiana.

"Where is the Eugene Debs of the 21st Century?" *Debs Foundation Newsletter* (Spring 2000). Debs' Foundation Archive. Terre Haute, Indiana.

The Drunk. Directed by William Tanoos and Paul Fleschner. 2014. DVD.

Weigel, John A. "Novelist Employs Eugene Debs as Central Character of Book." *The Dayton Herald*, 6 December 1947.

Zinn, Howard. "Debs Award Speech." Annual Debs Award. Terre Haute, Indiana, 1998.

10

KEEPING YOUR HEAD DOWN AT THE HYDE PARK BARRACKS MUSEUM

Adele Chynoweth

'Whip me! Whip me!'

Such is the elated exclamation of a school student, in middle childhood. For the purposes of this discussion, I will call him 'John'. John, fully clothed, presses himself, with arms raised, against a large wooden triangle, the kind of frame that was used for the flogging of convicts. John's classmate, 'Vicky' gleefully wields a cat-o'-nine tails[1] and gently slaps his back.

They laugh.

Vicky then insists, 'My turn!'

They change positions. John returns the 'favour'. The giggling continues.

John and Vicky are part of a group from a state government school that has travelled over three hours' duration by bus to participate in *Convict Sleepover* at the Hyde Park Barracks Museum in Sydney, Australia. It is a school learning programme for schools from remote and regional New South Wales.[2] The children's tour guide, an accomplished actor, skilfully inhabits and straddles dual roles of educator and guard. He tells the children, who have been assigned the roles of convicts, that if they keep their head down, work hard and stay out of trouble then they can get a ticket of leave.

Does the site of the Hyde Park Barracks Museum possess a working-class history? If so, is it represented in the Museum, and how? 18 months after my observation of *Convict Sleepover*, I return as a visitor to the newly refurbished site.

Historical background

Hyde Park Barracks is located in Macquarie Street, in Sydney's city centre, and is one of 12 museums that comprise Sydney Living Museums. The Hyde Park Barracks were built to house convicts and opened in 1819, having been designed by

DOI: 10.4324/9781003029519-14

convict architect Francis Greenway under the direction of Governor Lachlan Macquarie.[3] 1840 saw the end to convict transportation to New South Wales[4] and in 1848, the remaining convicts in the Barracks were transferred to Cockatoo Island, located in Sydney Harbour.[5] A total of 50,000 convicts had slept in the Barracks since its inception.[6] Prior to the establishment of the Barracks, convicts lived throughout Sydney, sometimes at their place of work or they slept rough, under trees or in makeshift shelters. Governor Macquarie built the Barracks as a dormitory for them. The Director of Heritage and Collections at Sydney Living Museums explains how Macquarie enticed convicts into the Barracks, 'He held this gigantic public luncheon with roast beef and rum and plum pudding and hundreds were invited in.'[7]

From 1848–1886, the Barracks became the Female Immigration Depot for single women.[8] In 1862, the top floor of the Barracks was allocated to the Government Asylum for Infirm and Destitute Women, in response to overcrowding at the Benevolent Asylum, also situated in the city.[9] In 1886, the site was used to accommodate courts and offices as part of the NSW Department of the Attorney General and Justice, including the NSW Registrar & Commonwealth Conciliation and Arbitration Court, and Industrial Arbitration Court, which are sites of significance to Australian labour history. 'Two landmark legal decisions were made at the site: in 1927 the basic living wage was approved, and in 1921 a case for equal pay for women was presented and rejected, but not granted until 1973'.[10]

In 1979, the Barracks was converted into a museum, which opened in 1984, overseen by the Museum of Applied Arts and Sciences. In 1990, the management of the Barracks was assigned to the Historic Houses Trust of New South Wales,[11] renamed Sydney Living Museums in 2013.[12] In 2010, the Barracks were included in the UNESCO World Heritage List. In 1981, as part of the site's conversion to a museum, the buildings that were added in the late nineteenth and early twentieth centuries were removed, in order to focus on the original structures. This marks the significant erasure, through the demolition of associated material culture, of twentieth-century industrial arbitration history. The destruction of these buildings denotes a disjuncture in the class history of the site and may be understood through the notion of Authorised Heritage Discourse (AHD), which 'deifies the great and the good, the beautiful and the old, the comfortable and the consensual'.[13]

In 1984, the building along the eastern wall of the Barracks was converted by the Department of Corrective Services into courtrooms for parole hearings and included a cell for prisoners. This area was transferred to the Historic Houses Trust in 2001. In addition, when the Museum opened, part of its exhibition content linked the site with the city's working-class history both on site and beyond its walls. One of the rooms featured a display of trade union banners but this was removed over 20 years ago.[14] However, part of the display in the Museum referenced the site's industrial arbitration history. This has since been removed, evident in the Museum's refurbishment having re-opened in February 2020. Instead, the current visitor experience focuses on the site's connection with the convict era and its subsequent function for housing women. This rationale for the recent interpretation of the site is a clear erasure of the site's contemporary working-class history.

Refurbishment

Sydney Living Museums wanted to attract more international tourists to the site by emphasising its convict history.[15] Sydney Living Museums ran a series of consultation workshops with external stakeholders in order to determine which historical narratives connected with the site would be chosen for representation in the newly refurbished Museum.[16] The decision regarding which stories should be told in the newly refurbished Hyde Park Barracks Museum was informed by a series of stakeholder workshops.[17] The Museum's Content Development Think Tank included: an Aboriginal Community Elder; academics from the fields of museum studies, archaeology and history; architects; professionals from other cultural institutions and representatives from local government.[18] No trade union organisers, members of the Labor Council of NSW or prisoner advocacy groups were included in the Think Tank.[19] This is a significant omission, given the site's purpose as a dormitory for convicts as well as its twentieth-century trade union history, evident in the noteworthy wage hearings that took place alongside the original Barracks building. Further, the fact that the original Hyde Park Barracks is still standing, in addition to several other historic buildings in Sydney, may be linked to working-class activism.

In the 1960s, the Hyde Park Barracks were threatened with demolition as part of inner-city development but a local campaign with federal support resulted in its conservation.[20] The site's subsequent transition to a museum was previously paved by a wider political context in Sydney:

> The campaigns, in the early 1970s, of residents' action groups to save historic sites and buildings threatened by inner-city development projects and the support offered those campaigns by the Builders Labourers Federation in banning work on those sites in dispute are the best indices of the degree to which the issue of conservation had acquired popular and democratic associations.[21]

However, this workers' union history was not reflected in the membership of the Hyde Park Barracks Museum Content Development Think Tank. Apart from the crucial inclusion of an Aboriginal Community Elder, the Think Tank's membership reflected Sydney's professional and cultural elite. It is not surprising, then, that the history of union campaigning that led to the approval of a basic living wage in the arbitration court is now absent in the Hyde Park Barracks Museum. Keep your head down and forget the workers.

A visitor's experience

The refurbishment of the Hyde Park Barracks Museum at a cost of $18 million was designed by Local Projects, a US 'experience design studio' based in New York.[22] The site is dominated by a 90-minute immersive audio experience in which visitors are given headphones and an accompanying digital device. A visitor's presence throughout the space triggers the relevant narrative recording to accompany a series of dioramas and object displays. The tour begins with a display inside the ticketing office of the 11 Australian Convict Sites that are included in UNESCO's World Heritage List.[23] The Museum divides the site's convict history into two periods: *Control 1819–26* and *Fear 1826–48*. The first period, *Control 1819–26*, positions convict history in the colony of New South Wales as a period of benevolent reform and rehabilitation under Governor Macquarie.

In one of the galleries, I am surrounded by a continuous animated display that depicts varying scenes where convicts labour. Through my headset I hear an enacted conversation between a convict in a stone quarry and his superior, revealing the policy, at the time, where, in addition to sentenced labour, convicts were also able to undertake paid work. The dialogue is essentially an argument, which the convict wins – telling his supervisor that he won't be back until next week. Another scene on the digitised animated landscape depicts convicts chopping wood. The character voice of the audio recording is that of a convict gang leader who tells his colleague that he doesn't have to chop timber today because no one is coming to check on them until Thursday. Another audio scene is a dialogue between two officers. One says that he rarely has to whip his convict servants. Another actor characterising a convict in an English middle-class linguistic register says, 'Pretty soon I realised if a man kept his head down, he could prosper here'.

This exhibition module refers to the colonial history of New South Wales in which male convicts were organised in work gangs. They were fed and clothed through government stores.[24] The work gang overseers were 'master tradesmen' who were, more likely than not, convicts themselves.[25] Historian Barry Dyster, in an article for the *Journal of the Royal Australian Historical Society*, has previously described the scene:

> Many of the gangs gathered each morning at the government Lumber Yard... which held the requisite benches, forges and toolsheds for various crafts. Woodworkers, metalworkers, leatherworkers, bricklayers, plasterers, plumbers and glaziers operated in or from the Lumber Yard. All of them were on the stores. So were the government quarrymen and stonecutters who met at the steep slopes of Cockle Bay (later called Darling Harbour); convicts dug other quarries close to building sites if stone lay near the surface there. Brickmakers congregated at the kilns beside the clay creek bottoms in present-day Haymarket... or at a lesser deposit of clay along the creek running into Woolloomooloo Bay.[26]

The convict working day started at daybreak and ended at three o'clock in the afternoon. However, after 1819, when convicts were moved into the Hyde Park Barracks, the working day extended to sundown and so any additional private contracted work would have been fulfilled 'under great strain'.[27] Yet the audio narrative that accompanies the diorama depicting convict work at the Hyde Park Barracks Museum is characterised by absences of both hardship and an analysis of power relations. The stories are struggle-lite. This perspective seemingly reflects recent revised historiography: 'The emergence of revisionist labour histories in the

1980s and 1990s transformed the historical debate by shifting the discussion away from the issues of whether convicts were victims or villains to the consideration of labour and labour relations'.[28] While convicts were working-class men and women who applied their skills to the development of the colony,[29] there are other discourses in harsh accounts of convict history such as David Hill's *1788: The Brutal Truth* (2008) and Robert Hughes' *The Fatal Shore* (1986). However, the latter are discredited in this historical revisionism, which also draws attention to narratives of entrepreneurship, including convicts who set up shops and the successful convict farms on the Hawkesbury River. All this is substantiated by the assertion that the colony of New South Wales was informed by an enlightened view 'that men of humble standing had a right to land'.[30]

While historical evidence supports this view, it is reasonable to contemplate whether wider discursive influences are at play. Australian historian Grace Karskens notes that the revision of early convict history as an example of positive, enlightened reform was published in the 1970s but was not widely acknowledged at the time.[31] Why its belated acceptance? Could the answer lie in its discursive alignment with neoliberalism and its belief in a free market economy as the means to prosperity and that 'enlightened avarice is the motivating incentive for the self'?[32] Commentaries of the successful hard-working, individual, entrepreneurial convict are compatible with the doctrine of neoliberalism.

The area within the Museum dedicated to *Fear 1826–48* displays objects such as the as a cat-o'-nine-tails whip and leg irons. The narrator's voice in the recorded commentary states that punishment of convicts became more severe after the 1830s: floggings, labouring in leg irons and/or banishment to remote penal posts. But in another room stands a tall and wide pillar featuring the reproduction of convict tattoos. The images are disembodied and clean, lines uninterrupted by skin texture. Poor chic meets naïve art in a display that looks as though it could feature in a brand meeting for skate clothing and urban streetwear.[33] The human elements of the tattoos are removed. It is as though I am being encouraged not to feel empathy for convicts. I conclude that this curatorial tone reflects the wider, current lack of acknowledgement and respect for working-class identity in our culture.[34]

This feeling of disconnection is exacerbated by my being encased in a headset, dominated by the audio narrative. One sees other visitors, who are also cut off by their headphones. Visitors co-inhabit spaces but are kept apart by a veil of sound. I manage nods of acknowledgement at other visitors but it is a recognition devoid of conversation. Any attempt to speak would interrupt the dominant audio linear narrative. Keep your head down and listen. The Museum's focus on the individual visitor's total engagement with the pre-recorded spoken narrative seems to show little cognisance of research that found that 'for most visitors, the museum experience first and foremost is a social one'.[35]

The top floor of the Museum is dedicated to the theme *Hope 1848–87* and includes displays pertaining to the site's function, from 1848–1886, as the Female Immigration Depot for single women.[36] I see frail remains of garments that belonged to the women who lived there, including young, homeless teenage

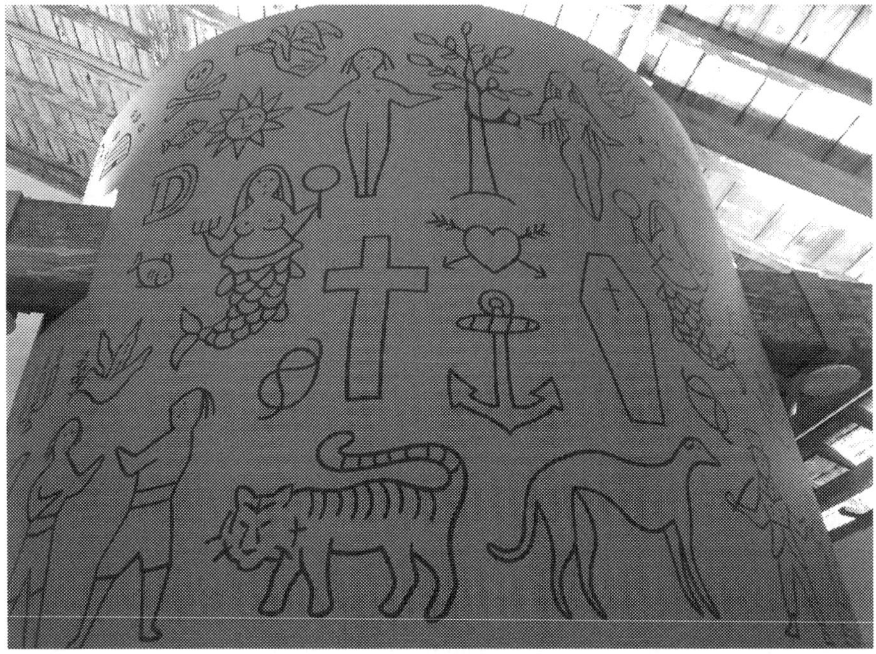

FIGURE 10.1 Poor chic meets naïve art: disembodied convict tattoos at the Hyde Park Barracks Museum. Artwork: Simon Barnard. Photograph: author.

women who came to Australia from Ireland under the Earl Grey scheme.[37] I hear the enacted narration of the young Mary Dunphy and I note that her name is included in the Australian Monument to the Great Irish Famine, opened in 1999, which stands outside on the perimeter of the site. Another room on the top floor is dedicated to the site's former reallocation, in 1862, to the Government Asylum for Infirm and Destitute Women. A series of object displays is accompanied by rudimentary, dormitory beds. Through my headset, Lucy Hicks, the matron, tells me that she is proud of the work that was done here, that they cared when no one else did. This is the first time during this visit that I am overcome with emotion and empathy. I feel for the desperate women who sought shelter here. I also note the absence of their voices and I am reminded of who records history as well as the role of celebrity in neoliberal, public history. Sydney Living Museums publicises Hicks as the paternal great- great-grandmother of Peter Garrett, singer in Midnight Oil and Member of the Parliament of Australia.[38]

Class and violence

The top floor of the Barracks building depicts a treacherous episode of violence in Australia's history in which a group of convicts turned on another community.

The Museum gallery *Violence at the Frontier – the Impact of Colonisation* represents the Myall Creek massacre in the area of New England in northern New South Wales.[39] On 10 June 1838, Australian-born settler John Fleming led a vigilante group which included convicts assigned from the Hyde Park Barracks. At least 28 Aboriginal men, women and children were brutally murdered. The two trials that responded to the massacre took place in the Supreme Court, located opposite the Hyde Park Barracks.[40] The first trial resulted in the acquittal of the 11 convict and ex-convict stockmen. It only took 15 minutes of deliberation for 12 wealthy jurors to return with a verdict of 'not guilty', which had been preceded, before the trial, by 'a tremendous amount of discontent in the community at the prosecution'.[41] John Plunkett, the Attorney General of New South Wales, remanded the 11 men on fresh charges.[42] The seven worst offenders were put on trial, convicted and sentenced to death.[43] The recorded narration in the Hyde Park Barracks Museum states, 'This was the first time that white men had been executed for murdering Aboriginal people'.

This exhibit excludes two facts. It was not only white men who were executed for the Myall Creek massacre. John Johnstone, a West Indian who lived in Liverpool, England, and sentenced to transportation to Australia for house robbery, was also tried and hanged for the murders at Myall Creek.[44] The ringleader, John Fleming, was never brought to justice.[45] As a free settler, he had freedom of movement and a supportive family network both within New South Wales as well as in Tasmania and Moreton Bay (Brisbane). An extensive search failed to locate him and later evidence suggests that Fleming hid on a property owned by his brother, located inland of Moreton Bay.[46] The Myall Creek massacre was undoubtably an act of racist-fuelled brutality. In addition, but no more importantly, a class-based analysis may support an understanding of the dynamics not only within the group of perpetrators but also of the means of their being brought to, or escaping, justice. It would not take much curatorial interpretation to assist visitors in understanding how the experiences of John Johnstone, of African descent, having arrived in Britain from a slave colony, may have led him to a life of crime. But in this gallery there is no reference to analysis such as Australian historian Manning Clark's conjecture concerning the influences on convicts, prior to their transportation, that had resulted in their becoming social outcasts and their criminal activity.[47] These crucial details would not serve to excuse murder but would bring much-needed nuancing to an otherwise superficial positioning of history cast on simplistic identity-based lines of division that exclude class.

Nevertheless, class is implied in the comparative semiotics of scale of the design throughout the Museum. By way of contrast, in a separate gallery, there is a depiction of the Blacktown Native Institution, over 40 kilometres away from the Barracks. The Institution was founded by Macquarie, as the Museum audio commentary tells me, to house Aboriginal children. Macquarie's insistence on 'civilising' Aboriginal people by stealing children from their parents' traditions and language was nothing less than attempted cultural genocide.[48] This genocide narrative is represented, in addition to the spoken narration, in a miniature model of the Blacktown Native Institution. Conversely, in the *Violence at the Frontier* gallery, the display is life-sized. I stand amidst tall thin screens that feature digital footage of trees and foliage. I am in the virtual bush – the site of the Myall Creek massacre. If the size of the elements within as part of the exhibition design serves as a means to interpret the discourse within the Museum, then convicts' crimes against the Aboriginal people are deemed greater than those committed by Governor Macquarie.

It is important to understand the role of convicts in the frontier wars in Australia, but also, the atrocious agency of free settlers and government officials. Instead, the Museum souvenir booklet positions Macquarie, in relation to transported convicts, as a benevolent reformer in that he viewed the colony 'not as a prison but as a place of rehabilitation for convicts. Through enterprise and diligence, they could re-enter civil society with the same rights as free men and women. Macquarie elevated convicts and ex-convicts to positions of authority and encouraged good behaviour with the reduction of sentences and grants of land'.[49] There is no mention, in the Museum, that Macquarie's compassion did not extend to female convicts as reflected in his assertion as noted elsewhere by historian Annette Salt, 'Female convicts are as great a drawback as the males are useful'.[50] Nor is there mention of, the former Female Factory at Parramatta, 27 kilometres from the Hyde Park Barracks, established in 1821, also built by Francis Greenway and accommodating up to 500 women convicts who produced goods for the colony.[51] The Female Factory was also a site that institutionalised children. Many of the mothers of the children were housed in the factory on site.[52] The Orphan School was a continuing site of childhood institutionalisation, later known as the Parramatta Girls Training School that closed in 1974, following an exposé of heinous child abuse and associated protests by women's groups in Sydney.[53]

There is no mention in the Hyde Park Barracks Museum of Macquarie's declaration of war on the Aboriginal people on 9 April 1816 through his instructions to Captain Schaw of the 46th Regiment:

> On any occasion of seeing or falling in with the Natives, either in bodies or singly, they are to be called on, by your friendly Native Guides, to surrender themselves to you as Prisoners of War. If they refuse to do so, make the least show of resistance, or attempt to run away from you, you will fire upon and compell them to surrender, breaking and destroying the spears, clubs, and waddies of all those you take Prisoners. Such Natives as happen to be killed on such occasions, if grown up men, are to be hanged up on trees in conspicuous situations, to strike the Survivors with the greater terror.[54]

There is no acknowledgement of the resonance of this throughout the international museum sector, in that 'the bodies of slain warriors were also decapitated, though in secret, and their heads sent off to museums in Europe'.[55] I could imagine that the Museum might justify this absence on the grounds that Macquarie's war crimes exist beyond the narrative and geographical scope of the history of the Hyde Park Barracks. So too is the Myall Creek massacre but that does not prevent the content managers of Sydney Living Museum from demonising 'white' convict labourers.

Legacy

The final gallery in the Museum displays video testimonies of the living who talk about the implications, for them, of the site's history. Aboriginal elders speak of the importance of reconciliation. Author Sienna Brown talks about the cultural link between Jamaica and transported convicts – a narrative conveniently placed in a separate room from the representation of the Myall Creek massacre. Descendants of convicts and female immigrants speak of their personal connection with their family history.[56] But the legacy of convict history has wider implications than personal ancestry and the site has a broader history than its former function, positioned in the Museum as seemingly benevolent accommodation for the poor and those who broke the law. Instead, there is an implied message in the Hyde Park Barracks Museum that the former residents should have all been grateful.

Whether the management of Sydney Living Museums acknowledge it or not, the legacy of the Hyde Park Barracks is clearly located within the history of the working and poverty classes and connected to a wider history in nineteenth-century Europe 'of institutionalised welfare policies and practices that emerged during the nineteenth century in the wake of the Industrial Revolution, which saw masses of people relocate to areas that grew into large cities. The growth of a pauper class prompted the formation of charitable organisations and new practices of state monitoring and attempts to control individuals and communities through social welfare agencies'.[57] Many residents of the Barracks came to Australia having had their lives scrutinised and controlled by such policies and practices. There were also child residents at the Barracks – child convicts and, later, young female immigrants. The imported practice, to Australia, of institutionalised and punitive welfarism also informed the removal of Aboriginal children. The Stolen Generations are part of this wider history, not separate from it. With respect to diversity in time, place and culture, the overarching lesson through history is that dislocation, displacement and institutionalisation have profound effects on all, not just one group. Yet, the interpretation of history at the Hyde Park Barracks Museum drives a wedge through the working and poverty classes with its construction of institutionalisation as benevolent opportunity for some and attempted cultural genocide for others. This discursive split is exacerbated by the Museum's erasure of narratives of activism of trade unions and women's groups, and its misplaced judgement of the contribution of skilled labourers in living history. Furthermore, the Hyde Park Barracks Museum's discriminatory fragmentation of the working and poverty classes has been applauded by Australia's peak museum body, the Australian Museum and Galleries Association, which in 2020 included the Museum in its prestigious awards. In the Australian museum sector, constructing, isolating and demonising the 'white' working class is a feather in a curator's cap.

Twenty-five years before the opening of a refurbished museum as the Hyde Park Barracks, cultural sociologist Tony Bennett, in his analysis of the representation of the penal past in Australia past, questions the 'tendency for the convicts to be cast in the role of enlisted migrants or early pioneers in order to provide an early point of reference to which the subsequent histories of settlers, squatters, miners and so on can be connected in a relationship of uninterrupted continuity'.[58] Further, in 'according the penal past the role of a foundational chapter in the history of the nation, that past is simultaneously detached from other histories to which it might be more intelligibly, certainly more critically, related – in particular, the broader and subsequent history of Australian penality'.[59] The Hyde Park Barracks Museum, could, as Bennett proposes, connect its penal past both synchronically and diachronically, 'synchronically, in relating prisons to other historically contemporary penal institutions – asylums, for example, or institutions for destitute women and their children – and diachronically in relating the penal past to present-day forms of punishment'.[60]

This quest for linking the site's discursive past with the present could readily be supported by the Hyde Park Barracks' immersion in the city that surrounds it. Unfortunately, Sydney Living Museums has its eye on the tourist dollar. One might ponder if this is result of external political influences but if so, here is a challenge for museum managers to stand firm. The comments of David Fleming, in 2014, in his then-role of Director of National Museums Liverpool, UK, serve as an example:

> The current obsession with tourism is very alarming.... There's nothing wrong with a policy that encourages overseas tourists, but there is something very wrong when we appear to have no other policy. This commercialisation of our culture is depressing, and it does not strike me as the intelligent policy for cultural activity that is needed if cultural organisations are to play their part in... helping promote the "national good".[61]

In addition to attracting tourists, what local communities could the Hyde Park Barracks Museum identity as potential sources of engagement?

In 1989, Australian journalist John Pilger wrote *The Secret Country* in order to draw much-needed critical attention to the lack of acknowledgement of contemporary history and the ridicule of black history. Pilger also paid heed to 'the silver and zinc miners of Broken Hill [who] won the world's first 35-hour week, half a century ahead of Europe and the United States'[62] and he mourned the death of this advancement, swindled through a new world characterised in Australia by politicians choosing mates from the rich and powerful, our resources being sold off amidst a deregulated economy, Australia's subsequent reliance on its tourist industry[63] and the emergence of 'a new Australian poor "living in massive deprivation."'[64] Pilger tells his reader that Sydney, the city in which he grew up, was, not so long ago, impoverished. Now, the slums are gentrified, selling for millions of dollars because Sydney is the gateway to Australian tourism.[65]

How might the Hyde Parks Barracks Museum be realised if, in addition to its bid for the tourist dollar, it acknowledged the site's connection with the poverty classes of Sydney, its current 'rough sleepers', the trade union activism that saved Sydney historic sites from demolition and campaigned for the fair wages that were brought formally to arbitration hearings on its site? Sydney was built by convict

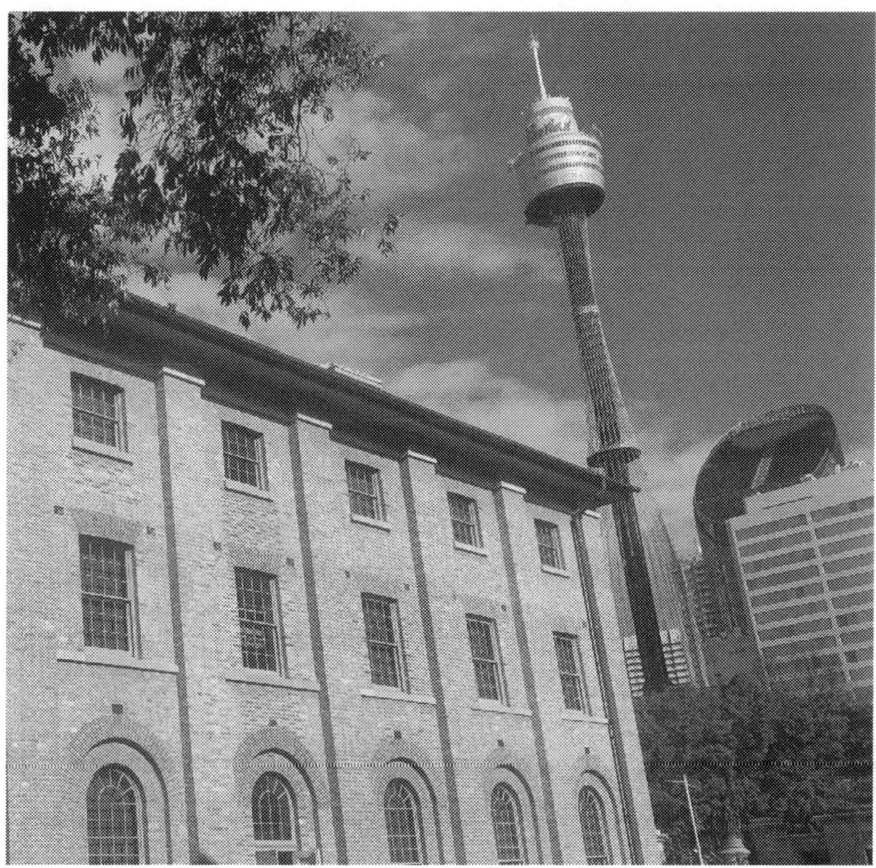

FIGURE 10.2 A side wall of the Hyde Park Barracks, showing the site's proximity to the Sydney CBD, the gateway to Australian tourism. Photograph: author.

skilled labourers. How might the Museum acknowledge the current skills shortage, seen as caused by government cuts to vocational education and big businesses that 'rort the temporary work visa system'?[66] How might the Museum acknowledge the current working poor and challenge the neoliberal myth that 'keeping your head down and working' comprises an exit from poverty? The Museum's *Convict Sleepover* was targeted at schools from remote and regional New South Wales. How might the Museum work with communities to address the effect of neo-liberal policies that have 'resulted in the withdrawal of services from the bush and subsequent job losses, which in turn have seen young people moving from inland rural towns'?[67] Regarding the Barrack's association with banished prisoners, could the Museum work with communities that are affected by penal institutions and current welfare practices that result in both Indigenous and non-Indigenous children being displaced in their own country today?

Following my exit from the Museum, on a nearby street corner, I stop to purchase *The Big Issue*, the independent fortnightly magazine that is sold by, and for, the marginalised.[68] Glenn, the vendor, spins my copy on his upstretched hand as he raises his head to the sky. We laugh. His selling post is located only one block from the Hyde Park Barracks Museum and yet the connection that I experience in that moment seems like a world away.

Notes

1 The cat-o'-nine tails is comprised of nine strands of rope, approximately 18 inches long, held together by a wooden handle, used to whip the back of an 'offender' (Harvey, "Of Flogging and Electric Shock," 87).
2 Sydney Living Museums, *Annual Report 2016–2017*, 5.
3 Rathbone, "Hyde Park Barracks." Greenway had been transported from England to the penal colony of New South Wales after he had been found guilty of forgery. Greenway arrived in the colony in February 1814 (Herman, "Greenway, Francis (1777–1837)") and one month later, he was granted a ticket of leave. In 1816, he was appointed government architect (New South Wales Government, State Archives and Records, "Francis Greenway, Architect & Engineer").
4 Ritchie, "Towards Ending an Unclean Thing," 144.
5 Davies, "Clothing and Textiles at the Hyde Park Destitute Asylum, Sydney, Australia," 3.
6 Rathbone, "Hyde Park Barracks."
7 Director of Heritage and Collections, interview.
8 Kyle, "Emigration of Women to Australia," 200.
9 Davies, "Clothing and Textiles at the Hyde Park Destitute Asylum, Sydney, Australia," 4.
10 Starr, "A Short History of the Hyde Park Barracks Museum."
11 Davies, "Clothing and Textiles at the Hyde Park Destitute Asylum, Sydney, Australia," 5.
12 Sydney Living Museums, "About Us."
13 Smith et al., "Introduction," 2.
14 Bennett, *The Birth of the Museum*, 125.
15 Director of Heritage and Collections, interview.
16 Head of Content, Strategic Projects, Sydney Living Museums, interview.
17 Head of Content, Strategic Projects, Sydney Living Museums, interview.
18 Director of Heritage and Collections, emailed list of members of think tank to author, 29 January 2020.
19 It is interesting to note that the stakeholder group that informed the direction of content in the refurbished Hyde Park Barracks Museum was called a 'Think Tank'. It is a term that is also used for those institutes that conduct studies in support of neoliberal policies (Harvey, "A Brief History of Neoliberalism," 44).
20 Bennett, *The Birth of the Museum*, 124.
21 Bennett citing Zula Nittim, *The Birth of the Museum*, 124.
22 Barlass, "Work in Progress."
23 One notable convict site that is excluded from this list and, therefore, from the Museum's display, is the Parramatta Female Factory Precinct.
24 Dyster, "Bungling a Courthouse," 3.
25 Dyster, "Bungling a Courthouse," 5.
26 Dyster, "Bungling a Courthouse," 6.
27 Dyster, "Bungling a Courthouse," 6.
28 Nunn, "Juveniles as Human Capital," 55.
29 Nunn citing Stephen Nicholas, "Juveniles as Human Capital," 55.
30 Karskens, "Convicts and the Making of Australia." This view is also represented in an exhibition at the Port Arthur Visitors Centre, in Tasmania, informed by the research of

historian Hamish Maxwell Stewart, which displayed 'how a place of terror and incarceration could simultaneously be a place of work, industrial negotiation and opportunity' (Karskens, "Banished and Reclaimed," 33). However, this policy was by no means equitable. Convicts and working people 'had a strong interest in the establishment of uncontested British rights to land in Australia' (Goodall, *Invasion to Embassy*, 48) without sympathy for Aboriginal rights. 'Women were also entitled to receive a grant of land - the first possibly being Ellenor Frazer on 20 February 1794' (NSW Government, State Records & Archives, "Land Rights Guide").

31 Karskens, "Convicts and the Making of Australia."
32 McGuigan, "The Neoliberal Self," 224.
33 'Poor Chic refers to an array of fads and fashions in popular culture that make recreational or stylish – and often expensive – "fun" of poverty, or of traditional symbols of working class and underclass statuses' (Bettez Halnon, "Poor Chic," 501).
34 See Moore et al., "Recovering the Australian Working Class."
35 Falk and Dierking, *The Museum Experience Revisited*, 171.
36 Kyle, "Emigration of Women to Australia," 200.
37 Sydney Living Museums, "Hyde Park Barracks," 60.
38 Sydney Living Museums, "Peter Garrett's Hyde Park Barracks Ancestor."
39 Tedeschi, "Murder at Myall Creek," xiii.
40 Crockett and Hise, "Hyde Park Barracks," 50–51.
41 Tedeschi, "Murder at Myall Creek," 114–15.
42 Tedeschi, "Murder at Myall Creek," 117, 146.
43 Tedeschi, "Murder at Myall Creek," 176–80.
44 Tedeschi, "Murder at Myall Creek," 96; Duffield, "From Slave Colonies to Penal Colonies," 30.
45 Crockett and Hise, "Hyde Park Barracks," 50.
46 Tedeschi, "Murder at Myall Creek," 117–18.
47 Cited by Nicholas and Shergold, "Convict Workers," 4.
48 Peter Read links the removal of Aboriginal children as an act of cultural genocide, *The Stolen Generations*.
49 Crockett and Hise, "Hyde Park Barracks," 35.
50 Salt, "These Outcast Women", 19.
51 Salt, "These Outcast Women," 16–28.
52 Ramsland, "Children of the Back Lanes," 57.
53 Parry, "Tracing the Past," 151.
54 Organ, "Secret Service."
55 Organ, "Secret Service."
56 Brown's novel, *Master of my Fate*, is based on the life of William Buchanan, who was born into slavery in Jamaica, was sent to England and was later transported to the colony of New South Wales and housed at the Hyde Park Barracks.
57 Chynoweth, "Goodna Girls," 4.
58 Bennett, "The Birth of the Museum," 154.
59 Bennett, "The Birth of the Museum," 155.n
60 Bennett, "The Birth of the Museum," 155.
61 Fleming, "What Does the Democratic Museum Look Like?"
62 Pilger, *The Secret Country*, 4.
63 Pilger, *The Secret Country*, 3.
64 Pilger, citing the-then Minister for Social Security in the Hawke Government, *The Secret Country*, 4.
65 Pilger, *The Secret Country*, 10.
66 ACTU, "Morrison and Big Business Could Fix Skills Shortage."
67 Chynoweth, "Rocking the Boat," 297.
68 The Big Issue, *The Big Issue Magazine*.

Bibliography

Australian Council of Trade Unions. "Morrison and Big Business Could Fix Skills Shortage." Media Release, 8 August 2019.

Barlass, Tim. "'Work in Progress': Hyde Park Barracks Closes for $18 million Transformation." *The Sydney Morning Herald*, 10 January 2019. Accessed 31 December 2020. www.smh.com.au/national/work-in-progress-hyde-park-barracks-closes-for-18-million-transformation-20190104-p50pm3.html.

Bennett, Tony. *The Birth of the Museum: History, Theory, Politics*. Abingdon and New York: Routledge, 1995.

Bettez Halnon, Karen. "Poor Chic: The Rational Consumption of Poverty." *Current Sociology* 50, no. 4 (2002): 501–516.

Brown, Sienna. *Master of My Fate*. Melbourne: Penguin, 2019.

The Big Issue. *The Big Issue Magazine*. Accessed 27 September 2020. www.thebigissue.org.au/the-big-issue-magazine/about/.

Chynoweth, Adele. "Rocking the Boat: The Hay Gaol Museum and the Disruptive Narratives of Forgotten Australians." In *The Palgrave Handbook of Prison Tourism*, edited by Jacqueline Z.Wilson, SarahHodgkinson, JustinPiché, and Kevin Walby, 295–318. London: Palgrave Macmillan, 2017.

Chynoweth, Adele. *Goodna Girls: A History of Children in a Queensland Mental Asylum*. Canberra: ANU Press, 2020.

Crockett, Gary, and Beth Hise. *Hyde Park Barracks*. Sydney: Sydney Living Museums, 2020.

Davies, Peter. "Clothing and Textiles at the Hyde Park Destitute Asylum, Sydney, Australia." *Post-Medieval Archaeology* 47, no. 1 (2013): 1–16.

Director of Heritage and Collections, Sydney Living Museums. Interview with author, 20 January 2020.

Duffield, Ian. "From Slave Colonies to Penal Colonies: The West Indian Convict Transportees to Australia." *Slavery and Abolition* 7, no. 1 (1986): 25–45.

Dyster, Barry. "Bungling a Courthouse: A Story of Convict Workplace Reform." *Journal of the Royal Australian Historical Society* 93, no. 1 (2007): 1–21.

Falk, John H., and Lynn D.Dierking. *The Museum Experience Revisited*. London and New York: Routledge, 2013.

Fleming, David. "What Does the Democratic Museum Look Like?" National Museums Liverpool. Accessed 25 October 2020. www.liverpoolmuseums.org.uk/stories/dr-david-fleming-what-does-democratic-museum-look.

Garton, Stephen. "The Convict Origins Debate: Historians and the Problem of the 'Criminal Class'." *Australian & New Zealand Journal of Criminology* 24, no. 2 (1991): 66–82.

Goodall, Heather. *Invasion to Embassy: Land in Aboriginal Politics in New South Wales, 1770–1972*. Sydney: Sydney University Press, 2006.

Harvey, David. *A Brief History of Neoliberalism*. Oxford: Oxford University Press, 2005.

Harvey, Holly. "Of Flogging and Electric Shock: A Comparative Tale of Colonialism, Commonwealths, and the Cat-O'-Nine Tails." *The University of Miami Inter-American Law Review* 24, no. 1 (Fall 1992): 87–119.

Head of Content, Strategic Projects, Sydney Living Museums. Interview with author, 2 November 2018.

Herman, Morton. "Greenway, Francis (1777–1837)." In *Australian Dictionary of Biography*. Accessed 22 January 2020. http://adb.anu.edu.au/biography/greenway-francis-2120.

Karskens, Grace. "Banished and Reclaimed." *Meanjin* 60, no. 4 (2001): 26–34.

Karskens, Grace. "Convicts and the Making of Australia." ANU School of History 2012 Allan Martin lecture. Filmed 15 May at the Australian National University. Accessed 28 July 2020. www.youtube.com/watch?v=vP-Li2vvdkA.

Kyle, Noeline. "Emigration of Women to Australia: Forced and Voluntary." *Descent* 37, no. 4 (2007): 198–203.

McGuigan, Jim. "The Neoliberal Self." *Culture Unbound* 6 (2014): 223–240.

McQueen, Humphrey. *A New Britannia*. St Lucia: University of Queensland Press, 2004.

Moore, Tony, Mark Gibson, and Catharine Lumby. "Recovering the Australian Working Class." In *Considering Class: Theory, Culture and the Media in the 21st Century*, edited by Deidre O'Neill and Mike Wayne, 217–234. Leiden and Boston: Brill, 2017.

New South Wales Government, State Archives & Records. "Francis Greenway, Architect & Engineer." Accessed 22 January 2020. www.records.nsw.gov.au/archives/collections-and-research/guides-and-indexes/stories/francis-greenway-architect-and-engineer.

New South Wales Government, State Records & Archives. "Land Rights Guide, 1788–1856." Accessed 11 October 2020. www.records.nsw.gov.au/archives/collections-and-research/guides-and-indexes/land-grants-guide-1788-1856.

Nicholas, Stephen, and Peter. R. Shergold. "Unshackling the Past." In *Convict Workers: Reinterpreting Australia's Past*, edited by Stephen Nicholas, 3–13. Cambridge: Cambridge University Press, 1988.

Nunn, Cameron. "Juveniles as Human Capital: Re-evaluating the Economic Value of Juvenile Male Convict Labour." *Labour History* 108 (May 2015): 53–69.

Organ, Michael K. "Secret Service: Governor Macquarie's Aboriginal War of 1816." 2014. Accessed 25 October 2020. https://ro.uow.edu.au/asdpapers/481.

Parry, Naomi. "Tracing the Past: The Find and Connect Web Resource." In *Silent System: Forgotten Australians and the Institutionalisation of Women and Children*, edited by Paul Ashton and Jacqueline Z. Wilson, 145–159. North Melbourne: Australian Scholarly Press, 2014.

Petrow, Stefan. "Claims of the Colony: Tasmania's Dispute with Britain over the Port Arthur Penal Establishment 1856–1877." *Papers and Proceedings: Tasmanian Historical Research Association* 44, no. 4 (December 1997): 221–240.

Pilger, John. *The Secret Country*. London: Vintage, 1989.

Ramsland, John. *Children of the Back Lanes: Destitute and Neglected Children in Colonial New South Wales*. Sydney: New South Wales University Press, 1986.

Read, Peter. *The Stolen Generations: The Removal of Aboriginal Children in New South Wales 1883 to 1969*. Sydney: NSW Department of Aboriginal Affairs, 1981.

Salt, Annette. "These Outcast Women: The Parramatta Female Factory." In *Silent System: Forgotten Australians and the Institutionalisation of Women and Children*, edited by Paul Ashton and Jacqueline Z. Wilson, 16–28. North Melbourne: Australian Scholarly Press, 2014.

Senate Community Affairs References Committee. *Forgotten Australians: A Report on Australians Who Experienced Institutional or Out-of-Home Care as Children*. Canberra: Commonwealth of Australia, 2004.

Smith, Laurajane, Paul A. Shackel, and Gary Campbell. *Heritage, Labour and the Working Classes*. London and New York: Routledge, 2011.

Starr, Fiona. "A Short History of the Hyde Park Barracks Museum." Accessed 28 June 2020. https://sydneylivingmuseums.com.au/stories/short-history-hyde-park-barracks.

Sydney Living Museums. "Annual Report 2016–2017." Accessed 27 September 2020. https://sydneylivingmuseums.com.au/sites/default/files/SLM_Annual_Report_2017_FA3_DPS_LR.pdf.

Sydney Living Museums. "Peter Garrett's Hyde Park Barracks Ancestor." Accessed 27 September 2020. https://sydneylivingmuseums.com.au/2016/09/29/peter-garrett's-hyde-park-barracks-ancestor.

Tedeschi, Mark. *Murder at Myall Creek: The Trial that Defined a Nation*. Cammeray, NSW: Simon & Schuster, 2016.

Tranter, Bruce, and Jed Donoghue. "Convict Ancestry: A Neglected Aspect of Australian Identity." *Nations and Nationalism* 9, no. 4 (2003): 555–577.

11

FROM FACTORY TO MUSEUM

The obliteration of the history of resistance

Meral Akbaş and Özge Kelekçi

(…)
i have been opened, closed, opened, closed, and seen
those who came as much as those who went,
(…)
if someone comes… sees… someone had come…
opened… stayed…
still staying with me.
(…)
i have seen it all, seen it all, the end of patience!
if someone comes… if someone sees…
now wind is shaking me…

(*Birhan Keskin,* Door)

Our discussion concerns a museum that was opened in 2016 on the premises of the old Izmit Paper Factory. The factory was originally founded in 1936 and is considered an important place of memory, representing Turkey's recent economic-social history. We ask, 'How and by which negligent and destructive methods is this history spatialised and visualised in this museum?' Although our study was initially limited to the space of the Museum, we knew that it would expand towards a larger field and that we would seek the story behind what remains of the factory today, from the expansive site, from all the different buildings within it, the machines, the workers, memories, old photographs, voices, and so on. Perhaps that's why we mainly searched for a 'door'; and why, when this study was concluded, as depicted in the photo in Figure 11.1 with a narrow road extending between rows of trees located on both sides, that it ended within emptiness.[1]

At the entrance of the Museum, a board outlining the chronological history of the factory welcomes the visitors, and includes the following 'milestone': 'On 18

DOI: 10.4324/9781003029519-15

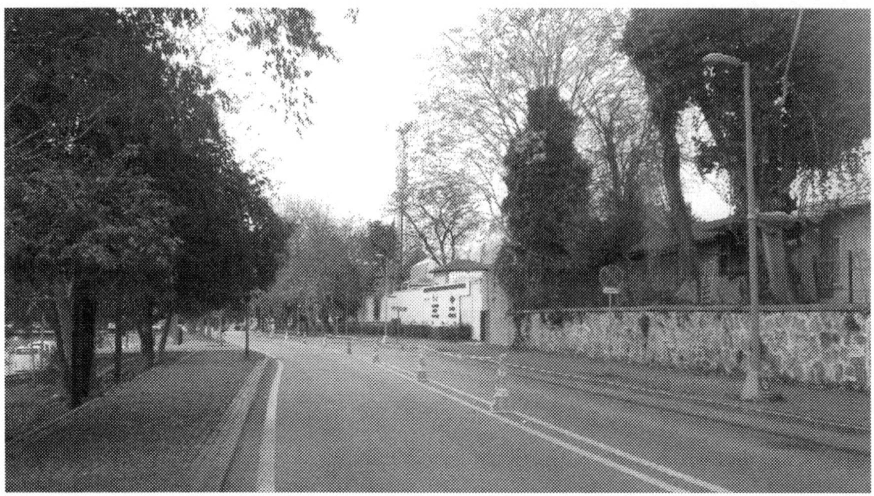

FIGURE 11.1 Main entrance of Izmit Paper Factory, named 'Cumle Kapi' (Main Gate), is no longer there!. Photograph: Meral Akbaş.

April 2015, the 79th anniversary of the first paper production at Sumerbank Izmit Paper and Cardboard Factory, the Kocaeli Science Center opened with the arrival of the guest of honour, 12th President Recep Tayyip Erdoğan'. This most likely was the reason that the Main Gate – which we recall in 2004 and 2005 was the site of resistance movements and occupation of the factory by the workers – was disassembled and destroyed, and replaced by the construction of the road as seen in the photo above. This grand opening as part of the Museum's history not only discloses the emptiness and void that informs our research but it also shuts down a history that is remembered and told by workers and makes all the experiences of workers invisible today.

In 2004 and 2005, the workers interviewed during the resistance and occupation movement in Izmit Paper Factory (SEKA)[2] were emphasising the very same thing. They repeatedly expressed their concerns about a long history about to be wiped out, and that they would be robbed of their home, history and identity if the factory were to be shut down. Therefore, SEKA meant much more than just a workplace. The SEKA resistance movement ended in 2005 when the factory was completely shut down and the factory estate was turned over to Izmit Municipality.

The then Prime Minister of the day said, 'We are presenting SEKA to the people of Izmit as a gift',[3] and proposed turning the estate into a green space like Hyde Park in London. In other words, he proposed a full evacuation and dehistoricisation of the site. Over a decade later, in 2016, Kocaeli Metropolitan Municipality opened SEKA Paper Museum here, stating, 'We want visitors to travel through time in these buildings which were once home to hardworking and honest workers'.[4]

The changing course of capitalism in Turkey

Throughout the 1930s of the Great Depression, in Turkey, the government announced a new strategy of etatism where the economy became internally focused, the State having adopted an economic policy favouring rapid industrialisation.[5] Thus, the State was now responsible for its own entrepreneurship, which preceded the development of capitalism within the borders of the nation-state. When the State began announcing its five-year development and progress plans, the first plan included the vision of establishing new factories. The Republican government adhered to this and started opening new factories one after the other in the upcoming years. Isparta Rose Oil Factory, Pasabahce Bottle and Glass Factory, and Zonguldak Coal Mining Incorporation were all founded during this time. Izmit Paper Factory was also established in 1936 as a part of this state-led industrialisation period in Turkey.

Turkey's socio-economic history marks the Great Depression, as the beginning of industrialisation in Turkey.[6] During this era, the State began establishing new factories in different Anatolian cities to improve the weak industry and invited the private sector into the market. Feroz Ahmad posits that the etatist politics of this era aimed to 'assist the improvement and development of the private sector by providing private enterprises with guidance and access to economic fields into which they could not afford to enter'.[7] While the government was initiating industrialisation projects that prioritised sectors such as glass, paper and textile, it also enacted a labour law prohibiting unionisation and strikes. For workers, '...this meant complying with the rules of a society where their interest would be safeguarded by a state-organisation around corporatist relations'.[8] The nation-state ideology in Turkey not only intended to construct society as a whole formed by the citizens sharing the same language, religion, culture and shared history, but also included the vision of a classless society.[9]

The government's economic initiatives of the 1930s in Turkey, where new factories were opened as state-owned enterprises, also show the government's desire to maintain social control.[10] Also, class-related characteristics of the market relationships during this developmentalist era were obscured through the creation of the myth of progressive government.[11] The implementation of etatist policies within a closed economy saw the government position itself as the one and only actor of development and improvement. Thus, the government created an 'extra-political' field where its economic actions could not be questioned.

Isparta Rose Oil Factory, Pasabahce Bottle and Glass Factory, Zonguldak Coal Mining Incorporation, and Izmit Paper Factory were all founded during the 1930s, amidst a myth of development led by the government. The social life of the cities was shaped around these newly founded factories. As Insel notes:

> These establishments... changed the sight of them [the cities]: well-maintained road networks allowing fast transportation of tools-equipment and the goods, shaded pedestrian pathways running along with green spaces... sanitary

> residences and gardens having water-electricity infrastructure... This way, the old cities... are gradually becoming modernized... improving economically and culturally.[12]

Indeed, one must see the factories not only as a production area but also spaces where a new way of life and a new culture are conveyed. The factories also brought new types of social relationships into the spaces where they were founded.

Museumification of social heritage: critical readings, methodological discussions

Critical social heritage studies emerged as an alternative interpretation and almost even as a form of intervention against the hegemonic heritage approaches which ignore the power relations and disregard the extensive and deep-seated relationship between cultural heritage, inequality and social injustice. These critical approaches see the social/cultural heritage sites, which recreate the past now, as a network of relationships rather than a sum of frozen objects.[13] Laurajane Smith posits that the hegemonic relationships formed around the great monuments, historical sites and aesthetically fascinating artefacts affect the memory in a way that the heritage of the local, oppressed and alternative is concealed. Thus, the Western-elitist cultural values are reformed and circulated in the social heritage sites.[14]

Those methods of knowing and remembering/reminding in critical fields such as class, gender, ethnicity and civil rights are mostly overlooked and/or disregarded by the hegemonic discourse.[15] This is evident in sites of industrial heritage. Either the memory and the history of the working class are disregarded or the subjectivity of the workers is sidelined, and the workers' narratives are assimilated. The UNESCO World Heritage List in its regard of factories and technical/technological equipment as heritage never considers the labour processes, social production relationships and class conflicts as cultural heritage.[16]

The memory of the working class as a form of collective remembering is also only possible as long as the togetherness and interaction among the bearers of that memory become continuous.[17] The likelihood of maintaining social memory and identity is reduced for the working class, whose sense of cohesion is becoming rapidly eroded, particularly as a result of neoliberalism.[18] While the industrial areas and, thus, the spatial memory of the working class are being destroyed globally, the discussions on how to protect these memories are becoming more and more important. In this regard, the notion of industrial heritage, which museumification and social heritage studies define in a limited way, needs to be redefined and critically discussed. First, what must be emphasised is the diversity of class memory in opposition to the dominance of a certain way of knowing. Secondly, it must be noted that the history and the heritage of the working class are essentially related to the protests, strikes and pursuit of social justice. Disregarding these social movements in the discussions on protection and reproduction of industrial heritage not only creates a simply static and frozen form of industrial heritage but also results in the obscuration of the truth about the most critical moments and spaces related to the memory and the history of the working class.[19] The heritage of the working class is beyond the physical remains of the factories, machines and production complexes; it is embedded in the cultural, political and economic traces of a social relationships network. Therefore, a critical re-definition and re-consideration of working-class heritage within industrial heritage may bring about a critical view and even a transformation of the entire social relationships network as well as the museumification process. As such, improving the visibility of the strike, uprising and resistance spaces is crucial. Acknowledging the spaces of social uprising and resistance movements as social heritage will be an achievement and a step towards making the memory of the working class visible as well as ensuring social justice.

The first encounter: '2005: SEKA was shut down and handed over to Kocaeli Metropolitan Municipality'

In the historical explanations on the walls of the Museum, the history of SEKA, which was privatised, shut down, handed over, downsized and occupied, does not reveal the identity of the ones who privatised, shut down, handed over, downsized and occupied it. None of these sentences on the Museum panels have a subject: they all are in the passive voice. Besides the liberal economic policies, the only sentence that indicates the performer of an act is as follows: '*All personnel was employed by Kocaeli Metropolitan Municipality*'. It almost sounds as if one day, all SEKA personnel decided to leave their jobs at the factory and started working in the municipality.

Charlotte Linde refers to these narratives which enable repetition, distribution and reproduction of the institutional memory as 'pretty tales'.[20] In different points of the Museum, the overall narrative depicts a pretty tale about a peaceful transformation, a work-life continuing elsewhere, the idea of a government as the architect of this continuity providing employment and protection. But, for example, what about the strike speaker's coat that is displayed in another part of the Museum? When and why was it worn? Perhaps it was in 2004 and 2005, when the workers struggled against the shutdown and occupied the factory, maybe mostly in the cafeteria, while welcoming their families, friends, visitors of the resistance, and telling this crowd about their struggle.

Everywhere and nowhere[21]

As our worker interviews point out, life in the factory, everyday relationships, experience and skills gained over time, and struggle cannot be explained without remembering and referring to them. Every worker we interviewed tells about which machines he operated, repaired and rested next to. However, the machines exhibited in the current state of the Museum are exhibited not only because they are not working, but also because they no longer carry the voices of those who operate them, those who stand by them for hours. Visitors walk around the huge machines and try to understand what they are used for by reading the information notes attached to them. Still, they cannot learn how these machines are embedded in human relations in the factory or how they are remembered and explained by the workers.

During our visits to the Museum, we sometimes followed the old workers who visit the Museum as visitors, listened to what they tell their relatives about the factory, and we learned which machine has a specific role in the factory and how they operate. We also learned that what remains from a huge factory and many machines is very little compared to the past. All paper machines were sold, a lot of machine parts were scrapped, and only a part of a machine is now exhibited in the Museum.

SEKA consists of five different factory buildings. Only one of these buildings, the First Paper Mill, was established as a museum; the second and third factory buildings stand empty. The fourth building, which includes the cafeteria, infirmary, cinema, cooperative, kindergarten and health centre, has been completely demolished, and now there is a bus stop and a car park in place of this factory building. The fifth building of the factory is hired by a movie company as a film set. The current state of the factory, which is reduced into a single machine in a single building, also prompts the workers to define their former workplace through a narrative of lack – no more machines, a large part of the factory is destroyed and there are no workers. The single machine on display in the main hall of the Museum, which was constantly maintained, controlled and with its oil changed by the former workers who are employed as experts by the Museum, stands there with its majestic presence as if it was a monument of a great absence and destruction. As we learned in the interviews, it was a machine that could not be stopped and worked 24 hours. Whereas now, once the machine stops, it does not work

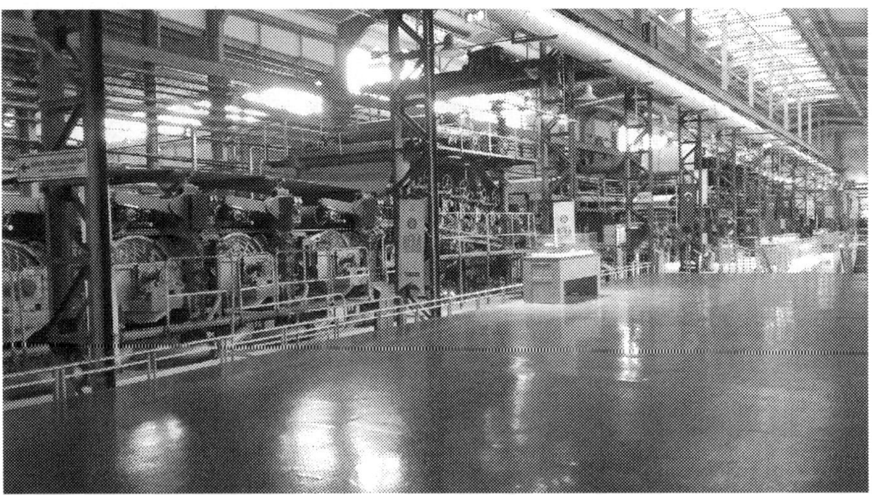

FIGURE 11.2 The paper machine exhibited in the Museum. Photograph: Meral Akbaş.

anymore. The workers we interviewed also often stated that the factory no longer had a voice. For them, when the machines stopped and the people left, the factory became silent. So the factory-museum defined in the leaflet published by Kocaeli Metropolitan Municipality as 'The Memory of Turkey' is like it is not a living or alive memory space; it is a recall in memory, which is constantly lost and destroyed, that survives in the memory of the workers and always reminds them of absence. It is as if a non-existent place was built instead of a destroyed place; in this place, where the workers claim to have their memories preserved, they always face the absence and escape from the present state of the factory.

The building used as a museum is being rebuilt in the silence of a single machine, while another building of the factory, the Fourth Paper Mill, has been completely demolished. This is one of the main centres of the factory occupation that lasted for 50 days in 2005. Workers gathered here, especially in the cafeteria; they held their meetings here. They also welcomed visitors here. If there were to be a march through the entrance door of the factory, the march would start from here, from the door of this building. Now there is some green space, a large toll car park and a bus terminal on that space. As one of the workers stated, the reorganisation of the factory area started with the demolition of this building of the Fourth Paper Mill, that is, with the destruction of the resistance memory of the workers. Tracing the absence of these destroyed places can provide important data in terms of working-class history and working-class memory.

In pursuit of a loud silence: women workers of SEKA as a story of absence

As you wander through the Museum, you come across an empty and spacious hall. After in all our meetings stubbornly and repeatedly asking questions about women workers, we were able to discover that women workers were working in this empty hall, where there were no photographs, explanations, or objects reminding visitors about the history of the machines and the factory, and where there were no items other than tables and chairs. The reason we describe our process of accessing this information as discovery is related to the excited and detailed answers of the former workers, who explained about the whole factory, the machines on display and the different parts of the Museum, with short and very limited information about women workers. It was as if men and women had never worked together in the same place. SEKA, as the family that is frequently mentioned and missed in our interviews, as the house that was destroyed, as the history that was constantly expressed by the workers, meant that for men, it did not signify a partnership, a sharing and solidarity area that includes women; men were again talking about men. In the oral history records made for the Museum's archive, we learned that there was not a single interview with women who had worked at the factory. The founders of the Museum seemed to prefer to ignore the women. While establishing this museum from an empty and abandoned factory area, they did not care about reaching women and recording their words, memories and histories. But we both knew that women were working in the factory. We had already seen some photographs in a very limited part of the Museum. One of these photographs was probably a photograph of a working woman who had no name, and therefore it was not clear why her photograph was found there. In addition, three photographs of women workers standing in front of their machines were also among the photographs exhibited.

Our interviewees spoke very little about women workers. None of our interviewees had any contact information to connect us with a female worker. However, in the workers' club where we held most of our interviews with male workers, our interviewees introduced us to other male workers, sometimes reaching them by phone and calling them to the club. So we started to look for and ask what parts of the Museum were the places where women workers had worked.

When we visited the archive of the Museum, we came across another photograph that was not exhibited in the Museum. In this photograph, probably taken during an official factory visit, women workers greet visitors and hundreds of paper stacks accompany them. Although we do not know whether this photograph was taken in the First Paper Mill, which is currently used as a museum, in such an area, women workers cut, weigh, pack, sort and prepare the paper stacks produced from the machines. This place is named the replenishment hall. Replenishment means completing something missing, improving, integrating, finishing. In a world where large machines work non-stop for 24 hours, women workers measure and calculate all the paper produced in the factory, and which comes out of the machines in large plates. They give the paper its final shape with their hands. In other words, they are the last ones to touch the paper. Our interviewees specifically stated that in the department where women had worked, there was no machine. Therefore, according to them, not including this area in the exhibition area of the Museum was not worth worrying about. What is interesting here at this point is that the male workers, who oppose the mechanisation of the space as one of the oppressive spatial strategies that established the Museum, and who said that the stories of the workers were left deficient in the museum space, stood in the same place with the dominant discourse created in the Museum. Two different positions, seemingly against each other, met in the masculine framework of the notion that an environment without a machine or with lighter, hand-operated machines need not be in the museum space. What was precious were machines, with all their glory and bulkiness; because it was these machines that produced the paper. On the one hand, this machine-based discourse of the workers, who operate, control and repair the machine, subordinates men's own labour to the machine. And at the same time, it makes invisible the presence of women, devaluates their labour and reduces their work to their 'nimble fingers'.

Turning the area, which is empty nowadays, where varying numbers of female workers worked for many years, long hours during the day into a place where visitors mostly can sit and rest, denotes an immense silence spread throughout the Museum. Doreen Massey points out that the contemporary hegemonic spatial realm is 'exclusivist', which tries to acquire a fixed, bounded and unproblematic identity. In the spatio-temporal reality of the factory-museum, this identity is the common male worker. Through the strategy of spatio-temporal emptification, the institutional memory of the museum petrifies the affective encounters with other gendered identities and redirects them onto common male experience. We again encounter a familiar story that feminist studies have told for a long time: women's memories are lost, falsified or completely erased.

On the other hand, while the hall tells the story of an absence with all its emptiness, it also contains information about what happened here in the past. What Linde calls 'noisy silences'[22] includes the friendships of the female workers, their fights, laughter, heartbreaks and the dreams they envision when they are tired. What had been discussed and hidden in this place, which has now been emptied and thus thrown out of history; what did women whisper in each other's ears; what did they stand up to, how did they slow down the work, what did they think, what did they feel, what did they do during the strike at the factory? Asking these questions, which seem a little nostalgic at first, means firstly recognising the presence and affiliation of women working in this factory, and hearing 'noisy silences' other than the sounds of the machines working in the factory.

Conclusion

Our analysis may be categorised under two main headlines: the history and its material traces of this history; and the discourses, subjectivities and narratives on which SEKA as a museum played a hard and strategic game with real consequences.

Three main historical periods and their material traces have been cancelled out, erased and ruined not only during its transformation to a museum but also during the establishment of the factory and also during the working life of SEKA. First of all, SEKA factory had been constructed upon the remains of Nicomedia Antic City in Izmit. The enlightened, industrialised Turkey shut out the Ancient Greek and the Roman Empire heritage of Izmit. Secondly, this history included material destruction of archives, documents, books and magazines. All the illegal leftist, revolutionary books were recycled following coup d'etats. All documents, including the top-secret state documents, counter-insurgency documents and shadow-state operations against leftist and Kurdish groups, were recycled at this factory. Even the pornographic materials that were once illegal to distribute in Turkey were recycled here. All these histories turned into tabula rasas in SEKA. And thirdly, it was a cover of the material traces of the cultural, socio-economic heritage of those industrial male workers, their surroundings, the urban environment that not only the workers but also their families had lived in and experienced, and gained opportunities or suffered all together. There were schools where the children of these workers were educated, there were paper industry schools, there were cinema halls, there were lodgings where all the families were habituated. All these cultural and social traces have been erased by the museumification process.

In terms of discourses and how they are represented, the machines and halls of SEKA display the voice and image of a male worker who mostly identified himself with the paper production machine. All these machines are huge and expensive so that what is represented in the Museum is the male worker who can deal with and handle these machines and his productive body. The museum space is constructed within a machine-based narrative of male factory workers. However, on the other side, where are the traces of resistance? Where are the voices of women? Where are the machines? Where is the Nikomedia Antic City? Where are the social and cultural halls of the workers?

This museum space does not represent the socio-political history of factory or labour history but simply the government's perception and representation of working-class and factory life. The narratives of resistance against the neoliberal politics of government in Turkey had completely been erased, although the Museum itself was a consequence and outcome of this strong resistance. It should be highlighted that the rebellious labour force is completely erased and cancelled out in the Museum, so the worker identity for government is there musealised as a passive, machine-dependent male worker. And so, there is no representation of women's voice in the Museum as a productive force; they might only exist in the realm of unproductive handy works. In this chapter, we tried to relate the space of museum with a highly different lens, with the situated knowledge of genders, classes, races and other under-represented groups but most importantly in a feminist archaeological way that might reveal the material and affective traces of the women labour force that globally is the first one to be sacrificed when it comes to the Museum.

After and throughout all these historical, material and discursive, symbolic destructions and reconstruction periods, these workers and families felt that they no longer have a home, history and identity here in SEKA Museum. This is the history and narrative of SEKA workers who occupy an absent presence in the SEKA Museum. This absent presence opens or maybe closes with and onto a gate, which always points to a threshold point.

> if it was up to me i would keep silent, but the rusty
> lock on my tongue might unlock,
> my secluded words might hum, the worms inside
> me might fidget,
> so i creaked exhaustedly.
>
> *(Birhan Keskin,* Door*)*

Acknowledgement

We would like to thank the Raoul Wallenberg Institute (RWI) of Human Rights and Humanitarian Law for their support of this research.

Notes

1 To elaborate, when the door was removed and this road was built, we talked to the men who were sitting at the cafe next to the road. One of the men angrily told us that he does not like this road at all, because before the arrival of President Recep Tayyip Erdoğan, the door of the old factory was removed and this new road was built. Even the road was washed and cleaned, and then trees were planted on its edges.

2 SEKA stands for Turkish Cellulose and Paper Factories Incorporation. SEKA had premises in different parts of Turkey, including Dalaman, Giresun, Caycuma, Bolu, Silifke, Kastamonu, Balikesir, Afyon, and Izmit. Hereinafter SEKA refers to Izmit Paper Factory.
3 Hurriyet Newspaper, "Erdoğan: Hyde Park instead of SEKA."
4 SEKA Paper Museum, "About Museum."
5 Osman Okyar defines etatism as a word 'derived from the French État (State) and denotes a situation in which the State takes an active and permanent part in economic affairs'; Okyar, "The Concept of Étatism," 98.
6 Keyder, *Türkiye'de Devlet ve Sınıflar* [State and Classes in Turkey], 124; Ahmad, *Modern Türkiye'nin Oluşumu* [Formations of Modern Turkey], 119.
7 Ahmad, *Modern Türkiye'nin Oluşumu*, 120.
8 Ahmad, *Modern Türkiye'nin Oluşumu*, 122.
9 A paper in *Ulku Journal* published by Ankara Community Center during this time includes an interesting sentence: 'In our country, there are no two classes as employees and exploiters. In Turkey... everyone works hard'; Karaömerlioğlu, "Köy Enstitüleri Üzerine Düşünceler," [Thoughts on Village Institutes], 61.
10 Insel, *Düzen ve Kalkınma Kıskacında Türkiye: Kalkınma Sürecinde Devletin Rolü*, 209–10; Keyder, *Ulusal Kalkınmacılığın İflası* [The Bankruptcy of *National Development*], 12.
11 Keyder, *Ulusal Kalkınmacılığın İflası*, 15.
12 D. Ronart as cited by Insel, *Düzen ve Kalkınma Kıskacında Türkiye: Kalkınma Sürecinde Devletin Rolü*, 220.
13 Harrison, *Heritage: Critical Approaches*, 15.
14 Smith, *Uses of Heritage*, 11.
15 Helaine Silverman as cited by Sather-Wagstaff, "Heritage and Memory," 197.
16 Smith, Shackel, and Campbell state that among the nine hundred in this list, only 33 are considered industrial heritage, see: Smith, Shackel and Campbell, "Introduction: Class Still Matters," 2–3.
17 Dicks, "Heritage and Social Class," 372.
18 Dicks, "Heritage and Social Class," 374.
19 Smith, Shackel, and Campbell, "Introduction: Class Still Matters," 13.
20 Linde, *Working the Past: Narrative and Institutional Memory*, 11.
21 In social heritage discussions, Bella Dicks emphasises that the working class is an 'absent presence' and uses this term to define absent/present class relationships: '"*Everywhere and Nowhere*" class relationships...', in Dicks, "Heritage and Social Class," 367.
22 Linde, *Working the Past: Narrative and Institutional Memory*, 220.

Bibliography

Ahmad, Feroz. *Modern Türkiye'nin Oluşumu* [Formations of Modern Turkey]. Istanbul: Kaynak, 2007.

Dicks, Bella. "Heritage and Social Class." In *The Palgrave Handbook of Contemporary Heritage Research*, edited by Emma Waterton and Steve Watson, 366–381. New York: Palgrave Macmillan, 2015.

Harrison, Rodney. *Heritage: Critical Approaches*. New York: Routledge, 2010.

Hurriyet Newspaper. "Erdoğan: Hyde Park instead of SEKA." Accessed 20 April 2017. www.hurriyet.com.tr/erdogan-sekanin-yerini-hyde-park-yapin-halk-elektrik-atsin-293637.

Insel, Ahmet. *Düzen ve Kalkınma Kıskacında Türkiye: Kalkınma Sürecinde Devletin Rolü* [Turkey under the Pressure of Order and. Development: The Role of the State in the Process of Development]. Istanbul: Ayrıntı, 1996.

Karaömerlioğlu, M. Asım. "Köy Enstitüleri Üzerine Düşünceler." [Thoughts on Village Institutes] *Toplum ve Bilim* 76, no. 2 (Spring 1998): 56–85.

Keskin, Birhan. "Kapı" [Door]. In *Kim Bağışlayacak Beni* [Who will Forgive Me]. Istanbul: Metis, 2011.

Keyder, Çağlar. *Ulusal Kalkınmacılığın İflası* [The Bankruptcy of National Development]. Istanbul: Metis, 2004.

Keyder, Çağlar. *Türkiye'de Devlet ve Sınıflar* [State and Classes in Turkey]. Istanbul: Iletisim, 2007.

Okyar, Osman. "The Concept of Étatism." *The Economic Journal* 75, no. 297 (March 1965): 98–111.

Linde, Charlotte. *Working the Past: Narrative and Institutional Memory*. Oxford: Oxford University Press, 2009.

Sather-Wagstaff, Joy. "Heritage and Memory." In *The Palgrave Handbook of Contemporary Heritage Research*, edited by Emma Waterton and Steve Watson, 191–204. New York: Palgrave Macmillan, 2015.

SEKA Paper Museum. "About Museum." Accessed 20 April 2017. http://sekakagitmuzesi.com/#hakkinda.

Smith, Laurajane. *Uses of Heritage*. New York: Routledge, 2006.

Smith, Laurajane, Paul A.Shackel, and Gary Campbell. "Introduction: Class Still Matters." In *Heritage, Labour and the Working Classes*, edited by Laurajane Smith, Paul A.Shackel, and Gary Campbell, 1–16. New York: Routledge, 2011.

PART IV

Answering back: Lessons from the working and poverty classes

In one of his stand-up sets, US comedian Chris Rock presents a segment about the difference between a job and a career. He says to those with careers that they 'need to shut the fuck up when you are around people with jobs' so as not to provoke resentment. 'Don't let your happiness make somebody sad'. His spoken self-portrait of his former role as a worker, where his days were spent fulfilling a repetitive, menial task, demonstrates that in a 'job', autonomy and time are forfeited in the interests of an income. Unlike those with jobs, those with careers can schedule their own work day. One of the differences between a job and a career is shown in who gets to speak and who is required to solely listen and follow instructions.

Part IV exemplifies both the potential and actual effects on museums and the lives of its communities when those with 'jobs' are listened to by those with museum 'careers'. What change can be generated when museums become the students of those from the working and poverty classes? And how can museums become good students?

The lessons learned throughout the following chapters may have been taught by some who now inhabit professional roles but they were raised in families headed by those in humble jobs, with minimal education, or with no experience of employment at all. For those with expertise in traditional skills as well as for members of Indigenous communities who work on country, their labour may not be recognised or valued by the tenets of late capitalism. Here, the museum has a complementary role to play in learning from the range of experiences. Those from the working and poverty classes are diverse and the museum should not drive an elitist preferential wedge between an already disparate precariat.

The chapters that comprise Part IV demonstrate ways in which those from the working and poverty classes have changed museums through their leadership in recreating memories, reviving traditional skills, story-telling (including personal accounts of disenfranchisement that demand to be heeded), generating research and

DOI: 10.4324/9781003029519-16

data collections, organising protests, staging interventions and emphasising that communities of practice provide a much-needed alternative to the neoliberal cult of competitive individualism.

Public museums were opened by those in power in order to teach working-class people how to behave. This volume closes with case studies of the working and poverty classes teaching museums how to better perform their civic duty.

12

LOOKING BACKWARDS, PLANNING FORWARD

Museum as Muck: Advocating for the working class in museums

Michelle McGrath in conversation with Adele Chynoweth

Museum as Muck is an advocacy organisation, established in 2018, for museum employees from working-class backgrounds – 'muckers'. Muckers not only support each other; they also lobby, through events and creative interventions, for systemic change in the museum sector. What follows is the written version of a conversation which took place in January 2020 between *Museum as Muck* founder, Michelle McGrath, and Adele Chynoweth.

Chynoweth: Michelle, it's wonderful to have the opportunity to talk with you. Can we begin with your role in *Museum as Muck?*
McGrath: I founded *Museum as Muck*, a network of working-class museum professionals that was established via social media. We started out meeting through social events and now we aim to apply our lived experiences to change the museum sector.
Chynoweth: What inspired the name of the network?
McGrath: *Museum as Muck* is taken from the historically derogatory phrase *'common as muck'* used to refer to someone deemed of lower social status. Us Muckers are common and proud. The name fits in with our approach of being subversive and not taking ourselves too seriously.
Chynoweth: Is it OK to talk about your background?
McGrath: Yes, absolutely. I was born in Ireland, in 1983, to 18-year-old parents. Both of them had grown up in poverty. It was my mother's idea for us all to move to London. She saw it as an opportunity. She'd seen her older sisters make the move with their children and, as a result, they had a good support system through social housing. Both my parents had left school when they were 13. They didn't have educational qualifications and, as young parents, they weren't working. They came to London, in 1985, when I was two years old.

DOI: 10.4324/9781003029519-17

Chynoweth: Your personal experience is recent. It challenges a constructed, sentimentalised nostalgia about the working class.

McGrath: Yes, exactly. This was 1985. This isn't about a romanticised image of men up north in the 1960s with their flat caps doing heavy labour in the mining industry. If we cling to images such as these, we miss out on so many working-class stories. And actually I don't come from a working-class background. I didn't grow up in a house where anybody was 'working', not after my father left the household when I was seven; he had brought money in as a bricklayer until then. My mother was part of the welfare system in the UK. You'd have your social housing. You'd have your rent paid and you'd have a weekly payment to survive. I remember my mum raising herself, me and my sister. Her money on the Thursday was £79 a week. Then she'd get £18 child support on a Monday and that was it. That was for everything – food, clothing, toiletries.

My mother inherited the use of the system from her parents who also survived from social support. I think her father did bits and bobs of labour when she was growing up but he was also an alcoholic, so there were mental health issues that probably influenced how the money would come in. Aspirations for young people were few. All she and her sisters knew about was having children because that's what women did in Catholic Ireland.

Chynoweth: How did that two-year-old in London go on to a path through education?

McGrath: Every working-class person has their own story. What helped me climb the ladder was the state schooling system. My sisters and I had to go to school. We couldn't just leave at 13 like my parents did. I was always good at school. I enjoyed learning myself but didn't visit any museums and galleries until I was an adult. I was just pushed through the education system. Because I did quite well, I ended up thinking about university, even though that was a real challenge financially. The only jobs that I was aware of were public service jobs like police, doctors, teachers. I enjoyed working with children and young people. So that's the vocation I chose.

Chynoweth: It's the classic social mobility degree – teaching or nursing – for working-class women.

McGrath: You're absolutely right. So I think I ended up becoming a teacher because I didn't have any other kind of role models or experiences.

I was the first person in my family to go to university and it was very much self-actualised. My mum wasn't sitting around helping me fill out application forms, I just did it myself. Mum, because of her own lived experience, couldn't guide us through education and the world of work, but she was very supportive of just anything that my sister and I did. So it was almost like we could have done the smallest thing, and to her it was incredible because she had so little opportunity and education. To her, just doing GCSEs and going to school was amazing.[1]

Chynoweth: How did you make the transition from teaching to museums?

McGrath: I qualified as a teacher in my early twenties and I knew that I wanted to work in education but the school environment felt too formal. Teaching's a bloody hard job. I thought, 'God! I don't know if I'm ready for this as a career.'

I wanted to explore the cultural side of things. I became really interested in creative ways of learning because I saw creativity as such a powerful learning tool for children and young people. Some of my peers were in the arts and interested in creativity too. Those external influences from friends also led me to understand that creativity and the arts are interesting, and from there I started to explore museums and galleries. Then I had this realisation that I could teach in museums! It was an absolute light bulb moment – knowing that I could combine my passion for education with my interest in the arts.

So I volunteered, which is a huge thing for working-class people, because obviously you're working for no pay, but I did it. I was either just working part-time, doing a bit of supply teaching, and then volunteering on the side, or at one point I was unemployed and had to receive benefits for a couple of months, but I was familiar with that way of life and so I still volunteered in museums. My first museum role was working front of house at the V&A Museum in South Kensington. I just worked my way up from the ground. But, interestingly, during my front of house role, I contacted the learning department numerous times, asking if I could volunteer, work for free, and they never gave me any support or opportunities in museum learning, even though I was a qualified teacher. I just wanted to volunteer and get some experience. I was already an employee but they didn't support that at all. So it was really hard. I ended up going to The Ragged School Museum in London's East End in order to get that learning experience. I volunteered there for around a year. Then what happened was, somebody left in the team there and they just offered me a position in the team, which I'm not sure is good recruitment practice now that I think about it, but really that was my break into a paid museum learning role.

I ended up staying there for three years because it was really hard then to get the next job. The sector is so competitive and I'd only had that initial experience. So it's been a long, long road!

I went on to taking museum learning posts at various museums including Royal Museums Greenwich and the British Museum. I am now Head of Education and Learning at Bow Arts, a registered arts and education charity that delivers arts and creative services across London.

Chynoweth: In some of *Museum as Muck's* promotional material, you describe yourself as 'benefits class'. What's the source of that term?

McGrath: I use that term to refer to receiving benefits in order to live. I don't use 'underclass' because it feels derogatory. But I acknowledge that some people do like to use it as a means of owning the word and taking back control. So it's really a question for the individual. Some use the term 'council class'. It means the same to me as benefits class. It means you're relying on the State. You're not working.

Chynoweth: In Australia, I know of sociologists who use 'poverty class'.[2]

McGrath: That's an interesting term. It feels quite like a strong reality statement. My mother grew up in poverty. It was actual poverty. It wasn't that times were a bit hard.

We need to crack open and blow up what working class is. It's important to make people aware that all of the people that identify as working class have different experiences. There is a wide spectrum to the 'working class' but there just so happens to also be shared experiences and crossover in living with low social, cultural and economic capital.

Chynoweth: I am challenged by some colleagues from middle-class backgrounds who demand that I define 'working class'. There seems to be a sense, for them, that the working class doesn't exist anymore, therefore it's not an issue and now, you're emphasising the pluralism of the current working class so that it can't be discounted by some constructed, historical singularity.

McGrath: Yes, you're right. Class can be ignored because it can be hidden. It's not like some of the other protected characteristics where it's something that you could just see by meeting somebody.[3] So, people can choose to ignore it. People who are working class are often riddled with shame, so they don't want to make it known to other people.

This embarrassment is worsened when people who aren't working class can say, 'It doesn't exist'.

Working-class people may not feel comfortable with challenging that because it may be hard to put themselves out there.

Part of *Museum as Muck's* mission is to give a platform for the working class – to get people talking about class and saying that it's real, it's alive, it's here. This is what it is. This is how it affects us. This is how it affects our careers. This is what it might look like to support working classes in museums.

Chynoweth: How do you get grassroots support for that? Where did you start?

McGrath: I'd started thinking about it maybe a couple of years before I actually did anything about it. I started *Museum as Muck* at a stage in my life when I was doing a bit of personal reflection, about where I was in life and how things were for me. I had experienced some changes in my life. I started putting the pieces together even though I'd always known that amongst my work colleagues, there weren't many who had a similar background to me: my class background is the most influential factor in my life. Not just in work, but in every facet of my being.

And then I got a bit fed up and angry, but in an energised positive way, and I thought, 'Sod it! I'm just going to throw this out there and see what happens!'

Chynoweth: How and what did you throw out there?

McGrath: I wanted to find other people in museums who were more like me.

In June 2018, I created a private Facebook page, where I said, 'Hey, this is a group for working-class museum people. I just want to make connections with you. See who's out there. It can be a closed space where we just chat and share experiences. We can have social meet-ups'.

So, it was going to start as more of a supportive social vehicle, which is still part of what we're doing now but I didn't anticipate, at first, how the group would evolve.

People responded, 'Oh my gosh! This is brilliant!'

There was so much enthusiasm. Other people in the network who I had connected with were so full of energy, so then we realised that we had to *do* something with all of this. We established a public platform on Twitter in order to raise awareness of the network and the need to pay attention to class-based issues in museums. That helped us to connect with people across the country. It's been really nice to bring that diversity of lived experience to the group. I don't know how I would have found other working-class people in museums without social media. There are now over 500 members in the Facebook group and an extra 50 members on our email list.

Chynoweth: Do you know about the representation of the working class amongst museum employees in the UK? How many?

McGrath: One of our concerns is that there is very little research and statistics – because most people don't care about class. So we attempted our own action

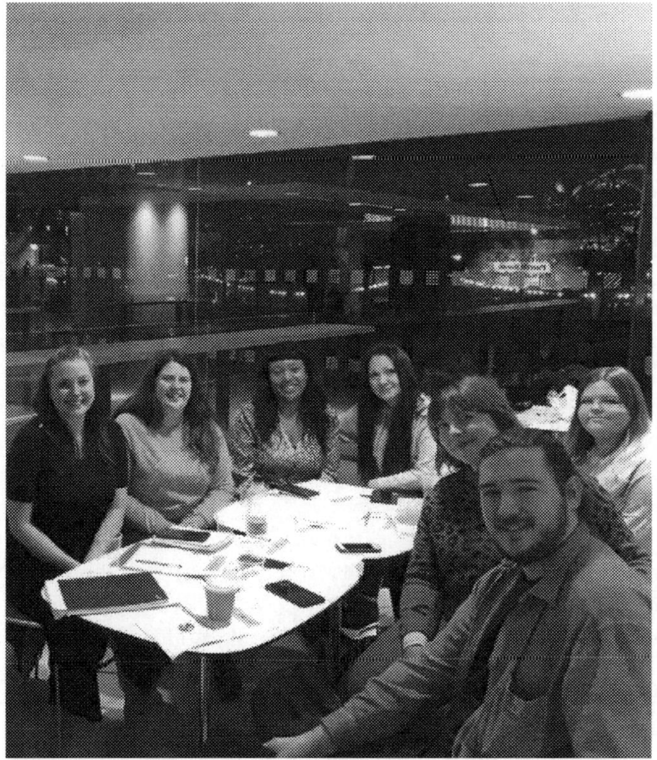

FIGURE 12.1 *Museum as Muck* Steering Group Meeting, January 2020. Photograph: Tracey Weller.

research at the 2018 Museums Association conference in Belfast. We set up a stall at the conference venue, signed 'Supermuckers', because we champion each other but the emblem also drew attention to our display of objects to reference museums that was also a supermarket experience. There were three parts to it. The first element was the objects acted both as museum objects but also products in a supermarket. The labels evoked museum text panels as well as price tags on a supermarket shelf. Each tag had a figure – a statistic – as well as an explanation about how many people receive free school meals, or how much people in certain positions get paid, for example. This was really powerful part because the labels included quotations from *Museum as Muck* members – their lived experience of certain workplace barriers.

Chynoweth: That sounds compelling.

McGrath: There were observations such as 'imposter syndrome' with the associated member's quote:[4]

> 'It's weird having a professional job but still considering yourself working class. You end up not feeling like you belong in any situation!'

Another hurdle is the stigma of having had free school meals:

> 'At Primary School once, I asked my Mum why I never had to bring money in little envelopes to school like the rest of the class. She told me she already paid the secretary. She was lying. She was embarrassed.'

In addition, is the experience of being an 'in-betweener'.

Chynoweth: What's that?

McGrath: Being an 'in-betweener' happens when you've professionally moved out of your class but you're still not a middle-class person. You don't suddenly, one day, become middle class. You've still got all of your background and differing social and cultural experiences. Just because you get paid some money now and probably not very much money, it doesn't mean that you're occupy a middle-class world. You feel like an in-betweener:

> 'I'm from East London and during my childhood experienced homelessness and the absolute s£!* show that is social housing in London. My parents are traditional working class, separated and still experiencing financial, welfare and housing issues. I struggle with balancing my background with the fact that I now seem to live a middle-class life – uni education, cultural activities, fairly good salary and a good local government job etc – definitely suffer from imposter syndrome which pushes me to try and achieve more'.

Chynoweth: How did you establish the class background of participants?

McGrath: We surveyed conference participants by asking, 'What job did the main earner in your household have when you were aged 14?'

It's the most effective measure of class background which we gleaned from Dave O'Brien's research.[5] I contacted him to ask about the best way to measure someone's class background. He advised, 'Don't ever ask people just to self-identify because people get it wrong.'

Instead, you ask them about their parents' occupation when they were 14 and then you look at the spectrum. We used the nine occupational categories as outlined in the PANIC report for participants to map themselves against:

1. Senior managers
2. Traditional professional occupations
3. Modern professional occupations
4. Middle or junior managers
5. Clerical or intermediate occupations
6. Technical and craft occupations
7. Semi-routine occupations
8. Routine occupations
9. Never worked and long-term unemployed

We also felt that it was essential to map which department and positions participants were occupying in museums in order to determine whether or not there was support for our hypothesis: that working-class people are less likely to be in directorial positions or roles in departments deemed as 'higher status' such as curatorial.

So we broke down museum jobs into sub-categories:

- Archives, curatorial, library, exhibitions and conservation
- Learning and education
- Finance, HR, IT and estates
- Directorate
- Consultants/freelancers
- Supportive/funding/universities

Therefore, respondents chose a colour sticky note that represented the department they worked in and placed it on the board that featured the spectrum of job roles so we could see not only their socio-economic background but also that position they occupy in the museum.

The conversations were great. Some denial, some confusion from delegates who thought they were working class. I found giving real examples and circumstances of less privilege helped them understand better. I had one quite difficult conversation where a museum director said she wasn't willing to talk to her staff about class as she believes they don't want to talk about it.

Chynoweth: Ye olde trick: those in positions of power feigning compassion in order to avoid controversy and debate. What were your research results?

McGrath: We found that of the 155 museum professionals we met across two days: 43 per cent were from the top three parental occupation backgrounds, the same amount were from the next three mid-tier occupations while only 14 per cent were from the 'lowest' three occupational backgrounds.

Those in directorate positions were most commonly from traditional professional backgrounds – category 2 (29 per cent), and none of the directorate respondents came from routine and service backgrounds – category 8. The archives, etc. category is dominated by category 6 and 3 and learning and engagement professionals are most commonly from category 3. The least represented in museum employment were those whose parents were unemployed or on benefits. That was four per cent and that was pretty much us – the Supermuckers – we entered ourselves in the survey responses. And our survey results showed that, at directorate level in museums, these employees came from middle to upper class backgrounds. The least represented in our survey were those museum employees whose background was retail and service.

Chynoweth: That's so interesting. Michelle.

McGrath: Yes, but *Museum as Muck* members are concerned that our survey respondents were conference participants who selected themselves, those who were already interested in engaging in this conversation. We also want to have these conversations with museum people who don't want to talk about class. Also, Museums Association conference participants are not likely to employed in entry-level museum positions or working in front of house positions because the museum employees who go to conferences are more likely those in other departments such as curatorial learning, or higher leadership positions. So we knew that our research is skewed but given that there are few statistics in this area, we've got to collect it ourselves.

Chynoweth: This is such important work, Michelle.

McGrath: I want to tell you about the final installation in the Supermuckers' stall – our till. It was just the same as a supermarket, except that we had a toy till with receipts, which served as a call to action for people who had participated in the Supermuckers' intervention. Each receipt had list of options for action to hep progress the conversation about class. It was our way of asking people to make a pledge. It could be anything from just telling a colleague about *Museum as Muck* to asking them to include a measure for class when monitoring staff diversity, or to aim to have working-class representation on their museum's board. There was also space for participants to enter their own pledge. So they walked away with a concrete takeaway action.

Chynoweth: There's such clever wit in that.

McGrath: Well, making things engaging, accessible and relevant is the work of museum educators. That's what I do in my job.

And while *Museum as Muck* uses humour and non-confrontational conversations, we are also deadly serious about what we stand for because talking about class is the most important conversation for museums to be having. That's not to the detriment of other represented groups because we're complete allies of other museum colleagues in sectors across the protected characteristics. But when you address class, you are also addressing all those protected characteristics because through class, you're going to hit race and you're going to hit gender and you're going to hit disabilities because class cuts across all of them. If you address class, then you can actually support people across all of those protected characteristics. Class is often the common denominator. It's like getting more bang for your buck. Put some effort into class and see lots of change.

So, getting back to the follow-up research, what is interesting is that, now, the Arts Council England are introducing this exact same question that we asked, 'What job did your parents have when you were aged 14?' in the annual survey about the workforce of the organisations that they fund (the National Portfolio Organisations – NPOs).[6] The Arts Council usually ask their NPOs to report back on their workforce in terms of the protected characteristics but now, they are also asking about class. But what *Museum as Muck* included in its survey at the Museums Association conference, in addition to participants' class background, was a question about where they worked in the museum. Because, anecdotally, our understanding of working-class employees in museums is that they mainly work in front of house, or cleaning, or in finance, for example. Because while it's great that the Arts Council are moving towards implementing this measure, it's not going to mean that much because what we found from our small survey is that 21 per cent of museum workers are working class, compared to a third of the general working population. That's obviously a disparity, but what's actually better to know is that this 21 per cent aren't hitting those leadership roles. They're not in roles of power. Museums can't address the issue of class until they know more about how this plays out in each particular organisation and this should not only be about the number of employees from a working-class background but what jobs they occupy. I want to speak with Arts Council England about this. I have already participated in a in a webinar panel discussion which was recorded by the Arts Council.[7]

Chynoweth: You say that you want to use your findings to talk with museums about class. How does *Museum as Muck* get a foot in the door?

McGrath: It's early days for this part of our work but in September 2019, we did host a breakfast at the British Museum and invited museum directors from all across the UK. To the nine directors who participated we presented statistics and ideas about how they might address class in their workplace. We are currently consolidating this into a more formalised approach where we offer to consult or lead activities and workshops with museum staff, concerning class issues, which we can tailor to specific museums and their workforce.

To assist with the development of this work, we applied for one of three Activist Museum Awards granted by the Research Centre for Museums and Galleries (RCMG), the School of Museum Studies at the University of Leicester, UK. The Award was part of the celebrations of the twentieth anniversary of RCMG with the aim of reflecting the ideas discussed throughout the book *Museum Activism* (2019), co-edited by Robert R. Janes and Richard Sandell. Along with Climate Museum UK and the International Slavery Museum, we were granted £1000 award funding. We will use this money to approach and bring together other working-class activists from across the Arts and Cultural sector to consult on the methodology and content for a future *Museum as Muck* programme. As part of the application, you were asked to provide a CV, so we included a tongue-in-cheek version:

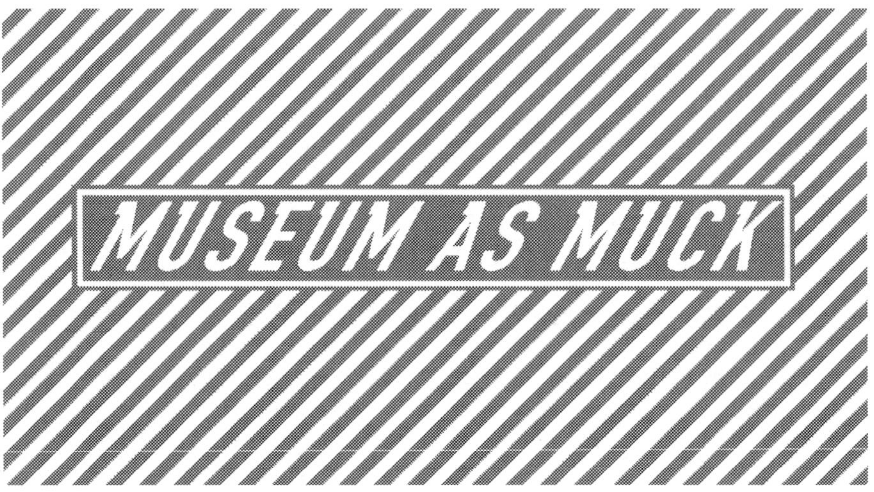

FIGURE 12.2 *Museum as Muck* logo, designed by Chris King.

CURRICULUM VITAE

Email: museumasmuck@gmail.com
D.O.B: June 2018
Address: UK wide

We are a network of working-class museum professionals looking to utilise our lived experience to affect change in the museum sector.

Key strengths

- Collective and activist approach to representing the voices of working-class workers in the museum sector
- Identifying systems of middle-class privilege in the sector and agitating for their removal
- Challenging stereotypes and promoting an intersectional approach to working-class identity
- As a working-class collective we aim to rise with our class, not above it

Activity

- September–November 2019: British Museum
    - Working Class Tea Party: Opportunity to meet the Muckers and hear direct from them regarding class in museums
    - AGM: First AGM for the network attended by 30 Muckers, consulted on plans for upcoming year
    - Directors' Breakfast: Senior Leaders had opportunity to interact directly with Muckers to reflect on their recruitment practice and organisational culture
- July 2019: Social History Curators' Group Conference, Edinburgh
    - Hosted workshop on poverty and working-class narratives
- May–July 2019: Museum Studies Department, University of Leicester
    - Consultation for Museums and Contemporary Issues MA module
    - Using lived experience and sector knowledge to inform content for new museum professionals
- Spring–Autumn 2019: Industry conferences
    - Individual steering group attendance at multiple industry events
- Spring 2019: Museums Association Conference
    - Application to participate in 2019 conference rejected
- November 2018: Museums Association Conference, Belfast
    - Supermuckers intervention at the Festival of Change
    - Conducted live action research into class make-up of sector
    - Spent emotional labour explaining privilege to museum delegates

Employment

- All areas of the museums and galleries sector
- Found in lower-paid roles
- Less likely to engage in self-promotion than middle-class colleagues
- Less likely to be promoted to management and leadership roles than middle-class colleagues

Education and qualifications

- First in family to attend university
- Less likely to have attended a Russell Group University than middle-class colleagues
- State school attendee and free school meals recipient
- Experienced in-year school transfer and disrupted schooling

Volunteering and internships
• Struggled to access the best volunteering and interning opportunities due to lack of family financial support • Inability to draw on family contacts in the cultural sector due to parents' occupation within C2DE social class
Membership of professional bodies
• Generally avoided due to anger management issues generated when assaulted by lip-service, whataboutism, gaslighting and the ennui of being trapped in an echo chamber of platitudes.
Skills
• Code switching and accent softening
References
• *The Panic Report*, 2018. • Kerry Hudson, author of *Lowborn*: *'Museum as Muck is Boss'*

This Curriculum Vitae was included as part of *Museum as Muck's* winning application for the 2019 Activist Museum Award.

Chynoweth: Oh that's great. Incisive, smart satire. Michelle, if you could sum up your work, what is the main message that *Museum as Muck* want the museum sector to hear?

McGrath: I think that *Museum as Muck* has encouraged the sector to talk more about class. There is a perception that working-class people don't have a culture. They do, but it's just not seen by the elite as high culture or the same as the culture that they're peddling. We've shouted so much now that people can't ignore the topic. If they are seen to be ignoring it, it would mark them out as terrible, terrible people. But we're not being aggressive about it because we don't want people to shut off from the conversation.

We don't want people to think, 'We don't want to talk about class because it's really difficult and people get angry and we're doing all the wrong things and we're scared and we don't know what to do.'

Everyone in the museum sector needs to be aware of their position, their privilege, their class, and how it can use that to help working-class people share that opportunity and that privilege that you have. For me, *Museum as Muck* is about giving back and sharing the privilege that I now have because it's not just about individual accomplishment in a vacuum. It's about remembering where I've come from and contributing to other working-class people. It's about looking backwards and using that view as an impetus for change.

Chynoweth: Thank you Michelle. The Muckers have embarked on a formidable movement.

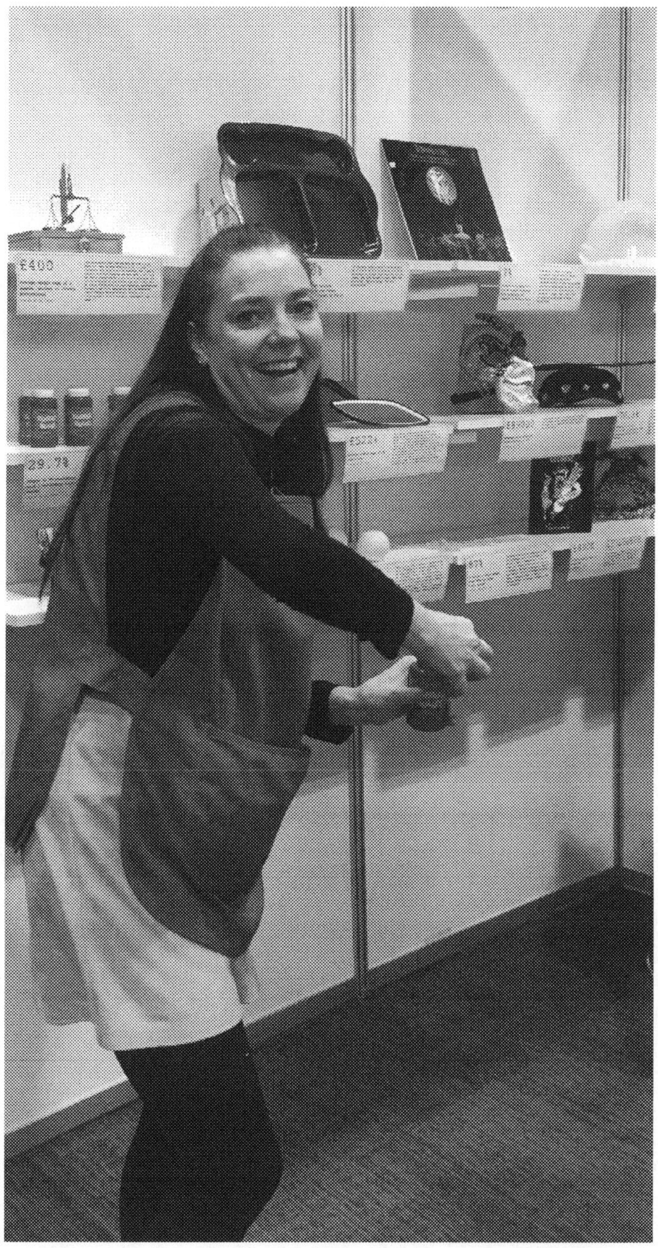

FIGURE 12.3 Michelle McGrath, founder of advocacy organisation *Museum as Muck*, at the 'Supermuckers' intervention stall, Museums Association (UK) conference, Belfast, 2018. Photograph: Kathleen Lawler.

McGrath: It's not just about the individual. It's about organising and sharing.

Chynoweth: So important. I look forward to learning more from you all. Thank you.

Notes

1 'GCSEs' refers to subjects taken as part of the General Certificate of Secondary Education, which is a secondary school qualification offered throughout the UK (except Scotland) to students aged 14–16 years.
2 Michell, Wilson and Archer, "Introduction," ix.
3 'Protected characteristics' were adopted as part of the UK Equality Act 2010 and are:

- age
- disability
- gender reassignment
- marriage or civil partnership
- pregnancy and maternity
- race
- religion or belief
- sex (man or woman)
- sexual orientation (Hepple, "The New Single Equality Act in Britain," 16).

4 Pauline Rose Clance and Suzanne Ament Imes coined the term 'imposter phenomenon' to refer to the personal experience of intellectual deception among high-achieving women, despite superior professional and academic achievements ("The Impostor Phenomenon in High Achieving Women: Dynamics and Therapeutic Intervention"). As a result of *Museum as Muck's* research, this experience may also be applied to class as well as gender. Michelle McGrath added, 'I believe all Muckers regardless of gender have felt some kind of imposter syndrome and some never get rid of it even when they have reached high positions.'
5 One of O'Brien's research projects (funded by the Arts and Humanities Research Council, UK) aimed to create 'public impact' through the project *Panic!* led by Create London (an organisation that commissions art projects that connect with people in cities). Dave O'Brien and his colleagues aimed to examine 'the scale of inequality' in the arts. In order to measure class, the research team applied the UK National Statistics Socio-economic Classification (NS-SEC), which divides occupations into eight categories. This mode of classification informed its survey of people employed in creative occupations. In order to determine respondents' class background, they were asked to indicate from the NC-SEC occupational categories which job their parents did when the respondents were aged 14 (Brook, O'Brien and Taylor, *Panic! Who's Missing From the Picture?*).
   In addition, the Office for National Statistics' (UK) *Labour Force Survey* (2020) addressed the issue of class by asking respondents to recall, when they were 14 years old:

- the city, town or village they were living in
- their family status (living with one or both parents, other family members, or in foster care, or a children's home)
- the main wage earner in the home and their main job (132–34).

6 Arts Council England, *Diversity*. Sociologist Susan Oman, in her role as Arts and Humanities Research Council (UK) Creative Economy Fellow, worked with Arts Council England to consider how to measure social mobility in relation to the cultural sector. Oman found that in order to address inequality in the culture and creative industries (CCIs), attention needs to be paid to class and social mobility. However, one of the challenges with the associated data collection is asking people confronting questions about their social origins. The quality of the data, Oman found, is dependent on people feeling comfortable about their data being collected. Oman made a series of associated recommendations, including the need for CCIs to 'work towards encouraging a positive diversity data culture within organisations through discussions, workshops and training on

the value of diversity data' ("Measuring Social Mobility in the Creative and Cultural Industries," 4; "Improving Data Practices to Monitor Inequality and Introduce Social Mobility Measures," 29–40).

7 Arts Council England, *#CreativeCase Live*.

Bibliography

Arts Council England. "#CreativeCase Live: Digging into Socio-economic Inclusivity." Accessed 23 January 2020. www.youtube.com/watch?v=c1RncRZbh5E.

Arts Council England. "Diversity." Accessed 23 January 2020. www.artscouncil.org.uk/our-impact/diversity.

Brook, Orian, Dave O'Brien, and Mark Taylor. *Panic! Who's Missing From the Picture?*, 2018. Accessed 23 January 2020. https://createlondon.org/wp-content/uploads/2018/04/Panic-Social-Class-Taste-and-Inequalities-in-the-Creative-Industries1.pdf.

Clance, Pauline Rose, and Suzanne Ament Imes. "The Imposter Phenomenon in High Achieving Women: Dynamics and Therapeutic Intervention." *Psychotherapy: Theory, Research and Practice* 15, no. 3 (1978): 241–247.

Hepple, Bob. "The New Single Equality Act in Britain." *The Equal Rights Review* 5 (2010): 11–24.

Janes, Robert R., and Richard Sandell. *Museum Activism*. London and New York: Routledge, 2019.

Michell, Dee, Jacqueline Z. Wilson, and Verity Archer. "Introduction: A Working-Class World-View in an Academic Environment." In *Bread and Roses: Voices of Australian Academics from the Working Class*, edited by Dee Michell, Jacqueline Z. Wilson, and Verity Archer, vii–xvi. Rotterdam: Sense Publishers, 2015.

Office for National Statistics. *Labour Force Survey: User Guide, Volume 2*, 2020. Accessed 9 August 2020. www.ons.gov.uk/employmentandlabourmarket/peopleinwork/employmentandemployeetypes/methodologies/labourforcesurveyuserguidance#labour-force-survey-lfs-user-guides.

Oman, Susan. *Improving Data Practices to Monitor Inequality and Introduce Social Mobility Measures: A Working Paper for the Cultural Sector*, 2019. Accessed 9 August 2020. www.sheffield.ac.uk/social-sciences/research/solutions.

Oman, Susan. *Measuring Social Mobility in the Creative and Cultural Industries: The Importance of Working in Partnership to Improve Data Practices and Address Inequality*, 2019. Accessed 9 August 2020. www.sheffield.ac.uk/social-sciences/research/solutions.

13

CHANGING LIVES AT THE SCOTTISH MARITIME MUSEUM

Martin Hughes

Real museum inclusion and diversity helps garner input from the working classes. And that commitment should come from the top. The most important thing for me is retaining vital skills and trades through community participation. In order to achieve this, museum board members and senior managers should get involved beyond accounting spreadsheets and actively engage with those 'on the ground', who run the place every day and work with the public. I have only ever met the board of our museum after annual general meetings. The majority of the board don't visit our boatbuilding workshop. That's a shame.

I grew up in a working-class family in Largs, on the Clyde Coast. I started working on boats when I left school at 16. It was one of these work experience programmes – six months over on the Isle of Cumbrae, which is just across the water from where I lived, and my boss there was Ian Boag who was from generations of boatbuilders. His father was the foreman of the William Fife boat yard in Fairlie.

I worked as bosun's assistant and the day I started the work experience programme, the boss Ian said, 'I don't agree with you being here!'

I thought, 'Oh great!'

But it turned out that he didn't like work experience schemes because after six months, the kids just left.

Ian said, 'But if you want to learn, I will teach you all I that can in the time that you're here.'

He took me under his wing.

My first job was painting the outside of the building – log cabins – and I thought, 'Oh, here we go. I'm just going to get used for slave labour here.'

Then he took me down to the workshop and one of the first things he taught me was steam bending wooden sail battens. He showed me how to do that. He was a brilliant man, a very skilled craftsman, and he instilled a passion in it for me. I managed to get an extension to work with him for another six months.

DOI: 10.4324/9781003029519-18

I then applied to do a course in Falmouth Marine School down in Cornwall. There were no boatbuilding courses in Scotland. This has been a bugbear of mine since I was 16. So at 17 years old I left Largs where I had grown up and left to study at Falmouth. It seemed that I was moving to the other side of the planet. In fact, when I first arrived in Cornwall I think some of the locals thought that was where I was from! I completed my City and Guilds in boatbuilding and national diploma in yacht design.

Two years and a mass of happy memories and I was now Qualified.

I have been fortunate to do a fair amount of travelling in my career, including living and working in Turkey for nine years, initially working for a yacht charter company before doing private work maintaining and repairing private yachts and skippering for charter. I eventually ended up skippering a small motor yacht for Turgut Ozal, the President of Turkey! I was lucky enough to buy my own yacht, which had been an ambition of mine since I was young and had set my target of achieving this by the time I reached 35. To own my own boat that I could live on and hopefully earn a living from was a dream and the full ownership papers arrived the day before my 28th birthday! I returned to Scotland in my 30s as I had a family and wanted to raise them at home.

In 1996, I began teaching boatbuilding at James Watt College. I built up the national certificate course and managed it for ten years. The students ranged from 16 year olds through to the oldest at 76 years. They were a diverse and interesting bunch of people to work with but eventually after a college 'review', the course was dropped by the management even although the course had a two-year waiting list. Accountants had decided that boatbuilding was not viable as the resources were high and the numbers were not. Apparently, there was a world shortage of beauticians and nail bar operatives so they concentrated on that. I was moved to deliver woodwork classes and construction drawing, which was fine but I was a boatbuilder, not a joiner. It was shortly after this that I moved to GalGael.

I've been boatbuilding for over 40 years now, including working up at the GalGael Trust in Glasgow.[1] It's a working community that puts the needs of people first. It started out as a protest. There was a plan to build a motorway through a public park in Glasgow. Folk were climbing the trees, trying to block it. The motorway ended up going through but the people demanded, 'Whatever trees you're taking down – they belong to us.'

They used the wood to build a boat.

GalGael contacted me and asked me if I would re-start the boatbuilding following the sudden passing of their founder Colin Macleod at only 39 years old. They had become a bit rudderless and my role was to try and help get things back on track. GalGael means 'foreign' or 'strange'. Gael and the meaning behind this is that no matter where you come from, at some point in your history you will have some foreign blood in you. So we are all 'foreign' or 'strange' and therefore equal.

The Scottish Maritime Museum

Scotland was a very big shipbuilding, boatbuilding, nation for hundreds of years. Almost every island in Scotland had a boatbuilder. Then modern techniques of fibreglass and steel took over wooden boats and then all the work went overseas. So there's very few traditional boatbuilders remaining in Scotland. There was a risk of no system for passing on the knowledge to younger generations and securing a future for traditional boatbuilding in Scotland, a coastal nation that historically has been immersed in traditional skills for centuries. That's why the Scottish Maritime Museum got involved. The Museum is one of several industrial museums in Scotland and is located in a big brick shipyard building with a glass roof that came from Linthouse, in Govan, an area in Glasgow. It was being demolished but a large portion of the building was saved and transported to Irvine and rebuilt as part of the regeneration of the town. Irvine was an old shipbuilding town and the area around it became very industrialised and then, of course, shipbuilding died out so there was a lot of unemployment. They had this idea, back in the 1960s, of regenerating Irvine and bringing in more industry and in the 80s they decided to locate the Maritime Museum there. The Linthouse was rebuilt in Irvine in 1991 and houses the national collection. There is also the other part of the Museum located in Dumbarton and this is the Denny Ship Model Experimental Tank building and houses the first hydrodynamic testing tank in the world along with other Scottish maritime history.

The Museum is fortunate to have strong leadership and a committed team of employees and volunteers who strive to ensure that the visitor experience is among the best available and we have received recognition for this with several national awards in recognition of their efforts. The Museum is a 2020 Travellers' Choice Winner in Tripadvisor's annual awards. That means that it's in their top 10 per cent of worldwide attractions.[2] There's currently a new project underway to regenerate Irvine yet again and that includes harbourside walkways and different visitor attractions round the harbourside and along the coast. David Mann, the Director of the Scottish Maritime Museum, plays a big role in promoting that and getting established. It's called the 'Irvine Maritime Mile'.[3]

Regeneration. It's like back in the 60s. The old area of Irvine was on the harbourside but it grew because of shipbuilding and was a big industrial area. At one point, it was Scotland's third port after Glasgow and Greenock. But when shipbuilding declined in the area, they came up with this idea of building new towns on the site of an old town to try and regenerate the old town.[4] So there's Irvine and then there's Irvine New Town, which is built slam bang in the middle of the old town, thinking that if you build that and you build industrial units it'll attract business.

'Oh, we'll just build a new town. That'll regenerate the area.'

It doesn't if they don't add the infrastructure to support the people who are there in the first place and where are they going to get employed?

'Oh, we'll just build factories and you can all work there.'

In my opinion, it generally makes the area worse because the employment tends to go to people outside the town, rather than people within it because they've already lost a connection with ongoing work. I know from working at GalGael, we were dealing with people alongside their addictions who were third-generation unemployed and second-generation addicts. Their parents were alcoholics, heroin addicts or whatever. You're looking at three or four generations of unemployment, which leads to addiction. It's a perpetual, ever decreasing circle. Don't get me wrong, it obviously does not apply to everyone but it is a massive problem in many post-industrialised cities globally.

So they got the building down there and it's now the Scottish Maritime Museum and alongside that there's an old building that used to be a forge and the Boatbuilding School occupies that. David and I sat down to write an application for two years' funding from the Coastal Community Fund. We wanted to set up a boatbuilding school and knew we could make a success of it. We got the funding. We set it up in a structured way so that people could get a qualification out of it. We're currently the only place in Scotland where you can get a full apprenticeship in boatbuilding.

The Museum has to show an income and I think from their point of view the opening up of the Boatbuilding School showed to their funders that you're actually doing something to change people's lives. The Museum has got a collection of old vessels, old wooden boats, and they had no one to restore them. So by setting up the Boatbuilding School, we could then take the Maritime Museum's collection and get it back into either a working condition or a condition so that it could be exhibited.

The Scottish Boatbuilding School

The Boatbuilding School has a scheme in partnership with Community Jobs Scotland to give people work experience. It's just pretty much the same as when I was young and started over in Cumbrae. In 2014, we recruited eight young people through Community Jobs Scotland, which was established to find training and employment for people aged 16 to 29 years with a focus on those most disadvantaged in the labour market. They were the first cohort to undergo formal training in boatbuilding for a number of years. At this early stage of the development, we were unable to offer a further education qualification in traditional boatbuilding. However, all the participants spent one year in our workshops and developed transferable skills in woodwork and boatbuilding. Four of our first intake went on to full-time employment with one being offered an apprenticeship in joinery with a local construction company.

The young people employed were predominantly from the local area, which is recognised as having one of the highest poverty rates in Scotland. Some of the young people had criminal records, while others came from complicated, socially exclusive backgrounds. We've got a boy at the moment who's got autism, so he comes in just a day a week, just basically to give him a space, if you like, somewhere to be where he's in the company of people. We also have volunteers who are pivotal to the success of what we do both in the School and in the Museum in general. At the School, we currently have six regular volunteers who provide their time and allow us to attain targets that we could otherwise not achieve. The roles all involve working on the vessels in the workshop and those we construct. In exchange for their efforts, we provide training in woodwork skills and the opportunity to have a space to work on their own projects.

One of our volunteers, Andy, joined us through the Garnock Connections programme.[5] He is 39 years old and has suffered from Asperger's syndrome from a young age but was undiagnosed for a long time. He has been through some tough times and had previously been homeless for two years, living on the streets and in homeless shelters when he could find a place. He began in the workshop learning basic bench skills before beginning work on the two Skiffs that formed the backbone of the Garnock Connections Programme. Andy grew in confidence as the project progressed and upon completion has remained with the Boatbuilding School as a volunteer.

The trainees leave us with a year of extra skills and that includes things like discipline and turning up for work at nine o'clock in the morning and working right through. For some folk, it's the first time they've ever had a job. It's a new experience for them. We've had some folk for two years. It depends on the funding. Och, if I can find the funding! But what we're doing is now recognised under the Modern Apprenticeship Scheme.[6] There was lot of effort and planning and sometimes it felt like banging your head off a wall. Eventually we got there and it's now been recognised as a dying skill. In March 2019, we took on Edel.[7] She's the very first Modern Apprentice in boatbuilding in Scotland.

It's something that I'm passionate about. I've got a good team – Connor, Edel, Gavin and the volunteers. Edel is great at communicating with the trainees and I think a lot of it's because they come from a similar background and through the one-year training. She's managed to achieve an apprenticeship and the new trainees can relate to that and understand a lot more than if it's with just me. You get a lot of people when they start who have a barrier to authority. They may be used to adults giving commands and being demanding of them whether parents, teachers, social workers or whatever.

They think I'm a person in power and I'm just going to be rubbish at it and not look after them but I have a team around me. It doesn't take them long to realise that you can't build a boat without being part of a team. They'll learn more from the team than just working with me as individuals.

The first boat we built was a St Ayles Skiff. The kids' parents didn't really know or understand what the group were doing.

We said, 'Well, bring them down to the workshop. Let them see what you're doing.'

Some of them did. Some of them didn't. But then came the day to launch the boat. The local newspaper was there. We were getting our photos taken and a lot of their parents turned up to see this 22-foot boat that their kids had built. They'd never done anything like it before in their lives. Their parents just couldn't believe it. They were gobsmacked that their kids were capable of doing something like that. That in itself instils a massive amount of confidence in a young person.

One of our trainees was Nicole, a young woman who had come from a rough background and had been in foster care from a very young age. She was stuck at home. She never went out. She had no confidence. When she started with us, she was quite withdrawn. She did boatbuilding for a year and I managed to get her extended for two years though unfortunately she was never going master the skills to be a boatbuilder. But being part of our team she came out of her shell. She started talking more and it turned out she was shit-hot at communicating to others about what she was doing. Whether she was doing it right or wrong, it didn't matter – she could talk about it. In fact, I don't think she's ever shut up! She's now a permanent member of Museum staff, in visitor services. She has just completed her national qualification (Scottish Vocational Qualification) in customer services. So she does the tours around the Museum – the shipyard workers' flat and the vessels down in the harbourside. It's been great for us because when she brings people over to the Boatbuilding School, she knows what she's talking about. Her life has changed dramatically. After working within a museum environment, her world's changed around 180 degrees and she's a wonderful, wonderful girl.

In addition to the young trainees, we have older volunteers who want to learn the same skills. We also have 'Graham' in our workshop. His father was a fisherman over on the east coast and 'Graham' became a really well-respected lawyer. He developed Parkinson's and retired early. He went to learn boatbuilding down in England, again because there was nowhere in Scotland. When he came back, he offered to volunteer for us. 'Graham' is older but he's not 'higher up the ladder'. So that breaks down work and social barriers – youngsters getting to realise that the person they're working with isn't above them or isn't their boss. That can be a big thing for those who have been 'looked-after' children or in an environment where adults have always been authoritarian figures.[8] When they end up somewhere and they're working alongside, rather than working underneath, then it builds respect and that's something that they take away with them. The young folk who find employment when they leave have done so because they have developed new skills and attitudes to work and it is all through being allowed to be creative. They have matured and come to realise that there is more out there for them, that their contribution is valuable and they have self-worth. They realise that what they can offer is more than sitting at home playing on the PlayStation or whatever.

I've got to have my heart in it. Otherwise I'd have given up a long, long time ago. I learned it from Ian, my boss. I remember I'd fitted a hatch cover and done a good job.

Then Ian opened it up and said, 'Yeah, but your screws aren't lined up.'

It's the finishing touch. It's a simple, wee thing. It doesn't make any difference to the performance; it just looks better and people subconsciously notice that it's good craftmanship. It's the icing on the cake. So that's something that I do all the time and teach my trainees at the School. One of the young trainees pulled up one of the older volunteers on this, telling him that his screws weren't lied up. For that he turned around, laughing, calling me a bastard for my perfectionism. But he had learned a valuable lesson!

If you give someone the skills to do something with their hands

I was consulted as part of the development of a national paper *The Craft Blueprint*. The aim of *The Craft Blueprint* has been to create a plan of action for developing the craft workforce across the UK. I spoke to them about the mental and physical benefits of being in a supportive environment and being allowed to be creative as an adult by using your hands to create objects from timber or other mediums.[9] The policy in the UK is to stick people with heroin addiction onto methadone. Their thought is you can just forget about them because they're on a methadone programme. But it's more addictive than heroin and the outcome's generally pretty much the same. We've had addicts in our workshop. We give them the tools. We teach them the skills. They get involved in boatbuilding. And when you create something, stuff is released in your brain.[10] The chemicals are similar to those you'd get from the false 'high' you'd get when taking drugs, only it's natural.

For most folk as they get older, they move further away from being creative, whether it's through study, career or family commitments. Time is always limited so the opportunity to 'create' is diminished and the 'buzz' is then replaced by a substitute, be it beer, wine or smack. Being creative is living.

When my kids came home from nursery or primary school and they'd made something out of plasticine or papier maché or done a painting, whatever, you get the biggest smile on their face because they've actually made something with their own hands.

When I worked at GalGael, we also had a facility where the trainees can make something for themselves. It's for them and they can take it away with them. Many have carved headstones for their friends that had passed away from addiction. They would go to the graveyard and would place this wooden carved headstone to commemorate their friends because they had been forgotten.

Others would make a wooden jewellery box or carve something and give it to their parents, 'I'm sorry for all the shit I've put you through.'

Giving addicts a space where they can be creative is immensely powerful. It doesn't work with everybody but I've seen an awful lot of people's lives changed through just being part of something, part of a group of people that are being creative. These skills aren't recognised for what they can give back. These skills should not be allowed to die out. Museums are a good way of keeping them alive.

Volunteers in museums come from all walks of life and many of the older ones have a wealth of untapped knowledge. They are probably best placed in society to pass old skills on to younger generations as many of them are retired and in a fortunate position of actually having 'free' time which they give to organisations all over the country. I think there should be a cohesive plan for museums to find their stories, skills and experiences and be a vehicle for allowing them to pass them on.

If you take the crafts away, if you take the art away, you take the spirit away from people and you take away the value from society.

Promoting and encouraging the craft sector, whether it be business or pleasure, is, I think, a critical path for development. I know there are thousands of other ways to be stimulated – gyms, walking, athletics, drink, drugs, whatever – but being creative and using your hands to turn a raw material into something of beauty that may also have a use or serve a purpose gives a massive rush and feeling of achievement and it doesn't matter how old you are. Creativity is a fundamental part of what makes us human and it should be encouraged everywhere.

I have been lucky enough to witness the effects of this and been fortunate enough to be involved in promoting it and being a part of people's lives, which have sometimes been dramatically changed by people taking part in the simple act of using their hands.

Next steps

At some point in the future, I want a new building because the one the School occupies is not really suitable but we're only five years into this and we've got to prove that it works. Success will attract funding and hopefully we'll get a purpose-built area that's specific for boatbuilding and it will be part of the exhibit of the Museum. At the moment, it's not the safest place for museum visitors to come through because it's an active industrial workshop. We do get visitors who are curious and we bring them over and give them a wee tour around but the idea is that we build a proper area with viewing galleries so that visitors can watch people building the boats, ask about the processes and engage with the folk in the workshop.

Establishing the Modern Apprenticeship in boatbuilding has probably been the biggest challenge as there were so many hurdles to jump to ensure that there would be a sustainable future for the craft in Scotland's future. It has been a massive commitment from a lot of people but now that it has been established and we are at the front of delivering it, it gives us a strong position to lead the way forward. Partnership work is the key to ensuring the future success of this exciting development; we are working with the University of the Highlands and Islands (UHI) to develop the apprenticeship scheme and encourage employers to give young folk a chance.

I'm very, very, very fortunate that I fell into boatbuilding because I didn't choose this as a career. It was just a job I got when I was 16 when I left school but my boss gave me a passion for it because he respected me when I was 16 and wouldn't ask me to do anything he wouldn't do himself. And I'm lucky enough that I can pass these skills on to folk and watch the difference it makes to see the smile on their face or the shock on their parents' faces when they see what their kids have created or whatever and see the pride that they take in it. Ian, my boss, is still my hero. Sadly, he passed away a few years ago. We're currently restoring a boat in the collection. *Golden Orfe* was built in Fairlie in 1923 at the Fife Yard where Ian's father was foreman and where Ian served his time. It feels that I've come full circle.

I'm restoring another boat just now. My ambition is to get it finished and go away with my wife, Susan, and live a simpler life – away from all the technology, hustle and pressure. We'll go and sail around the Mediterranean again, exploring: See how far I get before I snuff it.

Notes

1 GalGael, "Who We Are."
2 Scottish Maritime Museum, "Scottish Maritime Museum Makes Top 10% of Worldwide Attractions on TripAdvisor."
3 *Irving Times*, "Creation of 'Maritime Mile' and New Irvine Homes in North Ayrshire Development Plan."
4 The rebuilding of Britain after the Second World War included the creation of new towns, legislated in the New Towns Act 1946 (Lock and Ellis, *New Towns*, 5). The Clyde Valley Regional Plan of 1946 aimed to reduce the population of Glasgow. Several regional towns in the area were designated as locations for new towns, including Irvine in 1966 (Lock and Ellis, *New Towns*, 28). The legacy of the new towns policy is mixed. Deprivation statistics, relating to 'unemployment/lack of education/poor health and housing conditions', indicates that Irvine is ranked at 3, where 1 equals most deprived (Town and Country Planning Association, *New Towns and Garden Cities*, 25).
5 Garnock Connections is based in Renfrewshire, Scotland, 20 miles from Irvine. It engages with local communities to protect and promote natural and cultural heritage.
6 Skills Development Scotland, "Modern Apprenticeships."
7 Fotheringham, "First Boatbuilding Modern Apprentice Edel McCarthy Takes Up Position."
8 'Looked-after children' is the term used in the UK to refer to children who have been placed by authorities, either through a court order or voluntary agreement with their parents, to live in a setting away from their family, for example, with foster carers, in a Children's Home or with extended family members.
9 *The Craft Blueprint* was released in 2009 by Creative & Cultural Skills, an agency supported by Arts Council England to provide advice, training and research with the aim of supporting the cultural sector (Creative & Cultural Skills, "Creating a Fair and Skilled Cultural Sector"). In 2008, Creative & Cultural Skills released its Sector Skills Agreement – an action plan to support employers of cultural and creative industries. Creative & Cultural Skills' Creative Blueprint comprised a series of sector-specific workforce development plans (Creative & Cultural Skills, "Publications") and included *The Craft Blueprint* (Creative & Cultural Skills, "The Craft Blueprint, 2).
10 Psychologist Mihaly Csikszentmihalyi developed the theory of 'flow', which refers to the state of happiness resulting from a state of concentration or total absorption in an activity. Csikszentmihalyi observed that this is often experienced by those engaged in creative work (Csikszentmihalyi, "Happiness and Creativity").

Bibliography

Creative & Cultural Skills. "Creating a Fair and Skilled Cultural Sector." Accessed 23 July 2020. www.ccskills.org.uk/.

Creative & Cultural Skills. "Publications." Accessed 23 July 2020. https://web.archive.org/web/20100917062701/https://www.ccskills.org.uk/Research/Publications/tabid/81/Default.aspx.

Creative & Cultural Skills. *The Craft Blueprint: A Workforce Development Plan for Craft in the UK*. Essex, Belfast, Aberystwyth and Glasgow: Creative & Cultural Skills, 2019.

Csikszentmihalyi, Mihaly. "Happiness and Creativity." *The Futurist* (September–October 1997): 8–12.

Dyson, Kevin. "Creation of 'Maritime Mile' and new Irvine Homes in North Ayrshire Development Plan." *Irvine Times*, 24 April 2018. Accessed 5 October 2020. www.irvinetimes.com/news/16181022.creation-maritime-mile-new-irvine-homes-north-ayrshire-development-plan/.

Fotheringham, Ann. "First Boatbuilding Modern Apprentice Edel McCarthy Takes Up Position." *Glasgow Times*, 9 July 2019. Accessed 3 September 2020. www.glasgowtimes.co.uk/news/17757115.first-boatbuilding-modern-apprentice-edel-mccarthy-takes-position/.

GalGael. "Who We Are." Accessed 21 July 2020. www.galgael.org/.

Garnock Connections. Accessed 23 July 2020. www.garnockconnections.org.uk/.

Lock, Katy, and Hugh Ellis. *New Towns: Rise, Fall and Rebirth*. London: RIBA Publishing, 2020.

Scottish Coastal Rowing Association. "Award for Maritime Museum Skiff Builders." Accessed 14 July 2020. https://scottishcoastalrowing.org/2016/02/09/award-for-maritime-museum-skiff-builders/.

Scottish Maritime Museum. "Scottish Maritime Museum Makes Top 10% of Worldwide Attractions on TripAdvisor." Accessed 5 October 2020. www.scottishmaritimemuseum.org/scottish-maritime-museum-makes-top-10-of-worldwide-attractions-on-tripadvisor.

Skills Development Scotland. "Modern Apprenticeships." Accessed 16 July, 2020. www.skillsdevelopmentscotland.co.uk/what-we-do/apprenticeships/modern-apprenticeships/.

Town and Country Planning Association. *New Towns and Garden Cities: Lessons for Tomorrow (Stage 1: An Introduction to the UK's New Towns and Garden Cities)*. London: Town and Country Planning Association, 2014.

14

HOUSE OF MEMORIES

Care and equality in the UK museum sector

Kerry Wilson

Launched in 2012, *House of Memories*[1] is a multiple award-winning dementia awareness programme, led by National Museums Liverpool (NML) in the UK. Originally developed to support the health and social care workforce with funding from the Department of Health, an adaptation of the professional training programme, designed specifically for family members, friends and community volunteers who care for people with dementia, was launched at the Museum of Liverpool in 2016. The programme primarily promotes the use of social history collections and museum objects to stimulate and inspire enhanced communication and connection between carers and people with dementia, via dedicated museum-based training events and a range of supplementary resources including the *My House of Memories* app.

Live training events also include character-based documentary films about experiences of caring for people living with dementia, based on real-world testimony collected throughout the research and development stages of the programme. Following repeated investment from the Department of Health, and other commissions from national agencies including Health Education England (the training and development agency for NHS England), the programme has achieved unprecedented scale and reach as a cultural intervention in health and social care. By September 2020 for example, more than 12,000 health and social care professionals and family carers had participated in *House of Memories* training events in England and there had been more than 32,000 downloads of the *My House of Memories* app.

In the same month, a bespoke version of the app was launched in collaboration with the British Council and National Heritage Board in Singapore, representing the second international, licensed adaptation of the programme, following an earlier collaboration with the Minnesota Historical Society (MNHS) in North America. An organisational commitment to programme evaluation and building a

DOI: 10.4324/9781003029519-19

reliable evidence base has been crucial to NML's effective development and expansion of *House of Memories*. Successive evaluation studies,[2] undertaken at different stages of the programme's development since 2013, have shown consistent outcomes in three core areas. These include enhanced professional learning and development in person-centred dementia care; improved subjective wellbeing of participating carers; and evidence of social value and return on investment (cost benefit) for health and social care commissioners.

Specific outcomes under each of these themes include improved cognitive and emotional understanding of dementia and its implications; greater capacity to establish a sense of connection with people with dementia; and enhanced professional conscientiousness. Improvements to carers' subjective wellbeing include feeling optimistic about dementia care; feeling good about one's self as a dementia carer; feeling cheerful in role as a dementia carer; and feeling more confident as a dementia carer. As an example of the social value of *House of Memories* and cost benefit to commissioners, a social return on investment (SROI) analysis of the family carers' programme in 2017 showed that for every one pound invested in the programme, £18.73 of social value was generated over a projected five-year period (£1: £18.73).

This longer-term research partnership has facilitated an ethnographic approach to exploring the impact and value of the programme, enabling a more comprehensive observation and understanding of the strategic contexts and operational mechanisms that underpin its success. Pragmatically speaking, it is important as evaluators to analyse and communicate 'what works' (and equally what doesn't work). In this context, research has also identified effective practices and processes – alternatively described as 'design principles'[3] – including collaborative leadership; co-design and production; mixed funding models; and evidence-based advocacy, particularly with regard to promotion of the programme's social value. On a more interpersonal level, spending quality research time with the programme team, collaborators and extended networks has also enabled a more nuanced consideration of the programme's inherent values, and its relational, empathic and inclusive qualities, which underpin its more quantifiable success in enhancing person-centred dementia care practice within and across its multiple cohorts.

The most affecting and beneficial aspect of the long-term research partnership has been the time spent with people living with dementia and the care community that surrounds and supports them. As something that we are all likely to encounter in some form, with a family member, friend or neighbour, dementia is a powerful leveller. Carers taking part in *House of Memories* will often describe their fellow participants as 'people like us', and comment on the value of having the space to connect with them and support one another. Above all, *House of Memories* has retained a genuine community ethos, despite now working at considerable national and international scale, with 'people like us' continuing to learn from the shared human experience of living with dementia and its non-discriminatory implications and impacts. In this chapter, we consider how its policy responsiveness and strategic influence, collaborative nature and respect for working-class culture and communities, and subsequent enduring values as a cultural intervention in health and social care may translate and subsequently inform the future leadership of more inclusive, representative and culturally democratic museum services.

Health inequalities and museums as community assets: policy contexts

Contemporary public health debates and the accelerating arts and health agenda have undoubtedly facilitated a useful strategic space[4] in which *House of Memories* has effectively flourished. Public health strategies aiming to promote more preventive, community-based care agendas have created a useful rhetorical device for cultural sectors and leaders interested in a more integrated, cross-policy function and role for arts and culture. Emphasising the social determinants of health and wellbeing,[5] and the inequalities that arise based on material circumstances and the social and cultural contexts in which we live, greater attention is being paid, particularly at the local authority level, to asset-based approaches to healthier communities.[6] Asset-based Community Development (ABCD) as a public health strategy aims to 'promote and strengthen the factors that support good health and wellbeing, protect against poor health and foster communities and networks that sustain health'.[7] An important prerequisite is to recognise the assets available to achieve change, including the individual, organisational, associational, economic, *cultural* and physical resources available to communities. Furthermore, the more proactive regional administrations in the UK are ensuring that all departments – education, transport and housing – are contributing to health-based outcomes via *health in all policies* (HIAP[8]) approaches to policy-making.

Health inequalities have been exacerbated by sustained austerity-driven fiscal policies in the UK. Austerity measures have been distributed unevenly across government departments, creating differing levels of impact across different groups of society, with budget cuts being acutely felt by local government with real implications for public services.[9] Arguably, notions of the integrated public sphere, especially in relation to essential public services, have been born of necessity rather than choice, with increasing demands on third sector and charitable organisations to fill the gap left by reductions in core services. Previous research on community engagement work in the museums sector,[10] for example, discusses evolving 'practices of care' through a greater sense of networked allegiance with wider social care services, with an emphasis on cultural organisations providing an alternative to gaps in provision created by austerity measures.

Dementia care, as a public health priority, has further illuminated the need for community-level, asset-based approaches that can support people to live well, and to live independently with dementia, thus limiting the demand on acute health and residential social care services.[11] In response, there is growing momentum around arts and cultural commissioning from health and social services, with particular attention paid to people with dementia. There is a growing body of research on the value of museums in this context, based on their therapeutic value with positive social and cognitive outcomes for people with dementia and their carers.

House of Memories makes a unique contribution to the field, with its focus on the practice of dementia care and carers themselves. In an effective demonstration of cross-sector collaborative leadership – characterised by understanding stakeholder needs, distributed ownership and lateral decision-making[12] – the programme originated from a conversation with Department of Health representatives on the need for more creative approaches to training and development in person-centred dementia care. A comprehensive community of practice now supports the programme and its ongoing strategic development, including a range of national and international cultural organisations and agencies, local and national government representatives, and health and social care providers. NML as an organisation has established itself through this process as a valuable community asset, and subsequently helped to establish museums more broadly as anchor institutions in health and social care policy.

Sustaining a community ethos: collaboration, co-production and leading by example

The community of practice model[13] has been applied throughout the programme's development, including most notably through the active process of co-design and production in collaboration with people with dementia and their carers from traditional working-class communities in the city of Liverpool. The *My House of Memories* app, for example, was co-designed and developed in collaboration with Mersey Care NHS Trust, grassroots local charities and community organisations, including the Liverpool Service User Reference Forum (SURF). This approach served a practical purpose of course, in ensuring that resources were dementia friendly in accordance with the Disability Discrimination Act. The approach also ensured that the digitised social history collection made available through the app would have real resonance with people of the city.

Communities of practice as a concept[14] is derived from management theory on organisational learning, whereby the 'apprentice' becomes part of a professional or occupational community through a process of situated learning and appropriation of skills, routines, behaviours and values. The emphasis in the original concept therefore is very much on hierarchical forms of *practice* in specific vocational communities. This has been re-examined as work environments and contexts change, including for example work across multiple professional communities and the emergence of digital spaces. In the *House of Memories* example, the emphasis is on *community* learning, with equitable respect and gravitas for different forms of professional knowledge and lived experience between collaborators from health and social care and museum sectors, alongside community groups as co-producers.

Co-production has become a popular, and somewhat problematic, concept in public policy. Defined as joint working between people or groups traditionally separated into categories of user and producer,[15] co-production is especially suited to local, citizen-based innovation and practice and most commonly deployed in the context of public service development and delivery. The advance of co-production in public policy discourse has in turn contributed to a more explicit emphasis on lived experience[16] – that is, people and communities with direct experience of health, social and environmental issues – as a legitimate form of knowledge and expertise in public policy-making. The elasticity of the term, and its openness to interpretation, has led to some criticism of the ubiquitous adoption of the term co-production as a fashionable way of working, with some practitioners observing, '…most initiatives which use the term in the context of health and social care in the UK are not co-producing anything'.[17]

The active contribution of the lived experience and expertise of communities including the SURF group has ensured the quality, relevance and subsequent positive impact of all relevant *House of Memories* resources. The most significant outcome however – and one that exemplifies the authenticity of the programme's co-produced approach – has been the sense of ownership and pride felt by the people, families and community groups involved and the valued relationship that has developed and sustained between them and the team at NML. They regularly come together, for example, outside of ongoing research and development activities, for social gatherings and celebratory milestone events.[18] People with dementia and carers directly involved with the programme also independently act as advocates of *House of Memories* through their own networks, including for example the weekly #AlzChat discussions on Twitter.

These core values of localised collaboration, co-design and production have been replicated in regional roll-outs of *House of Memories*, nationally and internationally. In 2013 for example, the programme was delivered across the north of England in collaboration with Salford Museum and Art Gallery, Bury Art Museum and Sunderland Museum and Winter Gardens, and another regional programme was delivered in the Midlands in 2014 with Birmingham Museum and Gallery, Leicester Guildhall and Wollaton Hall in Nottingham. Each of these sites developed tailored, responsive training events and versions of the app in collaboration with local agencies and service users. In Minnesota, the *House of Memories* US app includes objects, photographs, music and video from the MNHS collection that were curated by people living with dementia and their caregivers, including African-Americans who selected items that connect to the black community.

Museum scholars have reflected at length on the relational qualities of collections and services with reference to the 'dynamic interactions of people with objects'[19] and the mediated materialisation of knowledge.[20] Through considering the evolution and impact of *House of Memories* as an equitable community of practice, it has been possible to observe the relational experiences between museum staff, collaborators and participants in the programme, and the extent to which the 'people like us' description applies to museum professionals as much as fellow carers and people with dementia. The Director of *House of Memories* is open about her own very personal motivations to develop the programme, linked to her mum's experiences of dementia and the emotional challenges of visiting her in her residential care home.

As a model of community working, the programme is rich with such empathic and personable qualities. This may seem like a glib observation for a social scientist, but the fact that NML team members are from the city area, have local accents and extensive local knowledge helps to root the programme in a familiar real-world context. The highly empathic facilitation of live training events, which are always emotive experiences, is also a powerful component of *House of Memories*. The emotional impact of the documentary films, for example, with real, relatable working-class characters, is often palpable and can be a confronting experience for participants. The *House of Memories* facilitator creates a safe and trusted space, enabling and supporting participants to share their reflections and their own personal experiences. Pilgrim et al[21] discuss the relationship between trust and ontological security – that being the extent to which we *belong* to places and situations – and the relative implications for experiences of health care. The sense of trust and ontological security developed between people with dementia, their carers and museums as community assets is a key outcome therefore for mutually beneficial professional practice across cultural and health sectors.

People like us: working-class culture and the city of Liverpool

The Museum of Liverpool (MoL), an iconic building on the Liverpool waterfront opened in 2011, is the birthplace of *House of Memories* and home for its regular live training events. The Museum invites visitors to explore 'how the port, its people, their creative and sporting history have shaped the city',[22] with gallery spaces including The People's Republic, dedicated to the 'diverse stories and unique identity' and 'everyday and extraordinary' contributions of people of the city throughout its 'turbulent history'. The Museum was a major capital development project, both for NML as a national museum group and for the city of Liverpool as a burgeoning cultural destination. The city was on the crest of a culture-led development wave on the Museum's opening, following its widely celebrated 'success' as European Capital of Culture (ECoC) in 2008.

Post-ECoC cultural policy in Liverpool has continued to be defined by spectacle events, including the Liverpool Giants, in collaboration with French theatre company Royal de Luxe,[23] and heavily incentivised by the visitor economy. A comprehensive evaluation[24] of Liverpool 08 and its yearlong cultural programme showed £130m of generated income; 9.7m additional visits to Liverpool in 2008; a 10 per cent rise in arts audiences each year in 2006–08; and press coverage encouraging a positive 'city image' in the national media. The economic impact of the event is often flagrantly misinterpreted and appropriated, however, by city spokespeople, with culture as the 'rocket fuel of the economy' becoming the catchphrase of the local administration. The ensuing rhetorical narrative that has come to define Liverpool – externally at least – as a successful 'cultural city' does little to convey or represent the real social characteristics and cultural fabric that define the everyday, working-class life of the city.

Researchers exploring the long-term effects of Liverpool 08[25] have made a concerted effort to contextualise any short-term impacts with the social demographic realities of the city, so that any longer-term changes in the city can be more accurately discerned and attributed to its ECoC status. During the mid to late twentieth century, the once great imperial commercial port had become a portrait of the 'devastating effects of deindustrialisation', including unemployment, poverty and urban disintegration. A steady recovery in the late 1990s and 2000s was challenged by the global financial crisis of 2008 and the subsequent impact of austerity measures and cuts in public expenditure on the city from 2010 onwards. As such, ECoC status has not significantly improved the creative infrastructure or cultural fabric of the city, with shrinkage in the publicly subsidised arts sector and relative stagnation in commercial creative industries, despite its promotion as a beacon of culture-led regeneration in Liverpool and beyond.

In short, there is little if any evidence to show that Liverpool 08 and subsequent event-led cultural interventions did anything to improve the social and economic prospects for people in the city, or indeed for their engagement with the city's arts and cultural assets. On the other hand, NML's *House of Memories* has done much to promote the relevance and value of the city's cultural institutions to its residents, with those taking part in the programme forming long-term relationships with MoL and sister venues. The connection here with the social history of MoL's collections, and how these are used in a reminiscence capacity as part of the *House of Memories* experience, is key.

Many of the collections used in museum-based sessions, and those objects digitised as part of the development of the *My House of Memories* app, speak directly to working-class culture and experience in the city. These include stories of its former industrial life and major employers, from the working docks and ship builders to notable factories and manufacturing sites including Tate and Lyle, Lever Brothers and Meccano. Working-class leisure and cultural activities are also widely represented, including cinemas, bingo halls and the fortunes of the city's football clubs. Somewhat bafflingly, formal approaches to cultural policy analysis in the city make an elitist distinction between 'art' and 'sport', despite the huge revenue generated by visiting football fans for an authority otherwise obsessed with tourist economy and visitor spend, and the extent to which football is woven into the cultural fabric of the city. In this context, *House of Memories* provides an important, evidence-based social value counter-balance to the market-driven philosophy of mega-event cultural policy in the city.

Enduring values and the culturally democratic museum

As debates rage in the cultural policy research community regarding persistent inequalities in who gets to work in, participate in and benefit from the cultural and creative industries, particularly where social class is concerned,[26] cultural democracy has re-emerged as an alternative agenda for cultural policy, subsidy and governance. Cultural democracy challenges 'the idea that art is only what artists do', guided by three central tenets: (1) that many cultural traditions co-exist in society, and that none should dominate as an 'official' culture; (2) that there is a cultural life in which everyone is able to participate; (3) that cultural life itself should be subject to democratic control.[27]

The culture, health and wellbeing sphere, with its emphasis on reducing health inequalities as per the policy contexts highlighted above, offers a platform for considering cultural democracy in action. We can see how the principles of cultural democracy are re-enacted at a grassroots level by the range of community-responsive arts, crafts and cultural activities shown to have a positive impact on physical and mental health.[28] In the UK, national networks are emerging to spearhead this work, including a range of constituent members representing different sectors, agencies and the lived experience and expertise required to enable real collaborative change. The Culture, Health and Wellbeing Alliance[29] (CHWA), for example, includes Strategic Alliance Members representing different arts and cultural organisations engaging in health and wellbeing work; Strategic Alliance Partners including Public Health England and NHS England; and the LENs lived experience network. The MARCH network[30] is one of eight national networks funded by UK Research and Innovation to further research into mental health. MARCH focuses on social, cultural and community assets – including the arts, culture, heritage sites, libraries, green spaces, community centres, social clubs, community associations and volunteer groups – and the role they play in enhancing public mental health and wellbeing, preventing mental illness and supporting those living with mental health conditions.

The principles of cultural democracy are also reflected in other, related contemporary debates and initiatives regarding the civic role of arts and culture and the value that arts organisations in receipt of public subsidy bring to communities. An inquiry led by the Calouste Gulbenkian Foundation[31] (UK) identified a number of characteristics shared by organisations that have a 'strong civic role', including being rooted in local needs; giving communities agency in developing artistic programmes; developing communities' skills and capabilities; building social capital; championing artistic quality; championing diversity; and challenging prevailing orthodoxies and ways of working. In terms of a civic cultural infrastructure, this has particular resonance for museums and libraries, as anchor civic institutions (and *statutory* public services in the case of public libraries in England), as they have been under increasing threat as a result of sustained austerity measures.[32] Historically, market-led policies and cuts in public expenditure have forced a retreat in egalitarian social aims in cultural institutions.[33]

In contextualising research on the impact and value of *House of Memories*, it was important to consider how the organisational values of NML supported the development of the programme as a health and social care intervention,[34] and subsequently how its success has shaped NML's organisational mission as a national museum group with a strong local identity. Its mission statement, 'to be the world's leading example of an inclusive museum service', was underpinned by values including a belief in the concept of social justice and in the power of museums to help promote good and active citizenship, acting as agents of social change. These values are enacted through management of the group's seven venues, including the International Slavery Museum, and through strategic initiatives within the wider professional community. These include a formative role in the creation of the Federation of International Human Rights Museums (FIHRM) and the Social Justice Alliance for Museums (SJAM).

The collective cultural leadership capabilities of the team behind *House of Memories* at NML therefore are also instrumental to its success. In relation to multi-agency working and collaborative leadership, NML has helped to position museums as the ultimate 'boundary spanners', characterised by the ability to engage with others; deploy relational and interpersonal competencies; and to acknowledge and value difference outside their own professional circles.[35] The culture, health and wellbeing agenda opens a space for re-examining and defining egalitarian cultural leadership, beyond pragmatic models of transactional leadership versus more charismatic, transformational modes of leadership practice,[36] in a more democratic, collaborative cross-policy capacity.

A more values-based, ethnographic approach to cultural policy research is needed to understand experience in the field and support its ongoing professional development. This will help to capture the complexities of the relationship between policy, the lived experience of collaborative cultural work and the mutually beneficial outcomes it aims to achieve, adding authority and authenticity to research via the collection of detailed professional narratives.[37] In another example of collaborative cultural leadership, the NML team has always ensured that independent researchers feel part of the integrated *House of Memories* community of practice. This is how museums can ensure that they remain relevant, connected and valuable to 'people like us' on a profoundly human level.

Notes

1 See NML, "About the Museum of Liverpool."
2 For summaries of individual, independent evaluation studies, and the research framework used throughout, see Institute of Cultural Capital, "Crossing Boundaries."
3 Wilson, "Community Spirit."
4 Wilson, "Better Together."
5 Marmot, *Fair Society*.
6 GCPH, "Putting Asset-based."
7 Ripon and Hopkins, *Head, Hands and Heart*, 3.
8 Public Health England, "Local Wellbeing."
9 Hitchen, "The Affective," 5.
10 Morse and Munro, "Museums' Community," 357.
11 Ganga and Wilson, "Valuing Carers," 3.
12 Wilson, "Collaborative Leadership," 521.
13 Wilson, "Communities of Practice."
14 Lave, *Situated Learning*.
15 Durose et al., "Generating Good Enough," 135.
16 Sandhu, "Value of Lived Experience."
17 Morris, "What is Co-production?"
18 For example, see NML, "House of Memories: A Celebration."
19 Bell, "Museums as Relational," 72.
20 Gosden, "Relational Museum."
21 Pilgrim, Tomasini, and Vassilev, "Examining Trust," 55.
22 NML, "About the Museum."

23 See "Giant Spectacular Liverpool's Dream."
24 Garcia, Cox, and Melville, *Creating an Impact.*
25 Crone et al., *Sustaining an Impact?*
26 Brook, O'Brien, and Taylor, *Culture is Bad.*
27 64 Million Artists, "Cultural Democracy," 4.
28 Fancourt, Warran, and Aughterson, "Evidence Summary."
29 See Culture Health and Wellbeing Alliance "Connecting Culture and Health."
30 See March Network.
31 See Inquiry into the Civic Role of Arts Organisations, "What is the Civic Role of Arts Organisations?"
32 Wilson, "Public Libraries."
33 Muddiman et al., *Open to All?* 22.
34 Wilson, "Political Value," 377.
35 Peck and Dickinson, *Managing and Leading.*
36 Burns and Wilson, "Trends in Leadership," 91.
37 Riessman, *Narrative Analysis.*

Bibliography

64 Million Artists with Arts Council England. "Cultural Democracy in Practice." September 2018. Accessed 24 November 2020. www.artscouncil.org.uk/sites/default/files/download-file/CulturalDemocracyInPractice.pdf.

Bell, Joshua. "Museums as Relational Entities: The Politics and Poetics of Heritage." *Reviews in Anthropology* 41 (2012): 70–92. https://doi.org/10.1080/00938157.2012.651072.

Brook, Orian, Dave O'Brien, and Mark Taylor. *Culture is Bad for You.* Manchester: Manchester University Press. 2020.

Burns, Susanne, and Kerry Wilson. "Trends in Leadership Writing and Research: A Short Review of the Leadership Literature." In *A Cultural Leadership Reader*, edited by Sue Kay and Katie Venner, 86–95. London: Cultural Leadership Programme, 2010.

Crone, Stephen, Rafaela Ganga, Tamara West, Michael Atkins, and Gayle Whelan. *Sustaining an Impact? Legacies of Liverpool as European Capital of Culture.* Liverpool: University of Liverpool, 2021.

Culture Health and Wellbeing Alliance. "Connecting Culture and Health." Accessed 24 November 2020. www.culturehealthandwellbeing.org.uk.

Durose, Catherine, Catherine Needham, Catherine Mangan, and James Rees. "Generating 'Good Enough' Evidence for Co-production." *Evidence & Policy: A Journal of Research, Debate and Practice* 13, no. 1 (2017): 135–151.

Fancourt, Daisy, Katey Warran, and Henry Aughterson. *Evidence Summary for Policy: The Role of Arts in Improving Health & Wellbeing*, April 2020. Accessed 24 November 2020. https://assets.publishing.service.gov.uk/government/uploads/system/uploads/attachment_data/file/918253/The_role_of_arts_in_improving_health_and_wellbeing.pdf.

Ganga, Rafaela Neiva, and Kerry Wilson. "Valuing Family Carers: The Impact of House of Memories as a Museum-led Dementia Awareness Programme." *International Journal of Care and Caring*. Published online 10 September 2020. Accessed 24 November 2020. https://doi.org/10.1332/239788220X15966470811065.

Garcia, Beatriz., Tamsin Cox, and Ruth Melville. *Creating an Impact: Liverpool's Experience as European Capital of Culture.* Liverpool: University of Liverpool, 2010.

GCPH. *Putting Asset-based Approaches into Practice: Identification, Mobilisations and Measurement of Assets.* Glasgow Centre for Population Health, Briefing Paper 10, Concepts Series. July 2012. Accessed 24 November 2020. www.gcph.co.uk/assets/0000/3433/GCPHCS10forweb_1_.pdf.

"Giant Spectacular Liverpool's Dream." Accessed 24 November 2020.www.giantspectacular.com.

Gosden, Chris. "The Relational Museum." 16 January 2009. Accessed 24 November 2020. https://materialworldblog.com/2009/01/the-relational-museum/.

Hitchen, Esther. "The Affective Life of Austerity: Uncanny Atmospheres and Paranoid Temporalities." *Social and Cultural Geography*. Published online 7 February 2019. Accessed 24 November 2020. https://doi.org/10.1080/14649365.2019.1574884.

Inquiry into the Civic Role of Arts Organisations. "What is the Civic Role of Arts Organisations?" Accessed 24 November 2020. https://civicroleartsinquiry.gulbenkian.org.uk.

Institute of Cultural Capital. "Crossing Boundaries: The Value of Museums in Dementia Care." Accessed 24 November 2020. http://iccliverpool.ac.uk/crossing-boundaries/.

Lave, Jean, and Etienne Wenger. *Situated Learning: Legitimate Peripheral Participation*. Cambridge: Cambridge University Press, 1991.

March Network. Accessed 24 November 2020. www.marchnetwork.org.

Marmot, Michael, Jessica Allen, Peter Goldblatt, Tammy Boyce, Di McNeish, Mike Grady, and Ilaria Geddes. *Fair Society, Healthy Lives*. The Marmot Review. London, February 2010. Accessed 24 November 2020. www.ucl.ac.uk/marmotreview.

Morris, Jenny. "What is Co-production? The Clue is in the Name – It Means Working Together to Jointly Produce Something." 29 September 2015. Accessed 24 November 2020. https://coproductionforchange.wordpress.com/2015/09/29/what-is-co-production-the-clue-is-in-the-name-it-means-working-together-to-jointly-produce-something/.

Morse, Nuala, and Munro, Ealasaid. "Museums' Community Engagement Schemes, Austerity and Practices of Care in Two Local Museum Services." *Social and Cultural Geography* 19, no. 3 (2018): 357–378. https://doi.org/10.1080/14649365.2015.1089583.

Muddiman, Dave, Shiraz Durrani, Martin Dutch, Rebecca Linley, John Pateman, and John Vincent. *Open to All? The Public Library and Social Exclusion*. London: Resource: The Council for Museums, Archives and Libraries, 2000.

NML. "About the Museum of Liverpool." Accessed 13 November 2020. www.liverpoolmuseums.org.uk/about-museum-of-liverpool.

NML. "House of Memories." Accessed 24 November 2020. www.liverpoolmuseums.org.uk/house-of-memories.

NML. "House of Memories: A Celebration." Accessed 24 November 2020. www.youtube.com/watch?v=ZKp1tdKbc1E.

Peck, Edward, and Helen Dickinson. *Managing and Leading in Inter-agency Settings*. Bristol: The Policy Press, 2008.

Pilgrim, David, Floris Tomasini, and Ivaylo Vassilev. *Examining Trust in Healthcare: A Multidisciplinary Perspective*. London: Palgrave Macmillan, 2011.

Public Health England. "Local Wellbeing, Local Growth: Adopting Health in All Policies." 17 October 2016. Accessed 24 November 2020. www.gov.uk/government/publications/local-wellbeing-local-growth-adopting-health-in-all-policies.

Riessman, Catherine. *Narrative Analysis*. Qualitative Research Methods Series 30. Thousand Oaks, Calif.: Sage Publications, 1993.

Rippon, Simon, and Trevor Hopkins. *Head, Hands and Heart: Asset-based Approaches in Health Care*. London: The Health Foundation, 2015.

Sandhu, Baljeet. "The Value of Lived Experience in Social Change." 3 August 2017. Accessed 24 November 2020. www.cloresocialleadership.org.uk/news-insights/the-value-of-lived-experience-in-social-change.

Wilson, Kerry. "Community Spirit, Global Impact: Sustainability and Scalability in Culture, Health and Wellbeing Programmes." 11 October 2020. Accessed 24 November 2020.

http://iccliverpool.ac.uk/?blog=community-spirit-global-impact-sustainability-and-scalability-in-culture-health-and-wellbeing-programmes.

Wilson, Kerry. "Public Libraries, Professionalism and the Civic Turn." 9 July 2019. Accessed 24 November 2020. http://iccliverpool.ac.uk/?blog=public-libraries-professionalism-and-the-civic-turn.

Wilson, Kerry. "Collaborative Leadership in Public Library Service Development." *Library Management* 39, no. 8/9 (2018): 518–529. https://doi.org/10.1108/LM-08-2017-0084.

Wilson, Kerry. "Better Together: Museums, Health Care and Collaborative Advantage." 11 November 2016. Accessed 24 November 2020. http://iccliverpool.ac.uk/?blog=better-together-museums-health-care-and-collaborative-advantage.

Wilson, Kerry. "The Political Value of Museums in Dementia Care." In *The Caring Museum: New Models of Engagement with Ageing*, edited by Hamish Robertson, 360–385. Edinburgh: MuseumsEtc, 2015.

Wilson, Kerry. "Communities of Practice as a Framework for Understanding the Professional Impact of Collaborative Cultural Work." July 2014. Accessed 24 November 2020. http://iccliverpool.ac.uk/wp-content/uploads/2017/05/CoP-lit-review-KWilson.pdf.

15

NGINTAKA SONGLINE TRACKS IN THE MUSEUM

Diana James

Museums of the twenty-first century in Australia are slowly emerging from an era where the colonial upper and middle-class European voice dominated the narration of history and categorisation of the art and cultures of the Aboriginal and Torres Strait peoples of this land. Decolonisation of museums is both a race and class issue, a challenge to relinquish the privileged class 'white expert' curatorial voice and allow other cultural views of history to be honoured. This chapter explores the challenges faced by traditional owners and workers of the remote Anangu Pitjantjatjara Yankunytjatjara Lands of Central Australia to have their voices heard in the national press that privileged a critique by powerful white experts who attempted to close the Anangu exhibition of the Ngintaka Songline.

On 28 March 2014, over 40 Aboriginal traditional Elders gathered outside the South Australian (S.A.) Museum in Adelaide to protest the threatened closure of their *Ngintaka Exhibition*. This multimedia exhibition of artworks, film and sound recordings told the ancient story of the Ngintaka Tjukurpa, the giant perentie lizard creation ancestor, of the Anangu Pitjantjatjara Yankunytjatjara (APY) lands in the north-west of South Australia. The exhibition had been curated by the Aboriginal traditional owners, artists, singers and dancers of the Ngintaka Songline who were now in Adelaide to open their exhibition. They were proud to be telling their story in the S.A. Museum in their cultural voice of story, song and art:

> Just as we hold our land strongly under freehold title, we hold our Law, our stories, our Tjukurpa – the songlines. We keep these stories strong by telling them over and over, through traditional practice, song and dance, and now through our artworks, books and film. It makes us very happy to share this story with all Australians.[1]

DOI: 10.4324/9781003029519-20

However, these Elders' voices were silenced by the powerful Murdoch press. A media storm generated around the rumour that 'men's secret sacred law' had been exposed threatened to close the exhibition before it opened. The front pages of *The Weekend Australian* and *The Review* of 22–23 March were headlined 'Desert Storm' and 'Culture War'[2] over images of senior Aboriginal men holding spears, supposedly outraged by the exhibition. Nicolas Rothwell, a 'usually reliable'[3] expert on Aboriginal art, declared the Ngintaka Exhibition a 'mortal threat to traditional Aboriginal law and culture'.[4] The Murdoch media privileged the voices of a few dissenting Elders whose fame and influence in the white middle-upper-class circles of fine art and politics was elevated to be much greater than the majority of Ngintaka Elders from the bush. The newspaper critique discredited the voices of the Anangu men and women whose leadership and agency were inherent in the exhibition. It fitted this narrative to paternalistically position the Anangu Elders involved in the collaborative research project as powerless victims of the white researchers, universities and museums. Issues of power, privilege and class were lost behind a *kupi-kupi*, a dust-devil, media spin that picked up rumours and whipped up public controversy. Under the threatening clouds of this media storm, busloads of Ngintaka traditional owners travelled thousands of kilometres from the centre of Australia to Adelaide to open their exhibition.

Exhibition opens under a media storm

On the morning of the scheduled exhibition opening, the Anangu Elders stood stoically outside the S.A. Museum until their voices were heard. Proudly standing their ground facing a feeding frenzy of reporters and flashing cameras, the Ananguku Arts and Cultural Aboriginal Corporation Board issued a clear statement in reply to the false accusations in the press:

> There is no secret sacred material in the Ngintaka story we are telling in this Exhibition. It is the open, public story that our parents and grandparents told us and we tell our children and grandchildren. Anangu Pitjantjatjara Yankunytjatjara (APY) Land Council approved this public version in 1996. This work is for future generations.[5]

That week, the Museum had been threatened with an injunction against the exhibition by one group on claims that were hotly contested by the other. The Museum Board, caught in a legal cross-fire, considered postponing the opening, which fuelled greater press frenzy as news websites across the country proclaimed: '*SA Museum forced to postpone Ngintaka exhibition featuring songline from the APY Lands*' and '*Songline exhibition pulled over culturally sensitive material*'.[6] Behind closed doors, lawyers acting for Ananguku Arts presented compelling evidence to the Museum that APY, the statutory body responsible for the protection of Aboriginal cultural heritage on APY Lands, had approved the research and exhibition of the public story of the Ngintaka Songline. The Songlines Project[7] had adhered to stringent Indigenous intellectual property protection protocols and informed consent approved by all Aboriginal partner organisations.

To the great relief of the Ngintaka traditional owners, the art centre managers, the researchers and co-curators, the exhibition opened on time! The Elders welcomed visitors and performed an opening ceremony of dance and song of the Ngintaka Tjukurpa. Anangu chairpersons of the supporting Aboriginal organisations spoke: Ananguku Arts, APY and the Ngaanyatjarra Pitjantjatjara Yankunytjatjara (NPY) Women's Council. The *Inma*, song and dance of the Ngintaka, was performed in the Museum courtyard by an Elder law man proudly leading a dance group of young next-generation Ngintaka custodians. As the song was sung, the sacred presence of the ancestors was called into the museum space to protect the tangible and intangible expressions of the Ngintaka Tjukurpa in the exhibition.

FIGURE 15.1 *Ngintaka Inma*, cover design for Ngintaka Songline Story and Song recorded at Angatja in 1994, published by Desert Tracks 1996. Image: Courtesy of Angatja Community.

Tradition of sharing the sacred not the secret

Anangu of APY Lands have a long tradition of sharing their culture through song, dance and art with the wider Australian community. The Ngintaka creation story was first published in *Brown Men and Red Sand* as told by the traditional owners of Angatja in the Mann Ranges to anthropologist Charles Mountford in 1948.[8] Anangu have since used this version of the story to document their carvings and paintings of this Tjukurpa sold from the Amata arts centre since 1974. An Anangu Elder, famous for his role in the struggle for APY Land Rights in 1981, published a version of the Ngintaka story in his autobiography of 1993.[9] The APY Executive approved the public Ngintaka story and song being shared with tourists to Angatja in the Mann Ranges since 1988. The Angatja Elders recorded the story and song cycle performance by over 30 traditional owners at a public Inma festival at Angatja in 1994. This recording was professionally edited and mastered to produce the Ngintaka Inma on CDs that were approved for sale by the APY Executive Board following the wishes and opinions of traditional owners in 1996. Anangu had enthusiastically shared the public story, song and dance of the Ngintaka Tjukurpa with thousands of mainstream Australians, art lovers and visiting tourists for 40 years prior to the exhibition in Adelaide in 2014.

The digital multimedia recording of the Ngintaka Songline during 2012–14 was inspired by the earlier cultural preservation work of the Angatja Elders. This collaborative research and recording project centred around multi-generational trips back to country led by the senior lawmen of the Ngintaka Songline. Some of these Elders were born in the bush before white settlement in the 1930s. Many of these revered old people, the living libraries of the ancient oral traditions of the Western Desert peoples, have since sadly passed. But their voices will be heard by future generations through these recordings now held in the Anangu-owned archive Ara Irititja. So those who follow them may walk with pride in their footsteps.

The 2014 public Ngintaka Exhibition was welcomed by artists across APY Lands as it celebrated their living oral and performing arts as well as the new Western Desert acrylic art generated by the story and song of Tjukurpa. The performance of their art and culture in major city exhibitions is a source of great pride to Anangu of the APY Lands. The exhibition did not need to reveal any men's secret law to present the beauty, depth and complex ontology of their Tjukurpa, the living creative force that inspires all their life and art. Senior Ngintaka traditional owners governed the research and exhibition curatorial process. They conveyed the sacred numinous landscape of the Tjukurpa through public story, song, art and dance, while maintaining a zone of silence over their secret law. The Ngintaka Tjukurpa is a complex multi-layered law with deep levels of secret cultural knowledge fiercely protected by the senior law men and avoided by women and children. Anangu have a sophisticated system of managing the secret sacred knowledge, ceremony and sites of both men and women with mutual respect. The level of story that those Elders born of the Ngintaka Tjukurpa chose to share in the exhibition was that open to families sitting around campfires: men, women and children.

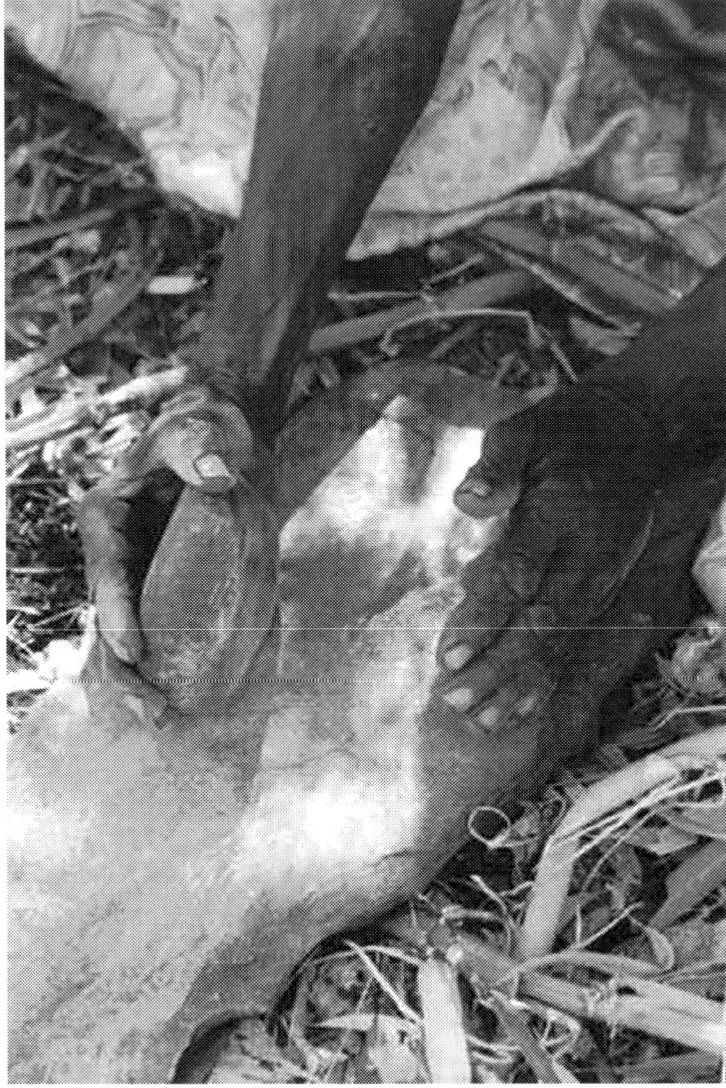

FIGURE 15.2 Nganyinytja grinding wild millet seed into flour on a traditional grindstone, like the one desired by the Ngintaka man. Photo: Diana James, Angatja 1999.

Indigenous cultural heritage: Communal rights versus individuals

The controversy that erupted around this exhibition brings into sharp focus several issues that have challenged Indigenous people and their interactions with museums and academic researchers, particularly anthropologists and archaeologists, for centuries. The media raised the spectre of past colonial plunder of Indigenous people's culture and secret sacred objects.

In Australia, this is recent history and institutions like the S. A. Museum have vast collections of Aboriginal cultural material and human remains, a legacy of colonial times. Unfortunately, the misuse of Aboriginal cultural heritage did not end then; there was still trespass in the late twentieth century. Within the living memory of the current Elders on APY Lands, anthropologist Charles Mountford published *Nomads of the Australian Desert* in 1976, an extensive account of desert culture including photographs of men's secret ceremony.[10] At that time, swift action by lawyers acting for APY lawmen had prevented further sale and reproduction of the book. Therefore, the aim of the Elders and the researchers involved in the Ngintaka research and exhibition was to build on lessons learnt from this experience and fully engage the APY Executive and traditional owners in research approvals and protocols.

The question for all Aboriginal groups, and for the museums and universities that seek to work with them, is: How to ethically share traditional communally owned culture? The seemingly obvious answer is to conduct research and exhibitions according to the wishes of the Traditional Aboriginal Owners of the culture that is being shared. However, as the events which unfolded through the Ngintaka Songlines Project illustrate, this is not as simple as it sounds. Gaining consent to publish communally owned intangible Indigenous heritage cannot be attained through standard university or museum ethical research consent forms. While individuals can consent to their image or words being published, they cannot individually authorise the public sharing of a traditional song, story or dance. Researchers must gain this approval from the large regional Aboriginal organisations holding the statutory authority and responsibility for the protection of the communally owned traditional cultural heritage of their people. Traditional Owner groups can safely express and resolve their different points of view within these appropriate cultural forums and reach agreement around what cultural heritage can be shared publicly, in what form and by whom. To expose Indigenous internal law and cultural debates to the harsh light of the western media is disrespectful and disempowers the processes of traditional consensus governance.

The Ngintaka Exhibition research was initiated and governed by Ananguku Arts and Cultural Aboriginal Corporation, the Aboriginal-owned organisation that represented all Anangu artists across APY Lands. Approval was given pursuant to the APY Lands Rights Act by the APY Executive Board, who had already listened to objections and adjudicated under traditional law the dispute over who had authority to share cultural material publicly in an exhibition. In 2011, the APY Executive considered one individual Elder's objection to the Ngintaka Project and affirmed the rights of the majority of traditional owners in matters of communally owned law and culture;

> One traditional owner does not have the right under Anangu traditional law to prevent other traditional owners from visiting sites to teach their children the Tjukurpa and telling and recording the non-secret public story version of their Tjukurpa.[11]

The APY Executive Board approved the research permit, following the wishes of the majority of Anangu Traditional owners, to travel and record story and song at public sites along the Songline with the exception of Wallatinna sites of the dissenting Elder.

The ethics of the Songlines ARC Project research and the Ngintaka Exhibition were further tested in the Supreme Court of South Australia and under traditional law on APY Lands by the APY Law and Culture Committee. While the media desert storm raged outside, the senior Ngintaka traditional owners who had authorised the exhibition attended a hearing of the case being brought against them in the Supreme Court in Adelaide.[12] Ananguku Arts was represented by lawyers with long experience on APY Lands; they were respectful of the complexity of working between two laws, languages and cultures. The Ngintaka Elders who sat in court each day defending their exhibition had a consistent message for the judge:

> Men's business is separate; we are following the track telling the story that we all understand, men and women. Everyone tells this story to their grandsons and granddaughters so the Tjukurpa will still remain.[13]

In his summation on 3 April 2014, Chief Justice Kourakis acknowledged that western law cannot adjudicate on a matter of Aboriginal traditional law.

> Courts have traditionally been reluctant to interfere in spiritual and religious matters. Courts have been reluctant, for example, to grant injunctions affecting the internal affairs of Christian churches. In my view, it is a very strong indication against the grant of a permanent injunction that the effect would be that, what I might loosely describe as 'colonial courts', would be making orders regulating and controlling the observance of Aboriginal law and custom.[14]

Kourakis found that on balance the majority of Ngintaka traditional Elders represented by Ananguku Arts presented the stronger case for the Ngintaka Exhibition in its entirety staying open. He commented on the difficulty that still exists in mainstream western society of understanding remote Aboriginal cultures, and the importance of being able to rely on the established protocols and processes of the statutory body, APY Land Council, its subcommittee the APY Law and Culture Committee, and representative Aboriginal organisations like Ananguku Arts and Culture Aboriginal Corporation.

Voice, power, privilege

Race and class

Issues of power, privilege, race and class that violently silenced Indigenous voices during the colonisation of the eighteenth and nineteenth centuries continue today.

In 1901, the new Commonwealth of Australia, ignoring Aboriginal people's existence or prior sovereignty, declared the 'White Australia' policy. This remained a fundamental government policy into the mid - twentieth century and contributed to the development of a racially insulated white society. Aboriginal people were not considered citizens of their own country until 1967 and many were forced to work as indentured labourers, or slaves, on rural properties and in domestic service. The legacy of these policies is social disadvantage across all western societal indices of health, levels of incarceration, morbidity, low levels of education, high unemployment, inadequate housing and the intergenerational dependence on welfare.

The western capitalist economic system defines the value of work in Australian society. Under this system, the paid work on remote communities is largely casual and irregular, fluctuating with government funding priorities defining 'essential' work. It is a precarious 'hybrid economy'[15] that depends on a combination of the traditional sharing economy with cash injections from externally funded jobs and welfare benefits. The exception is modern Aboriginal art, which has transcended cultural and class barriers, transforming traditional cultural skills into artworks highly valued by the elite western fine art market. The income from these 'products' does not elevate wealthy individuals; rather, it lifts the many as the artists share their income with their extended family. While the Australian brand is marketed on Aboriginal art and imagery, the artists of remote communities remain on the margins of this society's wealth.

In 2015, the then Prime Minister, Tony Abbott, blamed Aboriginal disadvantage in remote communities on their 'lifestyle choices'.[16] He justified axing Federal funding if the cost of services outweighed benefits. This was a continuation of the colonial policy of forced cultural assimilation: people must abandon their country to seek 'real work' as defined by the western economic system. The capitalist cost benefit analysis does not value highly Aboriginal traditional work that is generated by and sustains living on country. Their cultural work produces world-famous art and their environmental work manages vast regions of remote Australia: reducing devastating bush fires and feral species, while strategically monitoring Australia's sparsely populated regions. The Ngintaka Exhibition was a bold assertion by Anangu Elders of the value of their traditional work connecting people to country and maintaining the ecological balance and sustainability of the lands and waters of Australia.

Silenced voices

Aboriginal people in remote communities are more often spoken for by others than given the stage to speak for themselves. The voices privileged in the national cultural narratives of museums, universities, literature and the media are still predominantly middle-class 'experts'. Indigenous voices are still fighting to be recognised as the authority on their own history and heritage. Twenty-first-century museums, universities and national press need to include all First Nations voices and not continue to champion the voices of the powerful elite.

Marcia Langton, renowned Indigenous academic, speaks of this lack of Aboriginal voice on the national stage:

> Paradoxically, even while Aboriginal misery dominates the national media frenzy – the perpetual Aboriginal reality show – the first peoples exist as virtual beings without power or efficacy in the national zeitgeist. Political characters played by 'Aboriginal leaders' pull the levers that draw settler Australians to them in a co-dependent relationship.[17]

The APY Law and Culture Committee reasserted governance and cultural authority at a large regional meeting of 300 Anangu held at Umuwa on 12–13 May 2014. Both sides of the argument for and against the Ngintaka Exhibition and book were heard and responded to by the senior law men present. Unlike the western court, everyone could speak for themselves, be heard and allowed space to change their views and apologise to those they had offended.

Senior law men declared they were shamed that Anangu private business, the traditional law of their Ngintaka Tjukurpa, was being argued by whitefellas in the western press and courts. *The Australian* and *Weekend Review* articles were translated by the younger brothers of Elders greatly distressed that their images and quotes had been spread all over the front pages without their consent.[18] Images of men proudly holding spears at an Ananguku Arts workshop had been used to substantiate Rothwell's contention that the men were 'up in arms' against the Ngintaka Exhibition.[19] Unfortunately, journalists are not required to operate under the ethics required of academic researchers on APY Lands; they do not have to gain informed consent from those they quote or photograph. The APY Law and Culture meeting reasserted the authority of Anangu law and voice; a consensus was reached that the Ngintaka Exhibition was approved in accordance with the wishes of the majority of traditional owners of APY Lands.

Privileged voice of the press

Tragically, the Ngintaka media controversy was a brutal example of privileged middle-class 'Aboriginal experts' dominating the public narrative on Aboriginal law and culture.

Rothwell approached his discussion with the Amata Elders and the resulting articles from an established position against academic research into Aboriginal traditional culture. His *Quicksilver: Reflections*, delivered at the University of New England in 2011, derides '"two-way" research, respectful collaboration'[20] as a modern smokescreen for continued plunder of Indigenous knowledge. 'Hence the data transfer: a last-chance gold rush, as art historians, anthropologists and culture theorists rush to map the contours of indigenous beliefs'.[21]

He expounded this anti-humanities research position in his 2014 article 'Culture War'. Rothwell spared no one as he unleashed a sweeping fire storm that engulfed the researchers, the cultural institutions and their Indigenous advisory boards, the

Aboriginal partner organisations and the Aboriginal senior traditional owners of the Songline who initiated and governed the research and the exhibition. Rothwell intimated that the researchers had duped those Anangu who supported the project, '…their own strong local yes-team, … a man much given to vaunting his Ngintaka primacy'.[22] Rothwell appeared unable to acknowledge or was ignorant of the Anangu initiative and agency through APY and the Songlines Project Elders Consultative Committee governance of the research and exhibition. The approval process had been settled under Anangu traditional law and it was an affront to traditional authority that it was questioned in the press. It was a travesty that the exhibition became controversial in the western mainstream media arena of the politically and racially divisive 'culture wars' that continue to frustrate respectful debate of difference in Australia.[23]

Indigenising the museum

The Ngintaka Exhibition was the first time the S. A. Museum relinquished curatorial control and hosted an Indigenous exhibition. Anangu men and women from the remote APY Lands curated a dynamic twenty-first-century exhibition telling the public story of one of their ancient Songlines in multimedia formats of stunning audio-visuals, traditional carving and modern acrylic paintings. Visitors to the exhibition were led along a virtual songline following footprints of the ancestor on the floor as he strode through country creating landforms and bush foods of the spinifex rangelands of north-western South Australia. There were films of Elders telling the story; audio of the song and visuals of spectacular desert country linked the paintings of this hero's journey. This was a modern re-telling by the Anangu Elders of the Ngintaka epic Songline to the children and grandchildren of the city settlers.

Anangu successfully *indigenised* the western museum space; the story was powerfully told in their voices. The usual practice of museums to *represent* Indigenous culture with interpretation by museum curators was challenged by Anangu telling their story in their own language and cultural perspective. Borrowing a term from the Metis scholar David Garneau, the Western Desert Elders worked with the Songlines Project management to 'indigenise' academic research protocols and practice and 'indigenise' the resulting exhibitions of their culture, knowledge, art and sacred traditions. Garneau explains it thus:

> One goal of the Indigenous is to indigenize… to promote Indigenous ways of being and knowing that are better for our mutual continuance on this planet than the ways that currently rule us.[24]

This reversed the colonial role of the Museum: it was no longer the institution of empire displaying the 'exotic native' but rather the First Nations people were using the museum space to educate the colonisers about their culture. Anangu claimed the museum space as their own, sweeping away the old musty displays of their people as 'stone-age' relics, mute performers in white man's static panoramas of the past. The exhibition included an interactive installation that incorporated desert children's art, from the remote school at Kanpi in the Mann Ranges, into a dynamic 3D immersive artwork where city children could engage with the digital avatar of the perentie lizard.[25] The Ngintaka Exhibition was designed to introduce young and old mainstream society to the importance of the first cultural routes of this country, the Indigenous Songlines of Australia.

Indigenising research governance

Strong protection of Indigenous Cultural and Intellectual Property (ICIP) was key to the collaborative research design of the whole *Songlines of the Western Desert* (the Songlines Project), a major research project funded by the Australian Research Council (ARC)[26] and the sub-project the Ngintaka research and exhibition. The Songlines Project developed new standards of informed individual consent and communal consent to use communal-owned traditional knowledge in museum exhibitions and university research. ICIP protection of the intangible oral and performed traditional communally owned cultural heritage is more complex than ICIP developed for tangible arts and cultural objects. The aim of the Songlines Project multiple consent process was to ensure communal property rights were protected under western law and future use rights were conditional on traditional owner consent in perpetuity.

The process of gaining communal traditional owner consent was complex. Prior to the Songlines research commencing, the Elders on the Board of Ananguku Arts applied for communal approval through the APY Executive Board, the statutory body with responsibility to protect cultural heritage on APY Lands. The APY Executive consulted with all Ngintaka traditional owners across APY Lands before supporting the project on 13 October 2010.[27]

Final approval of a Ngintaka research permit was conditional on appropriate ICIP protocols and ethics. The Songlines Project did not commence until April 2012 after eight months of negotiation between the Aboriginal Partners and the ANU and NMA. The resulting Partners Agreement incorporated ICIP protection clauses that were much more stringent than those usually required by museums or universities. The Agreement ensured Aboriginal control of all ICIP material to be publicly exhibited or published during the term of the project and in perpetuity. The Songlines Project established an Elders Consultative Committee of Ngintaka traditional owners nominated by their peers.[28] Their approval was required prior to research or public use of any communally owned traditional ICIP in the Ngintaka Exhibition.

Individual participants in the research could review their input prior to it being used publicly. A unique *double consent* process of informed consent was developed for all individual participants. The *first consent* was signed by individuals happy to be recorded, photographed or filmed. Their *second consent* was signed after they had the opportunity to review the edited final versions of photographs, films, audio or other digital multimedia products, translations or captions designed to be used publicly. The context in which these materials might be used was explained: the exhibition, the web, advertising, publications or catalogue. All academic articles using Songlines research had to be sent back for approval by the relevant Aboriginal organisation or land council prior to publication.

These processes of communal and individual double consent were initially resisted by the Museum and the university. It is costly and time consuming to review consent and both institutions were used to owning the final copyright or having a licence to reproduce researched material without repeat consultation. However, the extended process of review and the opportunity for individuals to withdraw material before publication empowered the traditional process of communal consent. The Songlines research process was informed by the NPY Women's Council Action Research methodology developed in 2000:

> *Wangkara kulilkatinyi munu palyalkatinyi*
> Keep on discussing and reviewing what you make and design over a long period of time.[29]

Traditional owners of communal cultural heritage must have the right to control the context, interpretation and future use to which their knowledge may be put. The APY Executive Board, the Elders Consultative Committee and the 2nd Consents provided legal protection under western and Anangu law. The process protected the Ngintaka Elders, Ananguku Arts, the S. A. Museum and ANU throughout the media and legal storm.

Conclusion

Museums of the twenty-first century are emerging from their white middle-class colonial cocoons into multi-culturally diverse societies. The challenge is to recognise and accommodate the different cultural heritage values and ownership laws of different religious or ethnic groups within mainstream Australian society. To listen to the previously disadvantaged and disenfranchised classes and include their voices within the museum. Dawn Casey, the first Indigenous Director of the National Museum of Australia, courageously established a new vision for museums as a place of truth-telling, a meeting place for the voices of all peoples. Linda Tuhiwa Smith,[30] the Maori scholar, challenges us to relinquish the 'white expert' curatorial voice and allow other cultural views of history to be honoured. In Australia, there is not one Indigenous voice but many. Museums which have classically homogenised Aboriginal and Torres Strait Islander culture must now open to the diversity within the First Nations voices and the stories they want to tell. twenty-first-century museums must take risks, 'breaking new ground in redefining their national history, becoming more inclusive and accessible, and establishing themselves quite consciously as a forum for debate of contemporary issues'.[31] Empowering all voices to be heard will be challenging but necessary for museums committed to social justice, historical truth-telling and enabling greater social tolerance and equity in our multi-cultural multi-class society. Instead of museums being designed to educate the working class about the higher arts of the elite, museums could become places for educating the elites about the power, beauty and value of the cultural heritage of other classes and cultural minorities: a reversal of the colonial hierarchical perspective on class and culture.

The Ngintaka Exhibition was a bold break from tradition as the Aboriginal community, rather than the Museum, told their own story. This radical new approach was fundamental to the design of the collaborative Songlines Project: privileging the voice of the Elders Consultative Committee. The critical role of the APY Executive in ensuring communal approval by the majority of Ngintaka traditional owners was vital to the success of the project. The process ensured the exhibition was a source of great pride to the traditional owners. Robert Stevens spoke with pride of visiting the exhibition with his family and seeing white people paying attention to the story, music, films and artworks of his country. Comments recorded by visitors to the exhibition reflected their surprise and joy at being able, often for the first time, to gain some understanding of Aboriginal Songlines, the first cultural routes of Australia. Some visitors returned many times, bringing friends and family with them.

> And enthusiasm there ought to be for a project which has the potential to bring some of the complexities of the oldest surviving culture in the world in from the deserts to institutions like the S. A. Museum and, hopefully later, the National Museum in Canberra… They don't need to know all the details, but they do want the sense of the numinous that an exhibition like 'Ngintaka' offers. Indeed, I think there should be a permanent institution in every capital city that offers such opportunities to locals and tourists alike.[32]

Recognition of diversity of ideas and complexity of the ways in which Aboriginal people wish to engage with universities and museums is important for professionals in this space. Community engagement and consultation is an ongoing negotiation with individuals and their communities as they redefine the expression of their communal histories in museums. People empower objects with meaning and symbolism that is continually re-enlivened through the telling by each generation.

Dissonance and controversy are an inevitable healthy part of the cultural process of meaning-making by communities engaged in the tangled histories of colonialism and creating new multi-cultural societies that honour all voices. twenty-first-century museums, universities and the national press need to relinquish their power as arbiters of the voices privileged in our shared national history. Indigenous stories as told by Indigenous voices are a gift to the nation and the living cultural memory of the world.

> Nganampa mamaku tjamuku ngura, manta miilmiilpa nyangatja-
> Tjukurpa tjara.
> This is our fathers' and mothers', grandfathers' and grandmothers' country.
> Earth is sacred, full of Law and Dreaming.[33]

Notes

1 Ananguku Arts, Press Release.
2 Rothwell, "Desert Storm," 22–23.
3 Eccles, "Tragic Confrontation."
4 Rothwell "Desert Storm," 22–23.
5 Ananguku Arts, Press Release.
6 Gosford, "Ngintaka's Long Road."
7 *Songlines of the Western Desert* ARC Project Partners included Ananguku Arts, the Ngaanyatjarra Pitjantjatjara Yankunytjatjara (NPY) Women's Council, the Australian National University (ANU), the National Museum of Australia (NMA), Indigenous Heritage section of Department of Prime Minister & Cabinet (previously SEWPAC) and Australian Heritage Management Solutions. Supported by the Australian Research Council.
8 Mountford, *Brown Men*,148–58.
9 Lester, *Yami*.
10 Mountford, *Nomads*.
11 Bernard Singer, APY Chairperson, APY Executive Meeting, Minutes (unpublished), Umuwa, 6–8 June 2011.
12 The matter under consideration was *Lester v Ananguku Arts*, the Plaintiffs seeking an extended injunction against the exhibition.
13 Stevens, Press Release.
14 *Lester v Ananguku Arts*, 80.
15 Altman, *Sustainable Development*, 1.
16 Mehdora, "Remote Communities."
17 Langton, "Trapped in the Aboriginal Reality Show."
18 Burton, minutes of the APY Law and Culture Committee Meeting.
19 Rothwell, "Desert Storm" and "Culture War."
20 Rothwell, *Quicksilver: Reflections*, 9.
21 Rothwell, *Quicksilver: Reflections*, 9.
22 Rothwell, "Desert Storm," 8.
23 Johnson, "Ideas for Australia."
24 Garneau, "Indigenous Art," 326.
25 McGilchrist, "Ngintaka Interactive,"128.
26 *Songlines of the Western Desert* ARC Project.
27 Resolution of the APY Executive Meeting, Umuwa (unpublished), 13 October 2010.
28 *Songlines of the Western Desert* ARC Project.
29 NPY Women's Council Action Research Model, Alice Springs (unpublished), 2000.
30 Smith, *Decolonizing Methodologies*.
31 Casey, "Museums as Agents," 292.
32 Eccles, "Tragic Confrontation," 2.
33 Nganyinytja Ivy Ilyatjari, Ngintaka story recorded at Angatja, translated by Diana James, (unpublished) 1994.

Bibliography

Altman, Jon Charles. *Sustainable Development Options on Aboriginal Land: The Hybrid Economy in the Twenty-first Century*. Canberra: Australian National University, Centre for Aboriginal Economic Policy Development, Discussion Paper 226, 2001.

Ananguku Arts and Culture Aboriginal Corporation. "Statement in Reply to Nicholas Rothwell's Story in Weekend Australian." Press Release (unpublished), Adelaide, 26 March 2014.

Casey, Dawn. "Museums as Agents for Social and Political Change." In *Museums and Their Communities*, edited by Sheila Watson. London: Routledge, 2007.

Eccles, Jeremy. "Tragic Confrontation in the Desert." *Aboriginal Art Directory*, 8 March 2014. Accessed 30 December 2020. http://news.aboriginalartdirectory.com/2014/04/tragic-confrontation-in-the-desert.php.

Garneau, David. "Indigenous Art: From Appreciation to Art Criticism." In *Double Desire: Transculturation and Indigenous Contemporary Art*, edited by Ian MacLean, 311–326. Newcastle, UK: Cambridge Scholarly Publishers, 2014.

Gosford, Bob. "Ngintaka's Long Road to Adelaide." *Crickey Independent Inquiry Journalism*, 4 April 2014. Accessed 30 December 2020. https://blogs.crikey.com.au/northern/2014/04/04/ngintakas-long-road-to-adelaide/.

Johnson, Carol. "Ideas for Australia: Consensus versus the culture wars- getting the balance right." *The Conversation*, 12 April 2016. Accessed 30 December 2020. https://theconversation.com/ideas-for-australia-consensus-versus-the-culture-wars-getting-the-balance-right-56665.

Kunmanara (Hector) Burton. Minutes of the APY Law and Culture Committee Meeting (unpublished), Umuwa, 12 May 2014. [Kunmanara is used as a sign of respect for several years after someone has died.]

Langton, Marcia. "Trapped in the Aboriginal Reality Show." *Griffith Review Edition* (19): *Re-imagining Australia*. Griffith University, Brisbane, February 2008. Accessed 30 December 2020. www.griffithreview.com/articles/trapped-in-the-aboriginal-reality-show.

Lester, Yami. *Yami, the Autobiography of Yami Lester*, Alice Springs: Institute for Aboriginal Development, 1993.

McGilchrist, Jimmy. "Ngintaka Interactive, 2013–14 APY Lands and Adelaide SA Interactive projection, 25 × 25m, supported by Novatech." In *Ngintaka*, edited by D. James and E. Tregenza. Adelaide: Wakefield Press, 2014.

Medhora, Shalailah. "Remote Communities are 'Lifestyle Choices', Says Tony Abbott." *The Guardian*, 10 March 2015. Accessed 30 December 2020. www.theguardian.com/australia-news/2015/mar/10/remote-communities-are-lifestyle-choices-says-tony-abbott.

Mountford, Charles P. *Nomads of the Australian Desert*. Adelaide: Rigby, 1976.

Mountford, Charles P. *Brown Men and Red Sand*. Melbourne: Robertson & Mullens, 1948.

Rothwell, Nicolas. "Desert Storm: Songlines Suffering: Desert Men in Pain When Secrets on Display" and "Culture War: Songlines Project Sparks Indigenous Culture War." *The Weekend Australian/Review*, 22–23 March 2014.

Rothwell, Nicolas. *Quicksilver: Reflections*, Madwick Lecture, delivered at the University of New England, 2011. Accessed 30 December 2020. https://nicolasrothwell.com/2011/12/06/quicksilver-reflections/.

Smith, Linda Tuhiwa. *Decolonizing Methodologies*. Dunedin: University of Otago Press, 1999.

Stevens, Robert, Senior Ngintaka Nguraritja (Traditional Owner). *Ngintaka Project* (unpublished), Press Release, 8 May 2012.

Yami Lester and Ors v Ananguku Arts and Culture Aboriginal Corporation and Anor [2014] CJ No.392/2014.

INDEX

Page numbers in *italics* denote illustrations.

Printed in the United States
by Baker & Taylor Publisher Services